Anonymous

Permanent Record of Queen Victoria's State Visit to Derby

Anonymous

Permanent Record of Queen Victoria's State Visit to Derby

ISBN/EAN: 9783337097486

Printed in Europe, USA, Canada, Australia, Japan

Cover: Foto ©ninafisch / pixelio.de

More available books at **www.hansebooks.com**

PERMANENT RECORD

OF

QUEEN VICTORIA'S
STATE VISIT TO DERBY,

CONTAINING A COMPLETE, AUTHENTIC, AND NUMEROUSLY ILLUSTRATED ACCOUNT
OF THE VARIOUS CEREMONIES AND FESTIVITIES INCIDENTAL TO THE
OCCASION; TOGETHER WITH A

BRIEF RESUMÉ OF HER MAJESTY'S REIGN;

AN

HISTORICAL SKETCH of the DERBYSHIRE ROYAL INFIRMARY;

Biographies of

THE PRESIDENT OF THE INFIRMARY

AND

THE MAYOR OF DERBY;

AN INTERESTING ACCOUNT OF

FORMER ROYAL VISITS TO DERBY, &c., &c.

Derby:
W. HOBSON, "ADVERTISER" OFFICE, MARKET PLACE.

1891.

WITH THE GRACIOUS PERMISSION OF THE QUEEN,

THIS PERMANENT RECORD OF HER MAJESTY'S STATE VISIT TO DERBY,

TO LAY THE FOUNDATION-STONE OF THE NEW DERBYSHIRE

ROYAL INFIRMARY,

IS RESPECTFULLY DEDICATED TO HER MAJESTY

BY THE

Mayor of Derby (Sir Alfred Seale Haslam, Kt.),

UNDER WHOSE AUTHORITY THE WORK IS COMPILED AND PUBLISHED BY THE

EDITOR AND PROPRIETOR OF THE "DERBYSHIRE ADVERTISER."

PREFACE.

THIS Memorial Volume is issued in conformity with a numerously expressed desire, on the part of the loyal inhabitants of our town and county, for a permanent and authentic Illustrated Record of the Queen's State Visit to Derby on May 21st, 1891. The occasion in question far transcended in interest and importance any other Royal Visit recorded in our local annals; and it was felt on all sides to be only in accordance with the fitness of things, that to its history and description should be devoted a volume forming at once an artistic and enduring memento of the great event. The fact that the recent Royal Visit was the first State Visit with which Derby has been favoured by Her Majesty, imparted a uniqueness to the occasion which was the more marked and the more appreciated owing to the well-known rarity of such an occurrence. In a word, our citizens felt that they were the recipients not only of a great but an exceptional honour at the hands of their Sovereign; and they attested their sense of the distinction by affording Her Majesty a welcome which, it is no exaggeration to say, has never been surpassed, either in point of heartfelt loyalty or spontaneous enthusiasm. Moreover, the mission of benevolence—typical of Her Majesty's life—on which the Queen came amongst her devoted subjects in Derby struck a sympathetic chord in every heart, and shed additional lustre upon Her Majesty's sojourn in Derby on the memorable Twenty-first of May. The Derbyshire "Royal" Infirmary, as, by Her Majesty's gracious assent to the Mayor's application, the beneficent institution in whose behalf she visited Derby is now entitled, has at a time of grave difficulty and sore perplexity been favoured with the gracious presence and invaluable personal assistance of our Sovereign Lady the Queen. By consenting to come to Derby and lay the foundation-stone of the new Infirmary, so imperatively required for the welfare of our sick and suffering, Her Majesty gave such a stimulus to the scheme for erecting the new Institution as has already gone far towards carrying it to a successful issue. A considerable sum of money, it is true, still remains to be raised ere the total cost of the new buildings is fully provided for; and no efforts should be relaxed until the entire amount is forthcoming. At the same time, considering the very large sum required and the comparatively brief period during which the appeal has been before the public, the results already achieved are gratifying in the extreme, indicating, as they do, great liberality on the part of all classes of the local community, and an earnest determination to accomplish the object in view. It is, of course, neither possible nor desirable to assess in pounds, shillings, and pence, the precise extent to which Her Majesty's State Visit has already directly benefitted the building fund for the new Infirmary. But, as all who have watched the progress of the movement will gratefully acknowledge, Her Majesty's Visit—from the immediate date of its announcement—exercised a remarkably beneficial influence upon the scheme in whose behalf it was undertaken, imparting to it a powerful impetus, the value of which cannot be over-estimated. The new era in the history of our principal town and county charity, so graciously inaugurated by Her Majesty, cannot fail to be fraught for all time with such results as will cause the inhabitants of Derby ever to look back, with profound gratitude and delight, upon May 21st, 1891, as the most brilliant red-letter day in their local annals.

The various ceremonies and rejoicings so fully chronicled in this volume need no detailed comment in this introductory article. But this it is only right to say: their brilliant success was greatly due to the personal efforts and unstinted munificence of the Mayor of Derby (Sir Alfred Seale Haslam, Kt.), whose eminent public services received such distinguished recognition at the hands of Her Majesty. Sir Alfred expressed his determination that Her Majesty should be accorded a welcome second to none which she had ever received; and the loyal inhabitants of our borough followed his lead in a manner which left nothing to be desired. It is not too much to say that at this important epoch our ancient and loyal borough not merely upheld its best and most cherished traditions, but added a chapter to its history which will ever redound to its honour and credit.

The account of Her Majesty's Visit and the various proceedings incidental thereto which is furnished in this volume, has been reproduced, after careful revision, from the columns of the *Derbyshire Advertiser*. By general consent, the reports which appeared in the *Advertiser* formed infinitely the best and most graphically-written record of the Queen's Visit; and there can be no manner of doubt that their re-publication in this handsome volume will form a most acceptable permanent memento of the ever-memorable event. With reference to the illustrations and portraits with which this work is so profusely embellished, the Editor begs to express his acknowledgments to Mr. W. W. Winter, from whose photographs the great majority of them have been engraved, and to the other artists, including Mr. R. Keene and Mr. Scotton, who have allowed him the use of their photographs.

INDEX.

	PAGE
INTRODUCTION	1-11
SPECIAL MEETING OF THE TOWN COUNCIL	11, 12

THE ROYAL JOURNEY TO DERBY—

	PAGE
DEPARTURE OF THE QUEEN FROM WINDSOR	13
ARRIVAL AT BURTON	14
WAITING FOR THE QUEEN AT DERBY STATION	14
THE ARRIVAL	15, 16
THE SCENE OUTSIDE	17, 18
THE ROYAL ROUTE TO THE MARKET PLACE	19

THE VISIT TO MARKET SQUARE—

	PAGE
GRAND RECEPTION AND CEREMONY	20-26

THE ADDRESSES—

	PAGE
DERBY CORPORATION	26-30
THE MAGISTRATES OF THE BOROUGH	31
THE COUNTY COUNCIL OF DERBYSHIRE	31
THE MAGISTRATES OF THE COUNTY	32
DERBY BOARD OF GUARDIANS	32
DERBY SCHOOL BOARD	33
THE CLERGY OF THE DEANERY OF DERBY	34
THE MEDICAL PROFESSION OF DERBY	35
NONCONFORMIST CHURCHES OF DERBY	35
DERBY AND DERBYSHIRE NURSING ASSOCIATION	36
REPTON SCHOOL	36
DERBY SCHOOL	37
MASTERS AND BOYS OF TRENT COLLEGE	38
THE FREEMASONS OF DERBYSHIRE	38
UNITED TEMPERANCE SOCIETIES	39
DERBY CHAMBER OF COMMERCE	40
THE FRIENDLY SOCIETIES OF DERBY	40
THE TEACHERS OF DERBY AND DISTRICT	41
THE CEREMONY AT THE INFIRMARY	42-48
THE DEPARTURE—THE MAYOR KNIGHTED	48-50
THE QUEEN'S COSTUME	51

	PAGE
THE QUEEN'S BOUQUET	51
THE OTHER BOUQUETS	51
THE MAYOR'S RECEPTION ROBE	51
THE DRESSES OF THE MAYORESS AND THE MISSES HASLAM	51
THE OFFICIAL ACCOUNT OF THE QUEEN'S VISIT	52-54
GRAND MAYORAL BANQUET	55-65
THE DECORATIONS AND ILLUMINATIONS—	
THE APPEARANCE OF THE STREETS AT NIGHT	66, 67
THE INTERIOR OF THE RAILWAY STATION	68
THE FLORAL CORRIDOR	68, 69
THE ROYAL RECEPTION ROOM	71-73
THE ROYAL RETIRING ROOM	73, 74
THE STATION EXTERIOR	74, 75
THE MIDLAND HOTEL	75, 76
THE EVERGREEN ARCH AT THE MIDLAND STATION	76-78
THE MAYOR'S DINING MARQUEE	78, 79
THE ELECTRIC ILLUMINATIONS	79, 80
THE ROYAL PAVILION	80-82
MIDLAND ROAD	83-85
LONDON ROAD	85-88
ST. PETER'S STREET	88-92
THE CORN MARKET	92-95
THE MARKET PLACE	95-97
ST. JAMES'S STREET	97, 98
THE STRAND	98
CHEAPSIDE	98, 99
THE WARDWICK	99, 100
VICTORIA STREET	100, 101
NORTH LEES	101
STREETS NOT ON THE ROYAL ROUTE	102-106
THE VIEW FROM ALL SAINTS' TOWER	107-110
DISPLAY OF FIREWORKS AT THE ARBORETUM	111
THE EXCURSIONS	112
MILITARY AND POLICE	112, 113
GRATIFYING ANNOUNCEMENTS FROM THE MAGISTRATES	113
SIR ALFRED HASLAM IS PROUD OF DERBY	114
THE TOWN COUNCIL AND THE MAYOR	114-116
THE QUEEN'S CARRIAGES AND HORSES	117
BANDS AND STATIONS	117, 118
THE GENERAL ARRANGEMENTS	118, 119

	PAGE
ITEMS OF INTEREST	119-122
A CRIPPLE'S OFFERING—TOUCHING INCIDENT	123, 124
AMBULANCE STATIONS	124, 125
THE DECORATIONS COMMITTEE	125
DESCRIPTION OF THE CASKET	126-128
DESCRIPTION OF THE GOLD TROWEL	128
THE PULPIT AND THE QUEEN'S VISIT	129-134
THE PRESIDENT OF THE INFIRMARY—SIR WILLIAM EVANS, BART.	135-137
SIR ALFRED HASLAM, KT., J.P., MAYOR OF DERBY—A SKETCH OF HIS CAREER	138-149
DERBYSHIRE GENERAL INFIRMARY—DESCRIPTION OF THE NEW BUILDINGS	151-153
THE ARCHITECTS	153
THE NEW HOSPITAL AT DERBY	154
HISTORY OF THE INSTITUTION	155-158
THE MEDICAL STAFF OF THE DERBYSHIRE INFIRMARY	158, 159
A BRIEF SKETCH OF QUEEN VICTORIA'S REIGN	160-166
FORMER ROYAL VISITS TO DERBYSHIRE	167, 168
THE QUEEN'S FIRST VISIT TO DERBYSHIRE	169-171
THE QUEEN AND PRINCE ALBERT AT CHATSWORTH	171-174
HER MAJESTY REVIEWED THE YEOMANRY CAVALRY	174, 175
PRINCE ALBERT AT MESSRS. HOLMES' COACH WORKS	175-177
VISIT OF THE PRINCE AND PRINCESS OF WALES TO CHATSWORTH AND DERBY	177-182
THE PRINCE OF WALES' VISIT TO DOVERIDGE HALL AND DERBY	182-185
DERBY SCHOOL RECEIVES THE PRINCE A SECOND TIME	184
THE PRINCE AT BURTON-ON-TRENT	185, 196

INDEX TO ILLUSTRATIONS.

HER MOST GRACIOUS MAJESTY THE QUEEN	ii
SIR ALFRED HASLAM, KT., J.P., AND LADY HASLAM	xvi
THE PRESIDENT OF THE INFIRMARY—SIR WILLIAM EVANS, BART.	2
THE OLD INFIRMARY	4
THE MOST HON. THE MARQUIS OF HARTINGTON	5
THE NEW INFIRMARY	7
FLORAL CANOPY, CORNER OF ST. JAMES'S STREET	21
THE TOWN HALL, DERBY	23
THE RECEPTION IN THE MARKET PLACE	27
H. F. GADSBY, ESQ., TOWN CLERK	29
THE QUEEN LAYING THE FOUNDATION-STONE	47
THE QUEEN KNIGHTING THE MAYOR	49
INTERIOR OF THE ROYAL RECEPTION ROOM	70
THE QUEEN'S CHAIR	72

	PAGE
THE EVERGREEN ARCH, MIDLAND STATION	77
TRIUMPHAL ARCH, TOP OF ST. PETER'S STREET	89
THE ROYAL HOTEL	93
THE FREE LIBRARY	99
THE DERWENT FROM ST. MARY'S BRIDGE	103
THE ROYAL CROWN DERBY PORCELAIN WORKS	104
ALL SAINTS' CHURCH	107
THE OLD SILK MILL FROM DERWENT BRIDGE	109
OLD MARKET STONE, DERBY ARBORETUM	110
THE FOUNTAIN, DERBY ARBORETUM	111
LIEUT.-COL. DELACOMBE, CHIEF CONSTABLE	113
RAILWAY SERVANTS' ORPHANAGE	119
THE CASKET	126
THE GOLD TROWEL	128
THE HASLAM FOUNDRY AND ENGINEERING WORKS	143
THE MAYOR'S ARMORIAL BEARINGS	149
DERBY FROM THE LONG BRIDGE	150
THE PRESIDENT OF THE INFIRMARY AND THE MAYOR OF DERBY	151
THE ARCHITECTS	154
CAPT. PARRY, CHIEF CONSTABLE OF DERBYSHIRE	159
HIS GRACE THE DUKE OF DEVONSHIRE, K.G.	168
CHATSWORTH	170
DERBY SCHOOL	178
HARDWICK HALL	180

Lady Haslam.

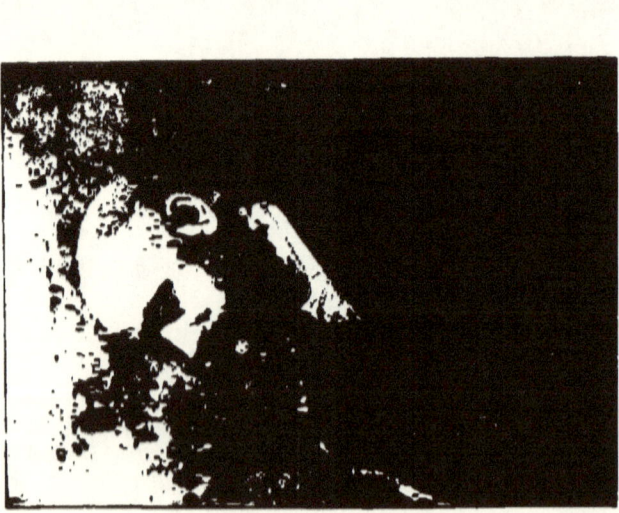

Sir Alfred Seale Haslam, Knt., J.P
(Mayor of Derby.)

From Photos. by) (W. W. Winter, Derby.

STATE VISIT OF
HER MOST GRACIOUS MAJESTY THE QUEEN
TO DERBY.

HURSDAY, MAY 21st, 1891, will ever be remembered with the greatest joy in the town and county of Derby. On that date Her Most Gracious Majesty the Queen honoured us with the State Visit which all classes had looked forward to with such unbounded pleasure. To say that the event realised the most sanguine anticipations of its success is but feebly to express the general sentiment of unqualified delight which the Queen's gracious presence evoked in the hearts of Her Majesty's devoted subjects in Derby. Many loyal and hearty receptions have, in the course of her prolonged reign, been accorded to Her Majesty in all parts of her dominions; but it is not too much to say that the welcome and ceremonies of Thursday, May 21st, in Derby, have never been excelled either in heartiness, brilliancy, or the spontaneity of their loyalty.

An observation of respectable antiquity runs to the effect that "great results from little causes spring." It is a little startling, nevertheless, to find that the visit to Derby of Her Most Gracious Majesty the Queen was due, amongst other reasons, to the mischievous destructiveness of the common rat. The chain of circumstance may be lengthy, but it certainly is unbroken. A number of the rodents in question, burrowing with the reckless pertinacity of their nature amongst the decaying brickwork of the drains under and around the present Infirmary building, contrived to riddle them with holes. The foul gases escaped and permeated the building. The institution designed for the purpose of restoring health became itself an originating centre of disease. A new building became necessary; and to lay its foundation-stone the Queen graciously consented to visit Derby.

Not the whole of the blame, however, is to be attributed to the industrious animal that has been mentioned. The case against the old Infirmary rests on other and further indictments of its sanitary condition, the extent and seriousness of which may best be put in brief form by stating that they are such as to cause an unanimous agreement as to the hopelessness of repair and the necessity of reconstruction. Costly though the scheme for building a new Infirmary may be, it is proved to demonstration that no other course is open. The citizens of Derby, therefore, with the inhabitants of the county generally, have addressed themselves to the task which lies before them in a hearty and cordial spirit, which leaves no doubt as to ultimate success, and suggests even that the hope may not be too remote that the operations may be so rapidly proceeded with as to render it possible for the Queen, who has now formally inaugurated the construction of the new building, to complete her gracious handiwork by again visiting Derby and assisting at the opening.

THE PRESIDENT OF THE INFIRMARY (SIR WILLIAM EVANS, BART.).
(*From a Photo. by W. W. Winter, Derby.*)

With the above observations by way of general summary, it may be useful here to give, in something like historical sequence, an account of the proceedings which led up to the splendid and successful pageant of Thursday, May 21st, 1891. We must go back then to the early part of 1890, when a serious outbreak of illness amongst the nursing staff of the Infirmary, culminating in the unfortunate death of one member, pointed to a defective condition of the institution. Sir William Evans, Bart., President of the Infirmary, took decisive action. Telegraphing to the Local Government Board for advice as to a competent inspector, that body recommended the employment of Dr. Seaton, who was promptly secured for the purpose of a thorough examination of the building. Dr. Seaton's survey occupied three days. It was of the most exhaustive character, and its result was such as to fill the President—quoting Sir William Evans' own words—with "astonishment and dismay." Dr. Seaton, in point of fact, condemned the building in the most unqualified terms, and darkly hinted at the insufficiency of any scheme of re-organisation and the necessity of re-building. The Governors, though astonished, happily did not allow themselves to be paralysed. They at once had the patients and nurses removed from the most dangerous parts of the building, and took what measures seemed to be practicable for the immediate repair of the most patent defects. Concurrently the advice of other experts was obtained. Sir Douglas Galton, K.C.B., D.C.L., F.R.S., an authority of high rank, and Mr. Rogers Field, a specialist in hospital construction, were in turn consulted, and for once doctors, notwithstanding a well-known saying, did not differ. The Infirmary stood condemned. It was an old building, erected in accordance with the best knowledge possessed at the time, and in its day and generation an admirable institution enough. Unhappily, the extensions, which from time to time had to be made to meet the growing wants of the population of Derby town and county, had, whilst increasing its accommodation, sadly impaired its efficiency. The fresh air supply at various points was cut off. A complicated system of ventilation and warming by means of flues carried inside the walls ceased to be understood, the key to it being lost as the years progressed and the *personnel* of the establishment altered. Repairs to those same flues being from time to time necessary, they were attempted by bricklayers of more zeal than prudence, with the deplorable result that drain pipes and ventilating pipes were confused, communication was established between them, and the very system which was designed for the admission of fresh and health-giving air became actively employed in the diffusion of foul and contaminated gases. In addition came the depredations of the rats, to which allusion has been made. Brick drains were carried under the basement—a method wholly disapproved of by modern sanitary science—and the bricks themselves being more or less porous, and the mortar having perished in the lapse of time, the rats found in the drainage system a happy hunting-ground for the exercise of their proclivities. As a consequence of all these causes, not only the subsoil, but the very walls of the building became penetrated with noxious matter. Any attempt at repair would be, in the opinion of the experts, enormously costly, and at the best of more than dubious permanent utility. There remained only the one alternative, to pull the existing building down, and to erect a new hospital altogether. "If that were done," Sir Douglas Galton said, "and if attention were paid to the details on which efficient management depended, there would be established a hospital not only satisfactory in curative details, but also economical to administer."

It will be easily conceived that the *dictum* of these authorities, pronounced in such unhesitating terms, and so far-reaching in its purpose, caused much anxiety to the Governors of the Infirmary. Nevertheless they faced the situation boldly, and the result of their deliberations was to accept the task devolved upon them, and to set about the erection of a totally new structure. A powerful Building Committee was formed, plans were sought for and scrutinised, and those of Messrs. Young and Hall, Architects, London, were approved. The resolve, in short, was taken. It next lay upon the Governors to secure that which alone could afford hope of a successful issue out of their predicament, to wit, the hearty, generous, and enthusiastic concurrence of the public. The Duke of Devonshire, as Lord Lieutenant of the county, was approached, and that nobleman, recognising that a great county undertaking was involved, to the promotion of which the honour and reputation of Derbyshire were committed, summoned a meeting of county and

THE OLD INFIRMARY.
(*From a Photo. by W. C. Keene, Derby.*)

borough residents for Thursday, the 9th of April, 1891. His Grace, himself, was unhappily unable from indisposition to attend and bear personal testimony to his interest in the project, though, as will be seen shortly, he adopted the most practical and munificent method of showing how warmly his sympathies were excited. His place at the meeting was occupied by the Marquis of Hartington, and the assembly, as was at the time remarked, was thoroughly representative of all classes of the community, "from peer to peasant, and from the merchant prince to the labourer and the artisan." Lord Scarsdale, the Bishop of Derby,

Sir William Evans, Bart., the Hon. W. M. Jervis, Brigadier-General Sir Henry Wilmot, Bart., Sir Henry Every, Bart., Mr. E. Miller Mundy (High Sheriff of the County), Sir Douglas Galton, the Mayor of Derby, and, as it appeared, almost every man of influence in the county was present at the meeting, together with many representatives of the trading and industrial occupations of the borough. The appearance of the Drill Hall, in short, bore ample evidence of the extent to which the new project had engaged the interest and the attention of all classes. The meeting was appropriately opened by the Bishop of Derby with prayer, after which Lord Hartington, in one of his most statesmanlike and convincing speeches, laid clearly before the gathering the leading circumstances of the case. He spoke

THE MOST HON. THE MARQUIS OF HARTINGTON.
(*From a Photo. by the London Stereoscopic Co.*)

of the good work performed by the Infirmary in the past, and explained how it came about that its capacities for further good were now impaired; and he dwelt upon the prime importance of keeping fully abreast of the age in regard to an institution of this character. His lordship also referred to the fact that Her Majesty the Queen had undertaken to lay the foundation-stone of the proposed new building; and although delicacy of feeling prevented the Marquis from explaining how it happened that so signal an honour came to be vouchsafed to Derby, many in the audience were able to solve the point, knowing that it was largely to Lord Hartington's own endeavour—exerted willingly in this, as in other directions, for the benefit of the town and county with which he is so honourably connected—that the visit of Her Most Gracious Majesty was due. What his lordship did feel at liberty to enlarge upon, however, was the stimulus to local effort which the presence of the Queen should afford. He made an earnest and eloquent appeal to the public for assistance in the work—an appeal which, being just as timely and appropriate now as then, we need not offer an apology for repeating. Lord Hartington then said he entertained not the smallest doubt that Her Majesty would receive from the county and the borough not only a respectful and loyal, but an enthusiastic welcome. But the most solid and substantial proof which could be offered to Her Majesty of the value which the people of Derby set upon her kindness lay in the amount of support which they were willing to give to the object for which she would visit the town. "Not the most enthusiastic cheers which Her Majesty could receive in the streets, not the most flattering expressions which could be laid at her feet in the addresses which would be presented to her, not the outward and visible signs of rejoicing which would meet her eyes in every quarter—none of these could tell the Queen so eloquently the appreciation of the honour which was being done to Derbyshire by her visit, as the assurance which he trusted they would enable the Governors to give to Her Majesty that, in great part owing to her auspicious presence among them, no difficulty had been found in raising the funds which would be required for the completion of this work of necessity and mercy."

It became the duty of Captain Reid, secretary to the Building Committee, afterwards to read the list of promised subscriptions. It opened right nobly. The Duke of Devonshire undertook to contribute £3,000; Sir William Evans, Bart., President of the Infirmary, offered a like amount; the Shareholders of the Midland Railway Co. headed the list with a magnificent promise of £5,000; and other promises were—Mr. Walter Evans, £1,500; Mr. T. H. Oakes, £1,000; Mr. Francis Ley, £1,000; Mr. G. H. Strutt, £1,000; Messrs. Boden & Co., £1,000. Numerous donations of £500 and lesser amounts were offered, and indeed it appeared that of the £64,000 or £65,000 required to complete the new Infirmary, a sum of £31,000 had been guaranteed in the short space of the fortnight during which the scheme had been before the public. The result was satisfactory in two ways. It was in itself a splendid evidence of the capacities of Derbyshire folk in the direction of charitable donation, and it demonstrated that the decision of the Governors to build a new Infirmary rather than reconstruct the old, had received most fully and amply the necessary *imprimatur* of public approval. As a matter of form, however, it was necessary that a formal resolution, committing the meeting to an endorsement of the Governors' action, should be duly passed, and this was moved by Sir William Evans and seconded by the High Sheriff of Derbyshire. It was supported by Sir Douglas Galton, who took the opportunity of informing the meeting, *ex cathedra* and in detail, of the defects of the old Infirmary and the impossibility of adequately overcoming them in the existing building. The resolution, on being put to the vote, was unanimously carried, as was also a further resolution, proposed by the Mayor of Derby (Mr. now Sir Alfred Seale Haslam), and seconded by Lord Scarsdale, by which the meeting pledged itself to the endeavour to raise the necessary funds.

Meantime the Mayor of Derby himself and the borough authorities had not been idle.

THE NEW INFIRMARY.

Meetings of the Corporation had been held. A proposal of the Mayor to vote £2,000 from the Corporate funds towards the cost of the Infirmary it had been found desirable, in the light of subsequent questions as to the legality of such a course, to withdraw; but His Worship's private and personal munificence was perhaps all the more fully expressed. Not only did he make a handsome donation to the building fund, but he charged himself with the cost of entertaining the royal and other guests upon the occasion of the Queen's visit, and with many of the other expenses involved in connection with the occasion—this liberality being all the more accentuated in view of the fact that the Mayoralty of Derby, unlike the case of many large towns, is a purely honorary office—and on the 21st April he presided at a large public meeting of the inhabitants of the borough held in the Derby Guildhall. Again there was absolute unanimity on the score of the necessity of the new building, and again there was evidenced an enthusiastic resolve on the part of the inhabitants to do all that in them lay to secure the success of the great object which lay to hand. This was shown by the most practical of all testimony. Not only were individual donations announced, which brought up the total building fund to more than half the required figure, but the co-operation of working men was indicated in a very excellent manner. It appeared that the *employés* in more than one large industrial establishment had undertaken to deprive themselves of one day's pay in order to present to the fund the amount so represented. There was every indication, moreover, that the example would be generally followed, and that the working classes, to the alleviation of whose sufferings infirmaries are mainly devoted, would thus show themselves praiseworthily prompt in recognising the responsibility that lay upon them. The main object of the town's meeting—to endorse the general policy of the Governors of the Infirmary—was accomplished in the adoption of the following resolution, which was proposed by Mr. W. G. Norman, seconded by Councillor Foulds, and supported by Councillor Jackson, Mr. Geo. Powell, Mr. W. J. Piper, and Mr. Alderman Bemrose, J.P.—"That this meeting recognises the necessity for re-building the Derbyshire General Infirmary in the interests of those members of the community for whom the institution exists, and approves of the course taken by the Governors." The resolution was unanimously carried, and the Mayor, turning to the second part of the evening's programme, made some interesting announcements as to the route to be taken on the occasion of the Royal visit, and also on the important subject of the decoration of the streets. These arrangements, in their details, had subsequently to be subjected to some slight modification; but on this score full information will be found in another part of this volume. It has here been our function to attempt to recapitulate the circumstances which led to the ceremony of Thursday, May 21st, and to do so in a brief and connected narrative which may be of service to Derby residents, and at the same time place the thousands of visitors from a distance in possession of information which may afford them all necessary comprehension of the pageantry they were privileged to witness.

Here, too, must be recorded the note of mourning which unhappily tinged the otherwise gladsome ceremonial. Derbyshire people are too closely allied with the house of Devonshire not to feel a calamity befalling it as one which comes nearly home to themselves. The death of Lord Edward Cavendish would have been lamented at any time; occurring as it did when the public mind was little attuned to tragedy, it came as a profound shock. Lord Edward, we may assume, would have been with us to share in the joys and hopes of the function of that memorable Thursday. His sudden and premature removal deprives both town and county of a figure of much prominence, and of a personality always welcome and agreeable. To the Duke of Devonshire, to Lady Edward Cavendish, and to Lord Hartington, many kind thoughts must silently have winged their way from the hearts of the masses of people collected in the streets of Derby, and the knowledge of this, let us hope, will be not without solace for a grief that must nevertheless, until time brings its anodyne, be poignant and intense.

For several days prior to the event, visual evidence of the most ample kind had been afforded of the determination of the inhabitants of Derby to do honour to the occasion. Decorative preparations were commenced early, and the wisdom of this was manifest as time went on, for when Thursday arrived there were not wanting amusing instances of the inconveniences of procrastination. Whilst most of the inhabitants whose places of residence or business lay along the line of route had by noon on Thursday completed the measure of ornamentation to which they had addressed themselves, a few were to be observed feverishly at work in the attempt to make up for time which had been lost; and as work under pressure of this kind is not always conducive to the maintenance of a philosophic temper, foolish virgins were once again the victims of a useful and time-honoured experience. As a whole, however, it must be said that everything was completed in an admirable manner. Thursday morning saw a vast change from Wednesday night. Finishing touches had been administered, and along the greater part of the route the citizens were able to enjoy, in a series of *coups d'œil*, many completed spectacles of singular picturesqueness and beauty. The general design of street decoration which is founded upon the erection of Venetian masts, has been subjected to some passing criticism as being conventional. It may be so; but contemners of the old would probably be placed in a predicament if they were required to devise a method which should be at once newer and better. There is always in this, as in other matters, a *carriere ouverté aux talents*: but as, meanwhile, the genius has not appeared who is to metamorphose existing methods, those methods may not only be still employed, but it may be observed of them that they are not one whit less effective than of yore. The suggestion which the decorations afforded the mind was certainly poetic. It was that the whole of the progress of Her Majesty lay through bowers of flowers and evergreens, the waving of thousands of flags adding brightness and joyousness to her path. It was a thousand pities that the weather proved dull and chill. Brilliant sunlight would have added just the one element needful. That, however, is a matter beyond the control of the ruling authorities of so ancient a borough as Derby, a borough which—as the antiquarian researches employed in the preparation of the Corporation Address to the Queen inform us—was "a place of importance" in remote Saxon times. From the moment of leaving the railway station Her Majesty, connoisseur though she must be in the matter of public decorations and festivals, could hardly fail to find that the endeavours of Derby in this regard would compare well with what has been witnessed elsewhere. The magnificent evergreen and floral arch in the station yard was a structure altogether out of the common. Although absolutely temporary in its purpose it was wrought out with an elaboration of design and with a perfection of finish that could hardly have been exceeded in the case of an edifice destined permanently to gratify the artistic senses. The Midland Road presented a vista of festoons of pink and white roses. The castellated gateway towards the extremity of this road, though in reality a mockery and a sham, which would have collapsed under the onslaught of an errant brewer's dray, fulfilled its purpose of looking massive, stern, and baronial. Turning into the London Road, the design of the decorations changed somewhat. The Venetian poles were linked together with double chains of evergreens, whilst the strings of roses crossing the thoroughfare gave place to bannerettes and flags of parti-coloured diversity. The scene at the Infirmary was one of extreme beauty. At this point the road is a fine, wide thoroughfare, and the effect of the flags in the roadway was helped by the decorations of the stands that had been erected for spectators, the visible portions of which were ablaze with the rich glories of the ever-useful crimson cloth. An evergreen arch, crossing the main road at its juncture with Castle Street, gave entrance to a stretch of roadway more circumscribed in its dimensions, though hardly so in the lavishness with which decorative possibilities had been called into play; but it was at the angle caused by the joining of London Road and Osmaston Road that a more complete wealth of display commenced. A most notable double arch, covering both the roads named, had been constructed, surmounted with figures of Britannia, and bearing upon its walls pictorial devices illustrative of the trades pursued in the town. Ornament, however, was not alone the object of this edifice. It served a double debt to pay, in that a band stand had craftily been devised as an integral part of its structure, from the elevated platform of which stirring music was discoursed during the afternoon to while away the tedium of waiting. Moreover, a fountain, cunningly arranged in a miniature flower garden, gave charm to the eye whilst the strains of music afforded it to the ear. Another device which is not to be forgotten was a huge floral canopy at the junction of the Corn Market with St. James's Street. Suspended in mid-air, this was a highly effective and artistic addition to the embellishments of the line of route, and one which gave a flourishing touch to a scheme of decoration which at this point was exceedingly handsome and complete. This canopy was in outline; that in the Market Place, under which it was arranged that the Queen's carriage should stay whilst the numerous addresses of welcome were presented to Her Majesty, was of more substantial proportions. It was covered over with a rain-proof roofing, very prettily designed in Moorish style, and showed in relief against the huge canvas-covered and handsomely decorated enclosure in front of the Town Hall, in which the Corporation and privileged spectators assembled for the purposes of the address-giving.

To do justice to the appearance of the town, the pencil of an artist would have been requisite. Words may be employed by a wielder of the pen able as Ruskin, but it is the eye rather than the mind which is the recipient of impressions, and to this end the artist puts the mere penman to the blush. Generalisation must be employed. Passing along the streets through which the Royal procession passed, the spectator everywhere beheld a vision of banners, of trophies, of streamers fluttering in the wind, and of flowers and shrubs deftly arranged by thousands of tasteful hands into designs full of grace and beauty. The joyous sound of bells filled the air, peals being rung during the day from six of the churches. The strains of music floated upon the breeze from well-nigh a dozen bands at various stations on the line of route. The great inspiration of the scene, however, was derived, as is always the case, from the masses of human beings who filled the streets throughout the day. An emotional magnetism prevails whenever a huge concourse of people is assembled for a common object which in itself excites individual and general interest. Loyalty is a sentiment usually dormant because seldom required to be otherwise. But the visit of the Sovereign or a member of the Royal Family at once supplies the spark, and the feeling leaps into flame, and expresses itself in eagerness and enthusiasm, and in the case of Her Majesty we will venture to say with real and warm personal affection besides. It was the possibility of an over-zealous demonstration of these feelings that alone rendered street barriers necessary, and required the restraining influence of the additional police who were drafted into the town; for nowhere in Her Majesty's dominions has a heartier welcome awaited her than that which was accorded on Thursday, May 21st, 1891, at the hands of the inhabitants of Derby.

SPECIAL MEETING OF THE TOWN COUNCIL.

At half-past three on the eventful day there was a Special Meeting of the Town Council. His Worship the Mayor, of course, presided, and the agenda stated that the meeting had been called " to affix the Common Seal to the Address to Her Majesty the Queen on the occasion of Her Majesty's visit to the town on the 21st of May, 1891." There were also present, Aldermen J. W. Newbold, W. Hobson, A. Woodiwiss, T. Roe, M.P., U. Sowter, Sir John Smith, W. B. Sherwin, and R. Russell; Councillors S. Evans, J. Grundy, I. Roome, G. B. Unsworth, T. L. Riley, R. W. Spriggs, A. Butterworth, E. C. Ellis, W. H. Marsden, S. Bennett, F. Stone, F. Ward, T. Sims, T. H. Harrison, G. Foster, T. H. Bennett, C. Wallis, T. Cox, F. E. Leech, J. F. Foulds, F. Duesbury, Dr. Laurie, W. Lowe, G. Bottomley, E. T. Ann, J. P. Doherty, P. Wallis, J. Jackson, Hon. F. Strutt, C. C. Bowring, W. Hart, W. Williamson, G. Dean, J. E. Russell, and W. Heathcote. The Mayor, who wore his robes of office, was accompanied by Sir W. Harcourt, Bart., M.P. (who was in Windsor uniform), Mr. Buszard, Q.C. (Recorder, in his robes), Sir Francis Burdett, Bart., and Lady Burdett. Aldermen Roe and Sir John Smith were attired in Court dress.

The Mayor said they had met there that afternoon to affix the Common Seal of the Council to the Address to be presented to Her Majesty the Queen. It would be in the recollection of all that, when he had the pleasure of making the announcement to the Council that Her Majesty had graciously consented to visit the borough, it was unanimously agreed that an Address should be drawn up and presented to her. The Address had been prepared, but it had been to a certain extent kept secret in order that their proceedings that day might not be detracted from. The Address, however, had now been set forth fully in the programme, and he thought it would meet with their unanimous approval. His Worship then made the formal motion.

Alderman Sir John Smith seconded the motion, and it was carried unanimously.

The Mayor, rising again, said he had now to refer to a solemn matter. The untimely death of Lord Edward Cavendish had cast a gloom not only over those proceedings, but over the county and over the entire country. Lord Edward was an exceedingly popular man in all classes of society. Politics made no difference whatever to him. Although he might differ from his friends on important matters of politics, it never made any difference in his private friendships. He was a gentleman who moved among all classes of men, and he (His Worship) ventured to say that no one act of his could have met with their disapproval. They had not only to deplore the death of Lord Edward Cavendish, but they had also that day been deprived of the presence of Lord Hartington, who had thrown his whole soul into those proceedings. We—added His Worship—sorrow in their great sorrow, and I think we ought to send a resolution of condolence. I move therefore the following proposition:—" Resolved, that the most sincere condolence of this Corporation be conveyed to Lady Edward Cavendish, his Grace the Duke of Devonshire, and the Marquis of Hartington upon the lamentable and untimely death of Lord Edward Cavendish, whose loss the Corporation feel to be one not only to his own family, but to the country at large, and especially to this county."

Alderman Roe, M.P., in seconding the motion, remarked that there was no man either in Derbyshire or in the whole country who would not support it. When they considered the loss which Lord Edward Cavendish would be to his noble parent and to the county, they could not but feel that such a resolution ought to be passed, even on an occasion of that kind when they were in the midst of so much excitement and joy at the thought of seeing the Queen. He was sure a proposition of that kind would meet with the unanimous approval of the town.

The resolution having been passed in solemn silence, the members of the Corporation proceeded to the Market Square ; and, as detailed elsewhere, entered the carriages provided for them by the Mayor, and, amidst the cheers of the crowd, took their departure for the station, in order to receive Her Majesty.

THE ROYAL JOURNEY TO DERBY.

DEPARTURE OF THE QUEEN FROM WINDSOR.

HE QUEEN, accompanied by the Prince and Princess Henry of Battenberg, with their children, Prince Alexander, Princess Victoria Eugenie, and Prince Leopold, left Windsor Castle at 1.35 p.m., for Derby. Her Majesty was attended by the Countess of Errol, Hon. Miss Ethel Cadogan, Miss McNeill, Miss Cochrane, Lord Edward Clinton (Lord-in-Waiting), Major Sir Fleetwood Edwardes, Hon. Alexander Yorke (Equerries), Sir Henry Ponsonby (Private Secretary to the Queen), Dr. Reid, Mr. Muther, the Right Hon. Henry Matthews (the Home Secretary), and Sir Henry Ewart. The Royal party drove to the Great Western Railway Station, where the Royal train—a London and North-Western one — consisting of sixteen saloon carriages, including Her Majesty's drawing-room and sleeping-cars, was in waiting. The railway officials in attendance were Mr. N. J. Burlinson, traffic superintendent of the Great Western Railway, who had charge of the train as far as Leamington, and Mr. J. W. Neale, traffic superintendent of the London and North-Western Railway, who took over the charge of the train at Leamington, and Mr. Fraser, station master at Windsor. Hundreds of spectators lined the route from the Castle to the station, and the Castle Guard turned out at the Henry VIII. gateway of the Castle, and presented arms as the Royal cortege drove down the grand drive from the Palace. The Queen, who drove in a closed carriage, the weather being showery, looked remarkably well, and bowed to the bystanders who saluted the Royal party. On arrival at the station the Queen and suite passed through the Royal waiting room and took their seats, the station precincts being guarded by detachments of London Metropolitan Police. The Royal train left Windsor at 1.40 p.m.

ARRIVAL AT BURTON.

The Royal train passed through Burton Station at 5.17, and at that time the station was strictly guarded. In compliance with the regulations issued, Superintendent Gilbride had a staff of police on special duty guarding all the approaches to the railway at the station. The station was closed to all excepting passengers who were about to travel in trains going in the opposite direction to the Royal one. In Burton many Royal Standards and flags were floating, whilst on many of the breweries and public buildings bunting had been used with a good effect for decorative purposes. Along the line upon which the Royal train passed, Messrs. Allsopp & Sons', Messrs. Truman, Hanbury, Buxton & Co.'s, and Messrs. Bass & Co.'s piles of beer barrels were very conspicuous in their decorations, and could easily be seen by the illustrious occupants of the carriages. The Royal train passed one minute late.

WAITING FOR THE QUEEN AT DERBY STATION.

The interval of waiting on the platform inside the station—and one had to be in position a good hour before the time—was rather a tedious one, for there was no band playing (as at the outside) for the entertainment of the waiters. Not that the gathering was a very large one, for—apart from the railway staff and servants of the company—the number of passes issued to privileged persons was of the most strictly limited character. This was rendered alike necessary by the stringent regulations of railway companies under such circumstances, and by the special desire of the Court authorities that Her Majesty's reception—at the station, at all events—might be of the quietest possible character. The "dreary drip" of arriving and departing trains was broken only by the arrival and departure of the various detachments of military and volunteers, with their respective bands, the Ashbourne corps (with whom the tall form of Lieutenant Matthews was noticeable) presenting a particularly fine appearance. The Guard of Honour, consisting of 4 sergeants and 100 rank and file of the 2nd Battalion Sherwood Foresters, were stationed on the platform, under the command of Major Carrington, with whom were Lieutenants White and Robinson, and were carefully inspected beforehand by Colonel Hooke, commanding the 45th Depôt, Captain Shaw, as his adjutant, being also very much in evidence. Amongst a host of railway officials present were Mr. G. E. Paget, chairman (in the uniform of a Colonel of the Leicestershire Yeomanry Cavalry), Mr. Chas. Thomas, deputy-chairman, Mr. W. U. Heygate, Mr. L. R. Starkie, High Sheriff of Nottinghamshire (in the uniform of the Yorkshire Yeomanry), Mr. G. Behrens, and Sir James Allport (in Court dress), Mr. John Noble, the General Manager (in the uniform of Honorary Colonel of the Railway Engineers Corps), Mr. W. L. Mugliston, Mr. T. G. Clayton, Mr. S. W. Johnson, Mr. W. H. Adams, Mr. G. H. Turner, Mr. McDonald, Mr. Argyle, Mr. Langdon, Mr. J. Pettifor, Mr. Pakeman, Mr. T. P. Osborne, Mr. Eaton, Mr. W. Towle, Inspector Loveday, Mr. Carr, etc. Presently a welcome telegram was read out by Mr. Mugliston, "The Queen left Leamington safely at six minutes past four," and from this time satisfactory bulletins continued to be received of Her Majesty's progress along the railway route from that place to Derby. Crimson cloth was laid down on the platform, time flew quickly on, and things began to present a very business-like appearance. A little before five o'clock the arrival of the Pullman express from London brought down a number of notabilities, and these were reinforced a little later on by the arrival of the Mayor and Mayoress (with their children) and the Reception Committee. Amongst those present at this time we noticed the Right Hon. the Earl of Latham, Lord Chamberlain of the Queen's Household (in Windsor uniform, carrying his white wand, and wearing his gold key of office), the Right Hon. Sir William Vernon Harcourt, Q.C., M.P. (in Windsor uniform), the Mayor of Derby, Mr. A. Seale Haslam, J.P. (in his gorgeous robes of office elsewhere described), the Mayoress and her children (whose dresses—elsewhere described in detail—were relieved with golden copies of the medal struck for the Mayor in honour of the occasion), Mr. Alderman Roe, M.P. (in Court dress), Alderman Sir John Smith, Knt., J.P. (in Court dress), the Recorder of Derby, Mr. M. C. Buszard, Q.C. (in his state robes and full-bottomed wig), the Bishops of Southwell and Derby (in black silk robes and three-cornered black hats), Colonel Hooke (in brilliant military uniform), the Right Hon. the Earl of Harrington (in the uniform of the Cheshire Yeomanry Cavalry), the High Sheriff of the county, Mr. E. Miller Mundy, J.P. (in the brilliant uniform of a Deputy Lieutenant), Sir Vauncey Crewe, Bart., Sir Andrew Walker, Bart., Mr. H. C. Okeover, J.P., and Mr. Fitzherbert Wright, J.P. (all in the uniform of Deputy Lieutenants), Mr. W. Harvey Whiston, clerk to the borough magistrates (in wig and gown), Captain Parry, chief constable of the county (in a handsome uniform, decked with three medals), the Under Sheriff, Mr. A. Grimwood Taylor, the High Sheriff's chaplain, Rev. E. Murray Robinson (in black gown, with Cambridge M.A. hood), Rev. Canon Knight (in black gown and Cambridge M.A. hood), Dr. Ogle (in the bright red robes of a doctor of medicine), and the remainder of the Reception Committee—mentioned in the carriages hereafter—the Duke of Portland, Lord Vernon, Lord Burton, Major Walter Boden, Sir T. W. Evans, Bart., and Sir Henry Wilmot, Bart., being conspicuous by their unavoidable absence. Colonel Hooke has already been mentioned, and that there were also with him a staff of military officers in brilliant uniform. At 5.20 the pilot engine arrived in charge of Inspector Piper, of the Locomotive Department, and this was, of course, a signal that the arrival of the august visitor was not to be long delayed.

THE ARRIVAL.

The train arrived punctually to the time appointed, the trumpeters blew a martial fanfare from their silver trumpets, and Her Majesty was helped to safely alight from her carriage by a Scotch and an Indian attendant. Her Majesty was received by the Mayor and Mayoress, the High Sheriff, and other dignitaries. The distinguished company forming the Reception Committee, who had been anxiously awaiting Her Majesty's arrival, formed in a line across the platform on each side of the carriage door, and the Queen walked between the lines, repeatedly bowing most graciously as she passed along. Her Majesty proceeded to the Reception Room, where she was followed by the Mayor and Mayoress and their four children, escorted by the sword and mace bearers, and accompanied by Mr. M. C. Buszard, Q.C. (Recorder of Derby), Mr. H. F. Gadsby (Town Clerk of Derby), Mr. Paget (Chairman of the Midland Railway Company), and Mr. John Noble, J.P. (General Manager of that Company). The Queen took up a position opposite the doorway, in about the centre of the room, where she stood ready to receive those who were about to be presented to her. The Lord Chamberlain (the Earl of Lathom) first presented the Mayor to the Queen. The first words which Her Majesty uttered at the close of this interesting ceremony, were words of respect and affection for the memory of Lord Edward Cavendish, who had died a few days previously, and of deep and sincere sympathy with His Grace the Duke of Devonshire, Lord Hartington, and Lady Edward Cavendish and her family, in their great sorrow and bereavement. Her Majesty also thanked the Mayor for having kindly invited her to Derby, and expressed her pleasure at being able to visit "her loyal people" in the town. The Mayor respectfully assured Her Majesty that the people of Derby greatly appreciated the honour and privilege she had conferred upon them by graciously consenting to be present on that memorable occasion. On their behalf he gave her a hearty welcome, and assured Her Majesty that a most affectionate and loyal reception would be accorded to her during her progress through the town. At this juncture His Worship presented Her Majesty with a gold medal (which had been struck from the same die as those supplied to the Reception Committee, the members of the Corporation, and 9,500 teachers and scholars)—having previously obtained permission to make this gift through Sir Henry Ponsonby, the Queen's Secretary. In accepting the gift, Her Majesty, in a few gracious words, expressed the pleasure it afforded her to receive so interesting a memento of her visit to Derby. The Mayor next had the honour of requesting the acceptance by the Princess Beatrice of a silver medal, to commemorate her visit to Derby. (This medal had been struck from the same die as that presented to Her Majesty.) The Princess graciously accepted the gift, and cordially thanked the Mayor for the solicitude he had displayed on behalf of the Royal party, and the fervent cordiality with which they had been welcomed. His Worship gracefully bowed to the Queen and Her Royal Highness, and then retired from their presence. The Earl of Lathom presented the Mayoress to Her Majesty, who was most gracious and condescending to her. The Mayoress was accompanied by her youngest child, Master Eric Seale Haslam, who was attired as a Highlander in a Royal Stuart Tartan, which suited him wonderfully well, and which was greatly admired by the thousands of spectators who subsequently saw him in the procession. The Mayoress requested Her Majesty's acceptance of a magnificent bouquet of flowers, composed of choice floral specimens—orchids: cattleyas, lelia purpurata, and odontoglossums, being the principal varieties used in its composition. The bouquet was in the "Standish," or flat style, which Her Majesty likes, as it can be put down at any moment without injuring the flowers. It was supplied by Messrs. John Standish & Co., Court Florists, of London. Her Majesty graciously accepted the bouquet, expressing her great admiration of the flowers, and commanded that the bouquet should be placed in the Royal train, so that the bright and beautiful component parts of it might not be injured during her progress through the town, and the performance of the various ceremonies assigned to her. Her Majesty showed her pleasure by allowing the Mayoress to kiss her hand, after which she took hold of Master Eric's hand, and graciously permitted him to kiss her hand. The Lord Chamberlain presented her two daughters, Miss Hilda Seale Haslam and Miss Edith Seale Haslam, to the Princess Beatrice, whose charming amiability immediately won their hearts. Miss Hilda presented the Princess with a lovely bouquet, which she gracefully accepted. Three bronze medals (struck from the same die as those previously presented) were also handed to the Princess for her three children, a thoughtful gift, with which she appeared very pleased. Mr. Buszard, Q.C., Mr. Gadsby, Mr. Paget, and Mr. Noble were then respectively presented to the Queen, at the conclusion of which ceremony Her Majesty proceeded to the Royal carriage, accompanied by the Princess Beatrice and Prince Henry of Battenberg. The procession was then formed, and the Royal party entered the town amidst the acclamations of the assembled multitudes who lined the streets, occupied numerous platforms, the windows and roofs of houses, and every available place from which a glimpse could be obtained of the Royal visitors.

THE SCENE OUTSIDE.

The keen interest taken in the Royal visit found exemplification in the fact that the various stands in the Midland Road began to find occupants so early as 2 p.m., and for a considerable period before that the barriers along both Midland and London Roads were lined two and three deep, notwithstanding that the afternoon's weather bore out the promise of the morning, and was the reverse of what is traditionally known as "Queen's weather." A dripping rain, in fact, fell continually out of the clouds which loomed up from the northeastern horizon before a wind which grew gradually more and more chilly. The meteorological conditions, however, damped not the ardour of the tens of thousands who lined the route, patiently passing the time until the hoisting of the Royal Standard on the Station front should proclaim the arrival of the train conveying Her Majesty and suite. As 3 o'clock drew near, the roads were cleared of pedestrians, and the long lines of humanity upon the pavements became thicker. Shortly after this time the children of the Railway Servants' Orphanage, who, with those from St. Andrew's Schools, shared a large stand in Midland Road, filed into their places in an orderly fashion; the other stands also gradually filled up. At this time rain came down rather more smartly, and the gloom overhead seemed to threaten a more copious downfall. As the drops came down umbrellas went up, until the whole of Midland Road was lined with them, and the stands seemed to be growing black mushrooms. Fortunately, the threats of Jupiter Pluvius were not carried into effect in their entirety, and the necessity for umbrellas became less. The weary interval of waiting was naturally spent in the admiration of the decorations, and those in Midland Road were of an exceptional character. The triumphal arch of greenery between the Midland Hotel and the Shareholders' Room came in for the greatest amount of attention, and to it was universally accorded premier honours. The decoration of the Station front was rather one of illumination than otherwise, and was seen at its best during the evening. The appearance of the street looking from the Station towards the London Road end came in for much appreciation, for beyond a fairyland of pink and white festoons was seen the castellated arch with portcullis, which must have reminded Her Majesty of the one beneath which she made her exit from Windsor early in the afternoon. The long period of inaction was suitably relieved by such little humorous incidents as are welcomed by the populace under similar circumstances. There was the inevitable "Derby dog," who scampered along the whole length of the course, frightened to madness by the roars of laughter which greeted its appearance. Twice did this unfortunate mongrel run the gauntlet. Then, again, peals of ironical laughter greeted the arrival of a corporation cart with sand for the roadway. Another incident which elicited much applause from the Railway Servants' Orphanage children was the appearance of the sword-bearer in the dignity of his uniform. Apart from the element of comedy the time passed pleasantly enough in the vicinity of the Band of the 2nd Volunteer Battalion Derbyshire Regiment, which occupied a stand at the Railway Station, and the Band of the Robin Hoods, who were located at the junction of Midland and London Roads. Then the Orphanage and St. Andrew's children rehearsed the National Anthem and Auld Lang Syne and practised volley cheering, and this caused an agreeable diversion. About 3.45 p.m. the men of the 2nd Battalion Cheshire Regiment marched from the station to take up their position on the route. It is worthy of note that each man wore a sprig of green oak in his cap. It may not be generally known that the wearing of this same sprig in the presence of Royalty is a privilege belonging to this particular regiment in acknowledgment of their having been instrumental in saving the life of King George the Second at the battle of Dettingen. Then came a troop of Derbyshire Yeomanry Cavalry, under the command of Captain Dugdale, and it is not too much to say that the troopers were very deservedly cheered for their soldierly bearing, and the smart appearance of both horses and accoutrements, and they did justice to their selection as a portion of the guard of honour. It was now 5.0 p.m., and the interest plainly began to intensify. The State coaches appearing at the top of Midland Road became the signal for renewed cheering, and almost simultaneously the remainder of the 2nd Volunteer Battalion Derbyshire Regiment came upon the scene from the railway station. Midland Road had up to this time been kept by the representatives of the civil power alone, but within a very few minutes the traditional "thin red line" extended on both sides of the way, the scarlet uniforms adding considerably to the picturesqueness of the scene. Another brief period and the civic procession hove in sight, preceded by the orthodox halberdiers and the borough banners, the carriers of which had a lively time of it owing to the wind. Time now passed rapidly and excitement intensified. Only fifteen minutes separated us from the Royal arrival. This was reduced to ten, to five, and then a burst of applause greeted the raising of the Royal Standard, announcing the arrival of Her Majesty and Suite. At 5.40 p.m. the civic procession entered their carriages, and moved away. The Mayor's carriage was a large and exceedingly handsome one, painted claret colour, relieved with red, and with an interior beautifully lined with morocco. That of the High Sheriff was also particularly fine. It was painted the family colour, blue, pricked out with red, and lined with cloth and morocco, embellished with the arms of the family.

THE ROYAL ROUTE TO THE MARKET PLACE.

Hardly had the Corporation procession reached the top of the street, and the plaudits by which it was again greeted had by no means died away in the distance, before the first of the escort of Dragoon Guards entered the road from the station premises, and a deep-bayed roar of welcome testified to the fact that the Queen had entered, at exactly 5.45 p.m., on her journey townward. The procession was marshalled in the following order:—

Mounted Police.
Distance between the Processions, 300 to 400 yards.

HER MAJESTY'S PROCESSION.

Lieut.-Colonel Delacombe, Chief Constable.
Escort of the 6th Dragoon Guards (Carabineers), accompanied by Major Parker, Capt. Massey, and Lieut. Francis.

FIRST CARRIAGE.

An Officer of Carabineers.

THE QUEEN.

T.R.H. Prince and Princess Henry of Battenberg.

An Officer of Carabineers.

Major-General Sir Henry Ewart, Equerry.
Major-General H. C. Wilkinson, C.B., Commanding N.E. District.
Capt. Birkbeck, Aide-de-Camp.
Col. T. Kelly-Kenny, Assistant Adjutant-General N.E. District.
Sixteen men of the 6th Dragoon Guards (Carabineers).

SECOND CARRIAGE.

The Countess of Erroll (Lady-in-Waiting).
The Honourable Ethel Cadogan (Maid of Honour).
Miss McNeill (Woman of the Bed-chamber).
Miss M. Cochrane (Lady-in-Waiting to Princess Beatrice).
Col. H. H. Hooke (Commanding Troops at Derby).

THIRD CARRIAGE.

The Right Honourable The Earl of Lathom, Lord Chamberlain.
The Right Hon. Henry Matthews, Q.C., M.P. (Secretary of State for the Home Department).
General The Right Hon. Sir Henry Ponsonby (Private Secretary to Her Majesty).
Lieut.-Col. Sir Fleetwood Edwards (Assistant Private Secretary to Her Majesty).

FOURTH CARRIAGE.

Lieut.-Col. The Lord Edward Clinton } Grooms-in-Waiting.
The Honourable Alexander Yorke
Dr. James Reid, C.B. (Medical Attendant).
Mr. Muther (German Secretary).

FIFTH CARRIAGE (closed).
Munshi Abdul Kerim and two Indian Attendants.

Remainder of Escort of the 6th Dragoon Guards (Carabineers).

Her Majesty's reception may be said to have been most hearty and spontaneous, and her progress was rightly characterised as uniformly and unequivocally magnificent. The National Anthem of course burst from the 2nd Volunteer Battalion Band as Her Majesty entered the scene, and this was repeated in turn by the Robin Hoods as the Royal coach passed, and then by the Band of the 45th Regiment at the Infirmary, the South Notts. Temperance Band in Traffic Street, the Band of the 2nd Cheshire Regiment on the Spot arch, the Burton Band at the Five Lamps, and lastly by the Grenadiers in the Market Square. It is to be remarked that the Royal carriages, notwithstanding that rain continued to fall slightly, remained open throughout the journey, the Queen and Princess Beatrice graciously and continuously bowing their acknowledgments, and it was remarked that Prince Henry appeared to appreciate the right hearty reception accorded them by the people of Derby. Her Majesty evinced much interest in the appearance of the Railway Servants' Orphanage Children, as indeed she did in the children's stands throughout the journey. The floral trophy at the junction of St. James's Street and the Corn Market attracted her attention as she admiringly drew the notice of Princess Beatrice to it.

THE VISIT TO MARKET SQUARE.

GRAND RECEPTION AND CEREMONY.

The hour of waiting for the important event of the day is always the most tedious. It is like "The children's hour," when one is able to rest from the busier occupations of the day and wait for the lighting of the candles. So it was in the Market Place as we waited for the advent of the Queen, only that the hour was extended to three, and so the suspense was correspondingly prolonged. But the vast concourse of spectators who formed a living fringe and border to the Market Square had come to see, and they were content to wait in patience. The period of waiting, however, was not unoccupied, nor the temper of the populace unduly strained. There is always an element of accommodation in an English crowd, and the mutual desire which is ever present to help each other to enliven the tedium of waiting does much to assuage the feeling of weariness that is apt on such occasions to creep over one. The official programme fixed the time of the Queen's arrival at a quarter to six o'clock, but before two o'clock had struck from the Town Hall Tower the vacant spaces on the stands and galleries had begun to fill and the barriers held back a multitude of gazers who crowded upon them in several rows. Fortunately the weather, though cold and rather cheerless, was on the whole fair and dry, and therefore the main element of depression was absent, and to state the converse, one of the main elements of success was present to the

Photo. by] FLORAL CANOPY, CORNER OF ST. JAMES'S STREET. [T. Scotton.

scene. In the earlier hours of the afternoon the spectacle was rather sombre in its appearance. The flags, which were floating from every house top and from the tower of All Saints' Church, displaying a profusion of Royal Standards, hung rather listless, and were only unfurled as a passing breeze caught their folds and revealed their various devices to the eyes of the spectators. The band of the Grenadier Guards, muffled up in their storm cloaks, and wearing the busby, occupied the stand erected in the centre of the square, and during the afternoon helped to relieve the *ennui* by a fine performance of the programme following:—

MARCH ...	"Laud auf, Laud ab!" ...	*Unrath.*
INVOCATION TO BATTLE	"Rienzi"	*Wagner.*
SELECTION	"Faust"	*Gounod.*
VALSE	..."Tout-Paris"	*Waldteufel.*
OVERTURE	..."Tannhäuser"	*Wagner.*
SELECTION ...	"The Gondoliers" ...	*Sullivan.*
VALSE	"Donau-Wellen" ...	*Ivanovici.*
MARCH ...	"Abschied von Foesani"	*Ivanovici.*
SELECTION ...	..."Lohengrin"	*Wagner.*
VALSE	"Toreador"	*Royle.*
FEST MARSCH	..."Tannhäuser"	*Wagner.*
SELECTION	"La Cigale"	*Audran.*
OVERTURE	"Rob Roy"	*Foster.*
MARCHE MILITAIRE	... ...	*Gounod.*

As the afternoon advanced the scene began to grow in animation and in beauty. One by one the windows surrounding the Market Square began to fill; then occasional faces began to appear on the various roofs, then the galleries by which the square was enclosed were occupied by the ticket holders, and with few exceptions by four o'clock not a seat was without its occupier, not a window but was alive with human faces, not a point of vantage but had its occupant. And still an hour and three quarters must elapse, at the least, before the object of our assembling could arrive and our curiosity be gratified. But as the hour advanced for the arrival of the Queen the tedium of waiting declined. It is the earlier hours that hang so heavily. The later ones become more full of animation, and the knowledge that the interval of waiting is growing shorter helps one to bear it in greater patience. And besides there is more to distract the attention and occupy the mind. So it was on this occasion. Shortly before four o'clock the guard of honour, formed of the men of the First Volunteer Battalion The Sherwood Foresters (Derbyshire Regiment), under the command of Captain Wheeler, arrived and took up their place. The Market Place was kept by a detachment of the same regiment, under the command of Lieut.-Colonel Corfield. The children of the various schools who were to take part in the welcome of song to Her Majesty, began to arrive about four o'clock, and quickly took up their positions on the stand erected for their accommodation. They arrived in quick succession, and included children from the Gerard Street, Orchard Street, and Ashbourne Road Board Schools, All Saints', St. Alkmund's, and St. Paul's, from the St. Michael's Church School, the St. Mary's Roman Catholic School, and the St. Anne's Church School.

Soon after four o'clock the carriages began to arrive by which the distinguished participators in the events of the day were to be conveyed to the railway station to be present to meet the Royal train, and for some time there was a scene of great activity. As the carriages came up one by one they were speedily occupied, and as they left the enclosure the occupants came in for a good deal of cheering, especially from the school children, who

THE TOWN HALL, DERBY.

probably had never before been privileged to witness so many scarlet uniforms and so much gold braid in the course of one afternoon. There were a few changes in the *personnel* of the procession as it left the Town Hall for the station, and it consisted of the following ladies and gentlemen :—

FIRST CARRIAGE.
A. Woodiwiss, Esq., J.P.
W. H. Whiston, Esq. (Clerk to the Justices).
W. G. Wheeldon, Esq.
J. Bailey, Esq., J.P.

SECOND CARRIAGE.
W. Turpie, Esq.. J.P.
W. H. Worthington, Esq., J.P.
Herbert Strutt, Esq., J.P.
Henry Swingler, Esq., J.P.

THIRD CARRIAGE.
H. H. Bemrose, Esq., J.P.
Lieut.-Col. Buchanan, J.P.
Walter Evans, Esq., J.P.
Rowland Smith, Esq., J.P.

FOURTH CARRIAGE.
Henry Boden, Esq., J.P.
W. Hobson, Esq., J.P.
Fitzherbert Wright, Esq., J.P.
W. Ogle, Esq., M.D.

FIFTH CARRIAGE.
Lieutenant-General Thomson. J.P.
U. Sowter, Esq., J.P.
Sir J. Smith, Knt., J.P.
Sir J. J. Allport, Knt., J.P.

SIXTH CARRIAGE.
Sir William Vernon Harcourt, Q.C., M.P.
Sir Vauncey Harpur Crewe, Bart.
Thomas Roe, Esq., M.P.
Lewis V. Harcourt, Esq.

SEVENTH CARRIAGE
Sir Andrew Barclay Walker, Bart.
Lord Scarsdale.
H. C. Okeover, Esq.
Captain Parry (Chief Constable of Derbyshire).

EIGHTH CARRIAGE.
The Earl of Harrington.
Sir Francis Burdett, Bart.
Lady Burdett.

NINTH CARRIAGE.
The Bishop of Southwell.
The Bishop of Derby.
Canon Knight.

TENTH CARRIAGE.
The High Sheriff (E. M. Mundy, Esq.)
The High Sheriff's Chaplain (Rev. E. Murray Robinson).
The Under Sheriff (S. A. Grimwood Taylor, Esq.)

ELEVENTH CARRIAGE.
The Recorder (M. C. Buszard, Esq., Q.C.)
The Town Clerk (H. F. Gadsby, Esq.)
Alfred Victor Haslam, Esq
Miss Edith Haslam.

Trumpeters.
The Mace Bearers.

TWELFTH CARRIAGE.
The Mayor.
The Mayoress.
Master Eric Seale Haslam.
Miss Hilda Haslam.

The costumes worn by the gentlemen who took part in the procession were brilliant in colour, and lent a variety to the scene. In the first carriage, Mr. Whiston, the Clerk to the Borough and County Magistrates, wore his robes of office; in the third carriage, Colonel Buchanan wore the uniform of the 1st Battalion Derbyshire Volunteer Regiment, of which he is the Colonel ; in the fifth carriage, Sir John Smith and Sir James Allport wore Court dress; Sir William Harcourt wore the Windsor uniform ; and Mr. Thomas Roe, M.P., wore Court dress. The Earl of Harrington was wearing the uniform of the Cheshire Yeomanry Cavalry. The Bishop of Southwell and the Bishop of Derby wore their bishop's robes. The High Sheriff (E. M. Mundy, Esq.) wore the uniform of a Deputy Lieutenant. The Recorder wore his Recorder's robes and a full-bottomed wig; the Town Clerk was attired in Court dress, and wore his robes of office. The Mayor was attired in his Mayoral robes, and the Mayoress wore the dress which our readers will find described elsewhere, whilst the sons of

the Mayor were very beautifully dressed, the youngest wearing a Scotch costume. The dresses worn by the daughters of the Mayor are referred to in detail on another page. Among those present on the gallery behind the Royal platform were the following :—
Sir James Allport, the High Sheriff (E. M. Mundy, Esq.), Colonel Cavendish, Mr. Alderman Kempson, Mayor of Leicester (wearing his chain of office and accompanied by the mace-bearer); Aldermen H. H. Bemrose, J.P.; J. G. Crompton, J.P.; W. Higginbottom, J.P.; W. Hobson, J.P.; G. Holme, J.P.; C. Leech, J.P.; F. Longdon, J.P.; J. W. Newbold, J.P.; T. Roe, M.P.; R. Russell, J.P.; W. B. Sherwin; Sir John Smith, J.P.; U. Sowter, J.P.; S. Whitaker; A. Woodiwiss, J.P. Councillors E. T. Ann, S. Bennett, T. H. Bennett, G. Bottomley, J.P., C. C. Bowring, J.P., A. Butterworth, G. Cholerton, W. Clemson, T. Cox, G. Dean, F. Stone, R. W. Spriggs, T. Sims, J. C. Russell, I. Roome, T. L. Riley, W. H. Marsden, W. Lowe, F. E. Leech, Dr. Laurie, J. Jackson, J. Hill, W. Heathcote, J.P., E. Haslam, W. Hart, T. H. Harrison, J. Grundy, Dr. Gentles, J. H. Foulds, G. Foster, G. Fletcher, S. Evans, E. C. Ellis, F. Duesbury, J. P. Doherty, Hon. F. Strutt, G. Sutherland, G. B. Unsworth, J. Walley, C. Wallis, P. Wallis, F. Ward, W. Williamson, W. W. Winter, J. Wright; Mr. W. Wheeldon; Mr. W. Bemrose, J.P.; Mr. W. Turner Shaw, J.P.; Mr. P. B. Chadfield; Mr. W. Cooper; Mr. W. Crowther; Mr. W. Haslam; Mr. Marshall; Mr. T. W. Coxon; Mr. G. Brigden; Dr. Sims; Mr. W. H. Whiston; Mr. Rowland Smith, J.P.; Mr. J. Bailey, J.P.; Mr. J. Wright Baker, J.P.; Mr. G. Frost; Mr. H. F. Gadsby; Mr. J. Wills; Mr. J. Sterndale Bennett; Mr. R. J. Fittall; Mr. John Close (the Borough Coroner); the Rev. J. S. Owen; the Rev. J. H. Askwith; the Rev. J. E. Matthews; the Rev. G. Hunsworth, etc., etc.

When the procession had left, there was a temporary adjournment to the Town Hall, where light refreshments were served to the ticket holders. The rain, which, notwithstanding many threatenings, had held off bravely, began to fall rather heavily for a few moments, and the stands in a moment became a mere conglomeration of umbrellas. The sun, however, struggled bravely, and so far overcame, that for the remainder of the afternoon the weather remained dry, if cold. There was little to break the slow monotony of waiting. Shortly after five o'clock, Mr. W. Crowther, the curator of the Derby Free Library and Museum, stepped to the front of the band stand, and the children sang "God save the Queen" and "Auld Lang Syne," by way of a dress rehearsal, accompanied by the band of the Grenadier Guards. In regard to time there was a good deal to be desired, but the youngsters sang splendidly in tune, and with characteristic nonchalance. As they rose in their seats to the invitation of their conductor the children presented a very pleasing and picturesque sight, but it was evident that their minds were with the brilliant uniforms and the moving throng, for the last verse of the old Scottish melody almost immediately was succeeded by a vigorous cheer for some passing notability. Still another half-hour to wait. The sun began to shine soon after half-past five, and with the brighter sky came a corresponding buoyancy all round. As six o'clock approached, the distinguished visitors who had left the square an hour before to welcome Her Majesty at the Railway Station, returned to take their places near their Sovereign while she performed the ceremony undertaken by her at the Town Hall. The band of the Grenadier Guards took up their position facing the dais. They had now divested themselves of their heavy cloaks, and their uniform of scarlet and gold shone in the somewhat fitful gleams of sunshine with a welcome brilliance. Just as the hour of six arrived was heard the distant cheering of the thousands who lined the streets all the way from the station. A moment afterwards came the order " Guard of Honour, shoulder arms," and the band and children rang out the commencing bars of the National Anthem, as the Queen's carriage emerged round the corner and drew up at the dais. Her Majesty, all smiles, bowed almost continuously to the acclamations of the people, and as her eye wandered from one side to the other, and she caught the strains of the children's voices, a perceptible indication of emotion passed over her face. Her Majesty looked remarkably well in health. The writer had occasion to see her immediately before her departure for the Continent early in the year, and remarked a great change for the better. She was accompanied by Her Royal Highness the Princess Beatrice and Prince Henry of Battenberg. As soon as the strains of the National Anthem had died away the right Hon. the Earl of Lathom, Lord Chamberlain, carrying his wand of office, stepped forward, and in turn introduced to Her Majesty the gentlemen whose function it was to present the addresses Her Majesty had consented to receive. First came Mr. M. C. Buszard, recorder of Derby, who read the address of the Corporation, as follows :—

DERBY CORPORATION.

To Her Most Excellent Majesty the Queen of Great Britain and Ireland.

May it please your Majesty,—

We, the Mayor, Corporation, and Burgesses of the borough of Derby, in Council assembled, desire permission to give public expression to our sentiments of loyal devotion, and to tender our most heartfelt welcome to your Majesty on the auspicious occasion of your first official visit to our ancient and loyal borough.

While our town has shared in no mean measure the national prosperity and progress which your Majesty, under the Divine guidance, has been enabled to secure for this nation and people by wise and beneficent government, it has likewise participated in the great awakening and growth of humanity and pity which has found expression in so many works for the relief and mitigation of human suffering, and which will be for ever associated with your Majesty's personal influence and name, ranking among the most glorious achievements of your illustrious reign.

Before proceeding to refer in particular to the immediate occasion of your gracious presence amongst us, with pardonable pride we trust we may be permitted to put your Majesty in remembrance of the fact that Derby was a place of importance in Saxon times, as attested by the Venerable Bede writing in 666, and was visited by King Edwin about the year 627. In 874 King Alfred the Great constituted it the metropolis of the county, and honoured it with his presence. About that time his brave daughter Athelfleda was in command of the forces and defeated the Danes in 918. In Domesday Book Derby is described as a Royal Borough of Edward the Confessor, and privileged with a Mint. Derby was made a corporate town by Henry I., who granted a charter about the year 1100. This charter was renewed and enlarged by Henry II., and confirmed about 1327 by King Henry III. In the year 1217 King John visited Derby, and granted a most important charter to the town, conferring great powers thereupon. In 1264 King Henry III. and his son, Prince Edward, visited the town. King Edward II. about 1322 visited the town with his army. In 1422 King Henry VI. granted a charter to the town. In 1466 King Edward IV. confirmed the charter. In 1488 King Richard III. also confirmed the said charter. In the year 1558

Queen Mary granted the town a charter. On January 13th, 1585, Mary Queen of Scots stayed a night in Derby. In 1624 James I. and Prince Charles were also a night in the town, and the King confirmed the old Town Charters. In 1635 and 1641 King Charles I. visited Derby, and in 1637 that monarch granted it a charter, and in or about 1680-82 King Charles II., granted the town our present and latest charter.

Returning with especial pleasure and pride to the ever-to-be-remembered event of this day, we crave permission to express our gratitude for your Majesty's kindly interest in one of the greatest and most important of our public charities—that of our Infirmary, on whose past work we look with pardonable pride and gratitude, and to whose future ministry we look forward with much regard and confidence.

We beg to assure your Majesty that the memory of this occasion will be cherished with pleasure and satisfaction in the annals of our borough and county, and we pray that, with the Divine assistance, the new building, to whose commencement your Majesty has this day accorded your gracious favour and welcome presence, may continue to dispense healing and succour to many generations yet to come. We venture to express our confidence that the sentiments of loyalty, gratitude, and pride associated with this auspicious beginning will furnish a powerful incentive to the furtherance of that work of mercy and humanity which is at once a public duty as well as a public privilege.

To this recognition of the special services rendered by your Majesty's visit to our town it is not unfitting that we should append some general expression of the deep and cordial sentiments of loyalty which animate us as your humble subjects.

The County of Derby, whose chief town we represent, has, we hope and venture to believe, never failed to furnish its due quota of favoured and trusty servants for the defence of your Majesty's realm, as well as for counsel and assistance in the arduous duties connected with the governance of this wide and glorious Empire, in the history of which your Majesty's happy reign forms the latest and most illustrious page; and we confidently hope that the future will show no diminution in that sense of public duty and loyal attachment to the person of your Majesty and the interests of the realm which we humbly claim for our borough and county in the past.

Not a few of those present to-day will remember the enthusiasm and affection evoked on the occasion of your Majesty's passage through the town in 1843 and 1849, in company with your Majesty's illustrious and lamented Consort; and of the subsequent visit, nineteen years ago, of their Royal Highnesses the Prince and Princess of Wales.

In the name of the whole body of loyal inhabitants of this borough, we embrace this opportunity of humbly expressing our sense of the many blessings we have enjoyed during your Majesty's long and glorious reign; and we earnestly pray that life and those marvellous powers of body and mind vouchsafed to you by Divine Providence, may long be preserved, and that your Majesty may continue to preside over the destinies of this nation for many prosperous years to come.

Given under the Common Seal of the Corporation of Derby, this 21st day of May, 1891.

(Signed)

Mayor of the Borough.

Town Clerk.

The address was written on ten pages of vellum, in German text with illuminated capitals and other adornments, bound together into a volume which forms a handsome quarto of 9 in. by 12 in., and was placed in a casket of gold and ivory, described hereafter. The full description of the address is as follows :—The first page opens with the commencement of the address. At the head are the Royal Arms of England, supported on the left by those of the borough, suspended from a stem of Tudor roses, showing the association of the borough and county in the great work inaugurated by Her Majesty, the rose being the badge of the county of Derby; and on the right by those of the Mayor, Sir Alfred S. Haslam. Passing to the second page, there are miniature views of All Saints' Church from Irongate, an old view of Derby— showing the silk mill and St. Mary's Bridge, and another view of the town from Burton Road ; the emblematic adornments being sprays of oak with silver acorns in golden cups, this for the Church of old England. Next we come to views of Chatsworth and Hardwick Hall,

H. F. GADSBY, ESQ. (*Town Clerk.*)
(*From a Photo. by W. W. Winter, Derby.*)

seats of the Lord Lieutenant of the County and the Marquis of Hartington—celebrated historic houses both. The decorative border is formed of roses heraldically treated, and intended to represent England. Following this is a view of Haddon Hall from the park, the romantic seat of the Duke of Rutland, and a view of the first court by moonlight. The border to this page is formed from the acanthus leaf, an ornamental interlude between the time when this kingdom had not yet become the United Kingdom. Turning to page five are found views of Bolsover Castle—a seat of the Duke of Portland, and Willersley Castle—a seat built by Sir Richard Arkwright, the founder of the cotton trade. The border is shamrock for Ireland. On the next page is an emblematic leek for Wales, the miniatures being views of Ilam Hall and a north view of Dovedale. Continuing, we find Matlock High Tor and the Ferry, Matlock, with acanthus scroll for border. After this Monsal Dale and another view in

Dovedale, with a thistle scroll border for bonnie Scotland, which came in last and so completed the United Kingdom as we now have it. The last page but one is formed of acanthus scrolls, and the last has a scroll of seaweed, intended to convey the idea of the silver streak which girds and protects these islands. Here the address ends, being signed by His Worship the Mayor and the Town Clerk, and is sealed with the fine old common seal of the borough. This magnificent work of art—alike happy in its inception, admirable in its taste and style, and exquisite in its workmanship—was designed and executed by our talented townsman, Mr. George Bailey, of 32, Crompton Street, Derby, whose antiquarian knowledge, great artistic skill, and long experience as an illuminator of the first rank, pre-eminently fitted him for the execution of the task which he has so well performed. The binding of the address is a beautiful specimen of gold tooling, after the manner of De Rome, early eighteenth century, with Harleian borders, the insides being in fawn coloured calf tooled to match ; the cover being in smooth crimson morocco leather—a beautiful work wrought with infinite pains by clever and careful workmen. This binding is from the well-known establishment of Messrs. Bemrose and Sons, of Derby and London. In painting this address the idea of the artist was not merely to ornament the pages but to make these ornaments tell the tale of the gradual growth of the United Kingdom ; a process that was the growth of many centuries. The parti-coloured rose was adopted at the birth of Henry VIII. in 1492, as issued from the red rose of Lancaster by his father, Henry VII., and the white rose of York by his mother Elizabeth of York. The trefoil or shamrock of Ireland was introduced at the union in 1801. Of the leek, for Wales, there are no precise data, but it may be reckoned from the birth of the first Prince of Wales, Edward II., at Carnarvon Castle ; whilst the thistle, for Scotland, was introduced in 1687 by James II.

The Mayor then stepped to the front, and presented the Address to the Queen, who received it in its beautiful casket with evident pleasure, and when the cheering had subsided graciously read the following reply, which was inaudible except to those who stood near to the Royal equipage :—

"I have received with much pleasure your loyal and dutiful address, and I highly appreciate the cordial welcome which has been accorded to me by my faithful people at Derby.

"It is with sincere satisfaction that I observe how largely your ancient borough has shared in the great prosperity and progress of my kingdom, and I feel encouraged in meeting the responsibilities that devolve on me when I know that I have the hearty support of my faithful subjects, and I am glad to be here to-day.

"I cannot but feel the greatest sorrow, which I am sure is shared by you all, at the death of Lord Edward Cavendish, who was so universally loved. I condole sincerely with his father and family, and I regret that this sad event should have deprived us of the presence of Lord Hartington on this occasion."

The other addresses were then presented in the following order, but Her Majesty simply received them, and they were handed over to the custody of Lieutenant-Colonel Sir Fleetwood Edwards, the assistant private secretary to Her Majesty, who waited by to receive them :—

THE MAGISTRATES OF THE BOROUGH.

The address from the Borough Magistrates was presented by Mr. Bailey, J.P. :—

To the Queen's Most Excellent Majesty.

May it please your Majesty,—

We, the Justices of the Peace for the Borough of Derby, beg to offer to your Majesty the expression of our deep loyalty and devotion on the occasion of your visit to this ancient and loyal town.

In common with all the inhabitants of the town and county of Derby, we gratefully recognise in the act which your Majesty graciously performs to-day at the County Hospital an instance of that personal interest in all that concerns the health and well-being of your people which has ever distinguished your Majesty's beneficent reign.

We thankfully acknowledge the many great blessings and privileges which, through Divine Providence, have been secured to this nation during your Majesty's reign, and we pray that your rule over the Empire may be long continued.

With every feeling of profound fealty and attachment to your throne and person,

We are,
Your Majesty's loyal and devoted subjects and servants,
(Signed)

W. HARVEY WHISTON, Clerk.

A. SEALE HASLAM, Mayor.
JOHN BAILEY, J.P.

The address was on a scroll of vellum, with a mediæval border, in which were introduced the arms of the borough of Derby, and the monogram "V.R.I.," mounted on scarlet silk with white fringe, the whole executed by Messrs. Bemrose and Sons.

THE COUNTY COUNCIL OF DERBYSHIRE.

The address of the Derbyshire County Council was presented by Sir Francis Burdett, Bart., as the representative of Sir William Evans, Bart., the chairman. It was as follows :—

To the Queen's Most Excellent Majesty.

May it please your Majesty,—

We, the Chairman, Vice-Chairman, Aldermen and Councillors of the Council of Derbyshire, humbly tender to your Majesty our grateful thanks for having so graciously acceded to the request that your Majesty would lay the foundation-stone of the Derbyshire New General Infirmary.

We beg to assure your Majesty that we deeply feel the honour that your visit will confer on us, and on all classes of the inhabitants of our county; and we are very sensible of the benefits which the Infirmary will derive from your Majesty's gracious presence and support.

We are also thankful that an opportunity is afforded to us—a newly constituted County Authority—of tendering to your Majesty these expressions of welcome to our county, and our profound loyalty to your Majesty's person. And we further earnestly pray that your Majesty may be long spared to reign over our country.

We are with deepest veneration your Majesty's loyal subjects and faithful servants.

By order of the Council,
(Signed) T. W. EVANS, Chairman.
W. HEATHCOTE, Councillor.
N. J. HUGHES-HALLETT, Deputy-Clerk.

This address was on a scroll of vellum, executed by Messrs. Bemrose and Sons. The ornamentation was very chaste and appropriate, consisting of a border, with the rose, shamrock, and thistle treated conventionally. At the corners, on shields, were the arms of England, Ireland, and Scotland, the two centre ornaments at the sides being the monogram, D.C.C. (Derbyshire County Council), and the seal of the Council. The scroll was draped in rich blue silk, with a white silk fringe and tassels, the whole enclosed in a casket covered with blue morocco, neatly finished in gold.

THE MAGISTRATES OF THE COUNTY.

Sir Francis Burdett, Bart., next presented the following address from the County Magistrates :—

To the Queen's Most Excellent Majesty.

We, your Majesty's Justices of the Peace for the County of Derby, present our humble duty to your Majesty.

We tender to your Majesty our grateful thanks for having so graciously acceded to the request that your Majesty would lay the foundation-stone of the Derbyshire New General Infirmary.

We assure your Majesty that we deeply feel the honour that your visit will confer on us and on all classes of your Majesty's subjects in our county; and we are very sensible of the benefit which the Infirmary will derive from your Majesty's gracious presence and support.

We are also thankful that an opportunity is afforded to us of tendering to your Majesty these expressions of welcome to our county, and our profound loyalty to your Majesty's person. And we further earnestly pray that your Majesty may be long spared to reign over our country.

We are, with deepest veneration, your Majesty's loyal subjects and faithful servants.

On behalf of the Justices of the Peace in the County of Derby.

T. W. EVANS, Chairman.

The address was a very elegant scroll of vellum, backed by red silk and gold fringe. The border was designed in fifteenth century Spanish style, the scroll fitted into a red morocco case of good design by Messrs. Bemrose and Sons.

DERBY BOARD OF GUARDIANS.

Mr. W. Harvey Whiston, accompanied by Mr. P. B. Chadfield, presented the address of the Derby Board of Guardians :—

To the Queen's Most Excellent Majesty.

May it please your Majesty,—

We, your Majesty's most faithful and loyal subjects, the Guardians of the Poor of the Derby Union, desire to approach your Majesty on the auspicious and happy occasion of your Majesty's visit to this ancient Borough, and to express our feelings of unbounded loyalty to the throne, and of warm attachment to your Majesty's person. We are encouraged to do this, knowing what a deep interest your Majesty always takes in the welfare of even the poorest of your subjects, and feeling sure that your Majesty will be gratified to hear that not only are the destitute poor well cared for in the Derby Union, but that there is also a spacious and well-appointed Infirmary attached to the Union, where a large number of sick poor receive every comfort and attention.

We desire to accord your Majesty a most dutiful and loyal welcome on this your visit to Derby, and to express the joy and pleasure which your Majesty's visit has created in this loyal Borough.

We pray that it may please Almighty God to spare your Majesty long to reign over us, and to continue to encourage us all by the noble example of your own life, to perform every man his duty to his Queen and country humanely and faithfully.

We are, your Majesty's most dutiful subjects.

Given under the common seal of the Guardians of the Poor of the Derby Union, this 21st day of May, one thousand eight hundred and ninety-one.

EDWARD HENRY ABNEY, Chairman.
PHILIP B. CHADFIELD, Clerk.

The address was on a scroll of vellum, lined with blue and white silk. The design consisted of a vignette of the proposed new Poor Law Offices and illuminated floral border, the whole, enclosed in a round morocco case, being executed by Messrs. Bemrose and Sons.

DERBY SCHOOL BOARD.

Mr. W. Turner Shaw, J.P., who was accompanied by Mr. William Cooper, presented the address from the Derby School Board :—

To the Queen's Most Excellent Majesty.

May it please your Majesty,—

We, your Majesty's most faithful subjects, the members of the Derby School Board, desire to approach your Majesty with the expression of our sincere and dutiful respect and gratitude on the occasion of the welcome visit of your Majesty to our ancient Borough.

We would humbly venture to remind your Majesty that the great work of the education of the rising generation, in which we are engaged, has, during your Majesty's benignant reign, greatly advanced and prospered ; and we, with all your faithful and loyal subjects, do not cease to remember the great and loving interest always manifested by your Most Gracious Majesty, and also by His late lamented Royal Highness the Prince Consort, not only in regard to the education of the young, but in everything tending to the enlightenment of the people of these realms.

Earnestly desiring for your Majesty, and all the members of your Royal House, continued life and happiness.

We are, may it please your Majesty,

Your most loyal and dutiful subjects.

Signed on behalf of The Derby School Board,

WM. TURNER SHAW,

WM. COOPER, Chairman.
Clerk to the Board.

The address was in book shape, elegantly bound in blue morocco, the tooled portion being specially cut from Hindu-Persian designs. The address was profusely illustrated with carefully executed water colour vignettes of Gerard Street Higher Grade, Ashbourne Road, St. James's Road, and Traffic Street Schools, with eight smaller vignettes. The illuminated borders were floral, with suitable royal and scholastic emblems introduced. The volume was enclosed in a blue morocco casket. The whole of this elegant production was executed by Messrs. Bemrose and Sons.

THE CLERGY OF THE DEANERY OF DERBY.

The Bishop of Derby (Dr. Were) and the Rev. Canon Knight presented the address from the clergy of Derby, the text of which was as follows:—

To the Queen's Most Excellent Majesty.

May it please your Majesty,—
We, your Majesty's most faithful subjects, the Clergy of the Deanery of Derby, beg leave to approach your Majesty with feelings of deep loyalty to your person, and profound attachment to your throne.

We desire to express our gratitude to Almighty God that He has secured to the English people, by the long duration of your Majesty's reign, those blessings which naturally spring from the continuance of good and wise government.

Chief among these blessings we venture to account the high example of social and domestic life which your Majesty has ever set before your people; an example which, we are convinced, has had an elevating and purifying influence upon the tone of English society.

Nor would we, especially on this occasion, omit to mention with peculiar gratitude the unvarying interest which your Majesty has shown in every effort for ameliorating the distress and elevating the intelligence of the poorer classes in this land. To the interest and to the wise counsels, both of your Majesty and of your ever-lamented Consort, we can without hesitation attribute a large share in that great outgrowth of manifold agencies for the exercise of philanthropy and the increase of intellectual culture which is so striking a feature of your Majesty's reign.

We cannot help noticing the immense increase which has taken place during your Majesty's reign in the population of the country, and especially of the towns. We are profoundly conscious how great a responsibility is laid upon the clergy of the Church of England, and upon all who have the moral and spiritual welfare of the people at heart, to spread the principles of the Christian faith among rich and poor alike.

With the fervent prayer that your Majesty may yet long be spared to reign over a godly and contented people, we beg leave to subscribe ourselves, with fervent sentiments of loyalty and devotion.

Your Majesty's most dutiful subjects.

Signed on behalf of the Clergy of the Deanery,

E. A. DERBY,
Bishop Suffragan and Rural Dean.

The address was a very neat scroll, draped with pale blue cloth, executed by Messrs. Bemrose and Sons.

THE MEDICAL PROFESSION OF DERBY.

Dr. Ogle, Senior Physician of the Infirmary, next handed to Her Majesty's representative the following address from the medical profession of Derby:—

To Her Most Gracious Majesty Victoria, Queen of Great Britain and Ireland.

We, the undersigned members of the Medical Profession in Derby, desire most respectfully to approach your Majesty and to tender to you our grateful thanks for this your most considerate act of regard for the welfare of the sick poor by coming to lay the foundation stone of a new hospital for this town and county.

That your life of unceasing sympathy with all who are in trouble may long be spared, and that you may be granted the blessing of health and strength to rule over a loyal and united people is our constant and earnest prayer.

J. WRIGHT BAKER, WILLIAM OGLE, JOHN W. LEACROFT, WILLIAM LEGGE, F. BOROUGH, WALTER G. COPESTAKE, FRANK ILIFFE, WILLIAM GRAFTON CURGENVEN, C. A. GREAVES, ALFRED O. FRANCIS, T. LAURIE GENTLES, HENRY F. FOULDS, W. ILIFFE, J. A. SHARP, EDMUND VAUDREY, E. COLLIER GREEN, F. CASSIDI, ROBERT LAURIE, R. W. GENTLES, J. LISTER WRIGHT, GEORGE RICE, HENRY BARRETT, H. B. S. CURLL, S. RUTHERFORD MACPHAIL, JOSIAH C. CASTOR, C. B. DALTON, THOMAS HIGHTON, W. PATTERSON, J. H. HODSON, R. M. WILSON, G. R. SIMS, T. HENDERSON POUNDS, FREDERICK L. MOORE, W. BENTHALL, A. BELL, GEORGE D. MOON, C. H. HOUGH, WILLIAM HENRY WRIGHT, J. ACTON SOUTHERN, CHAS. W. FLETCHER.

The address, executed by Messrs. Bemrose and Sons, was on a scroll of vellum, with a border of forget-me-nots and jessamine.

NONCONFORMIST CHURCHES OF DERBY.

The Rev. I. Dorricott (Primitive Methodist Minister), presented the address on behalf of the Nonconformist Ministers of Derby. It was as follows:—

To the Queen's Most Excellent Majesty.

May it please your Majesty,—

We, the Ministers of the various Nonconformist Churches of Derby, gladly avail ourselves of your Majesty's visit to our town to declare to your Majesty our humble and hearty loyalty.

We rejoice in your Majesty's prosperous and beneficent reign of 54 years, in the blessings of peace, the increase of commerce, the growth of freedom, and the spread of religion, which your Majesty's great Empire has enjoyed.

We acknowledge with much gratitude the ready aid and encouragement your Majesty has ever given to works of philanthropy and mercy. And we pray that it may please Almighty God to spare your Majesty long to reign over a loyal, free, and happy people.

And we beg to subscribe ourselves,

Your Most Gracious Majesty's Dutiful Subjects:—

REVS. W. T. ADCOCK, S. ANTLIFF, D.D.; S. A. BARRON, J. BIRKS, F.G.S.; ISAAC DORRICOTT, F. ELTON, P. GIBBON, W. F. HARRIS, F. E. HEAPE, GEORGE HEPPLEWHITE, W. HILL, T. W. HODGSON, A. L. HUMPHRIES, B.A.; G. HUNSWORTH, M.A.; F. JONES, A. LLEWELLYN, D. MACDONALD, M.A., B.D.; W. MARWOOD, A. MILLS, G. PAGETT, F. PLATT, R. ROBINSON, T. STRINGER, A. UNDERWOOD, W. UNSWORTH, T. WILKES, W. WILLANS, J. P. WILLIAMS.

This address, which was in scroll form, had a blue silk back, and was trimmed with white silk fringe, in case. It contained a mediæval heading, with capitals set in gold tablets, which gave it a very effective appearance. The body part was engrossed, and was followed by twenty-eight signatures. The side-piece was composed of conventional flower ornaments, which looked remarkably pretty and tasteful. It was executed at Messrs. Carter's, and was the work of Mr. J. B. Eley, of Franchise Street.

DERBY AND DERBYSHIRE NURSING ASSOCIATION.

The address from the Derby and Derbyshire Nursing Institution, presented by Mr. Rowland Smith, J.P., read as follows :—

To Her Gracious Majesty Victoria, Queen of Great Britain and Ireland.

The Nurses of the Derby and Derbyshire Nursing Association, 51 in number, mindful of your Majesty's great interest in the work to which their lives are devoted, most respectfully desire to express their deep sense of indebtedness to your Majesty for the encouragement that you have in so many ways given to them in their arduous and responsible duties. Her Royal Highness the Princess of Wales on the occasion of her visit to Derby became our Patroness, and it is our humble petition that a similar token of favour may now be granted to our Institution by your Majesty.

(Signed)   ROWLAND SMITH, President.
           ALICE WOODHEAD, Lady Superintendent.
           WILLIAM OGLE, Hon. Secretary.

The address was on a scroll of vellum, lined with crimson silk and gold fringe, neatly illuminated and enclosed in a crimson leather case. It was the production of Messrs. Bemrose and Sons.

REPTON SCHOOL.

The Rev. W. M. Furneaux presented the following address from Repton School :—

To Her Most Excellent Majesty the Queen of Great Britain and Ireland.

May it please your Majesty,—

We, the Masters and Boys of the Ancient School of Repton, once the capital of the Kingdom of Mercia, humbly beg that we may be allowed to offer the loyal expression of our devotion to your Majesty's person and throne on the happy occasion of your Majesty's visit to the borough of Derby.

And we earnestly pray that it may please God to spare your Majesty's life for many years to come, that your beneficent reign, which has been marked by such wonderful material progress, and by such manifold blessings to the people of England, may also be remembered as the longest in the annals of English history.

Signed, on behalf of the Masters,
           W. M. FURNEAUX, M.A., Oxon,
                      Headmaster.

Signed, on behalf of the Boys,
           M. C. C. SETON,
                 Head of the School.

The address was on a scroll of vellum, backed by purple silk and gold fringe, with mediæval border, in which were worked four views of Repton School, church arch, etc., enclosed in a neat leather case, the whole being the production of Messrs. Bemrose and Sons.

DERBY SCHOOL.

The address from Derby School was presented by the Head Master, Mr. J. Sterndale Bennett, who was accompanied by Mr. C. E. Heath, the senior præpositor.

To the Queen's Most Excellent Majesty, Most Gracious Sovereign,—

We, the Governors, Masters, and Scholars of Derby School, desire this day, in common with all other dutiful and loyal subjects belonging to this town and county, humbly to express our devotion, affection, and zealous attachment to your Royal Person, and to join in the general expression of gratitude for the great honour now paid by your Majesty to this town, of which our school is one of the most ancient institutions.

That we should approach your Majesty on this day of all others is an auspicious omen for our future prosperity. It was on this day, 337 years ago, that the Charter was signed by your Royal Predecessor Queen Mary, reconstituting and providing in perpetuity for the old school which has alone perhaps of all other English schools rung its Curfew Bell since the time of the Normans. Founded A.D. 1160, in the reign of Henry II., by that great Prelate, Walter Durdant, Bishop of Lichfield, it has for centuries educated the sons of Your Majesty's loyal subjects of Derby and Derbyshire. Within its walls was educated John Flamstead, the first Astronomer-Royal, at whose suggestion and under whose direction Your Majesty's Royal Observatory at Greenwich was first erected. The name of Flamstead is but one from the long list of distinguished *alumni* who up to the present time have continued to do honour to their school and to the town of Derby.

The School, for want of sufficient endowment, languished during the first half of the present century, but during the last 25 years has regained its position among the leading schools of the country.

Twice during that period has it been considered worthy of the high honour of a visit from members of Your Majesty's august family.

In 1872 their Royal Highnesses the Prince and Princess of Wales visited the School and distributed the prizes, and 12 years later His Royal Highness again came to inspect the new building raised to commemorate the honour paid to the School by the former visit of their Royal Highnesses.

God grant that the presence of your Majesty on this anniversary (remarkable to us as the day on which a former Queen of England gave by her signature new life to Derby School) may mark the beginning of a new era of prosperity and usefulness for this ancient foundation, and that in years to come your Majesty's royal favour now shown may be reverenced and jealously guarded by Derby boys as their most cherished tradition, encouraging them to noble thoughts and deeds as worthy citizens of that great Empire over which your Majesty so gloriously reigns.

Given under the seal, &c.   T. W. EVANS.
J. STERNDALE BENNETT,
Head Master.
THOMAS LIONEL CHADWICK,
Captain of the School.

The address was contained in a banner scroll, the words of it being written on vellum in engrossed style, with title and illuminated capitals, with the arms of the school at the head, and their mottoes. The arms were quarterly, 1st and 4th, borough arms, a stag lodged; 2nd and 3rd, See of Lichfield, with a bishop's mitre for crest; motto: *Literis mors est vita hominis sine*, also *Regia Schola Derbiensis*—which latter is simply the Latin designation of the school. The scroll was surrounded by scrolled borders, and a central device of Royal Arms, and floral emblems on the right side. It presented a very handsome appearance, being upholstered in striped silk, with fringes and bands of the school colours, presenting a quite unique appearance, and was further enclosed in a case of the before-mentioned colours, stamped with the arms of the school, and signed by the Chairman of the Governors and the Head Master and Captain of the school. It was very tastefully designed and illuminated by Mr. George Bailey of Derby.

MASTERS AND BOYS OF TRENT COLLEGE.

The Rev. W. H. Isaacs and Mr. C. B. O. Symons, the senior prefect of the school, presented the following address from Trent College :—

To Her Most Gracious Majesty Victoria, Queen of Great Britain and Ireland.

We, the Masters and Boys of Trent College, established in the year 1866 on the principles of the Protestant and Reformed Church of England, desire to welcome your Majesty on the occasion of your Majesty's visit to the town of Derby.

It is our earnest prayer that as supreme Head of Church and State, your Majesty may live long to rule over a happy and united people, and that from the public schools of this country there may continue to spring forth year by year a harvest of young Englishmen ready to acknowledge as the gift of Almighty God the blessing of freedom—political, moral, and religious, which they enjoy, and to defend that freedom by their service, unselfish and untiring ; by their obedience, faithful and intelligent ; and by humble and uncompromising loyalty, to your Majesty, and to that religion, the religion of progress and enlightenment, of simple faith in God's Holy Word and God's Holy Spirit, of which your Majesty is the acknowledged champion.

The address consisted of a scroll of vellum, mounted on crimson silk with white fringe. The border of acorns, with a vignette of Trent College introduced, was delicately painted. It was executed by Messrs. Bemrose and Sons.

THE FREEMASONS OF DERBYSHIRE.

Mr. H. C. Okeover, J.P., D.P.G.M., and Mr. W. Naylor, P.G.S., next handed in the address from the members of the Derbyshire Provincial Grand Lodge of Freemasons. It was as follows :—

To the Queen's Most Excellent Majesty.

May it please your Majesty,—

We, the members of the Provincial Grand Lodge of Freemasons in Derbyshire, humbly desire to approach your Majesty, and to assure you of our loyal attachment to your throne and person.

The object of your Majesty's visit to this town is one in which we take a deep interest; the cause of charity being at all times one of the leading principles of our order.

We rejoice that your Majesty, as Grand Patroness of the Royal Masonic Institution for Girls, and also of the Royal Masonic Institution for Boys, is directly connected with our fraternity, and we earnestly pray that your Majesty may be long spared to rule over a loyal and united people.

Given under the seal of the Provincial Grand Lodge.

      (Signed) HARTINGTON, P.G.M.
             H. C. OKEOVER, D.P.G.M.
14th May, 1891.   WM. NAYLOR, P.G. Sec.

The address was on a scroll of vellum, lined with blue silk and gold fringe. The border was mediæval in character, and in it were introduced the masonic emblems and county arms. The scroll was enclosed in an elegant leather casket with masonic emblems worked in gold outside, the whole being the work of Messrs. Bemrose and Sons.

UNITED TEMPERANCE SOCIETIES.

The address from the United Temperance Societies was presented by Mr. W. Hall and the Rev. J. H. Askwith :—

To the Queen's Most Excellent Majesty.

May it please your Majesty,—

We, the undersigned members and workers connected with temperance organizations in Derby and the district, desire to express to your Majesty, on this auspicious occasion, our sincere devotion and loyalty to your person and your throne.

The object of your visit to the town of Derby, to lay the foundation-stone of our new Infirmary, is of itself another proof of the great interest your Majesty has always taken in matters affecting the poorer classes in the land, and we recognise with profound thankfulness the manifold proofs of the social advancement and higher intelligence of the people, which are largely attributed to the benign influence of your Majesty's personal example and beneficent reign.

The gracious patronage extended by your Majesty to the Church of England Temperance Society, we are convinced, has done much to advance the cause of temperance, which also derived much benefit from the public utterances of the ever-lamented Prince Leopold, and it is our pleasure to inform you of the great progress which is being made in this and the surrounding districts, where young and old are being taught and trained in the principles of sobriety and virtue, which are so essential to the material prosperity and social and moral welfare of your people.

We trust that the life of your Majesty may long be spared, and that the remaining years of your long and successful reign may be rendered happy and enjoyable by the continued loyalty and unswerving devotion of all your subjects, and the peaceable relations existing with other nations.

We are your Majesty's loyal and devoted subjects and servants.

Signed on behalf of the United Temperance Societies—

Derby Temperance Society :
WILLIAM HALL, President.
MARY BODEN, President of the Women's Auxiliary.
GEORGE SHIRES, Secretary.

Church of England Temperance Society :
GEORGE SOUTHWELL, President.
R. J. KNIGHT, Chairman of Committee.
ELIZABETH OKEOVER, President of the Women's Union.

Derby and Derbyshire Band of Hope Union :
JOHN WILLS, President.
J. W. AVERY, Secretary.
LL. M. COOKE, Agent.

This address, the work of Mr. J. B. Eley, of Franchise Street, had an Old English heading with side panel, representing the county emblem (rose), and had been very nicely executed. In the centre of the side panel were the borough arms, surrounded by the conventional roses ; while the body of the address itself was engrossed. It was backed with old gold silk and fringe to match, and showed up very neat and effective. The case itself was of calf.

DERBY CHAMBER OF COMMERCE.

The address from the Chamber of Commerce was presented by Mr. H. M. Holmes, the President, and Mr. G. Bottomley, J.P. :—

To Her Most Gracious Majesty Queen Victoria.
May it please your Majesty,—
We, the Members of the Derby Chamber of Commerce, humbly desire, on the happy occasion of your Majesty's visit to this borough, to express our heartfelt loyalty and devotion to your Majesty's person and throne, and our appreciation of the honour you have done the town by consenting to perform the initial ceremony in the erection of a new Infirmary.

As representatives of the various branches of trade and commerce in Derby, we beg to recall the fact that during your Majesty's auspicious reign the population has trebled, and the wealth and prosperity of the inhabitants have proportionately increased under that happy union of individual freedom and legal authority which has peculiarly distinguished the long period of your Majesty's wise and beneficent rule.

We earnestly pray that your Majesty may long continue to reign over a prosperous and united people, and may by the blessing of Almighty God be spared to witness a further advancement in that material, moral, and intellectual progress which will ever be associated with your name.

Signed on behalf of the Derby Chamber of Commerce, this 21st day of May, 1891.

HERBERT M. HOLMES, President.
ALFRED SEALE HASLAM, Vice-President.

The address was on a scroll of vellum, with richly illuminated border, in which were introduced a view of the Old Silk Mill at Derby, specimens of Derby Royal Crown China, a Locomotive Engine, and several Mining Instruments. The whole, enclosed in a suitable morocco case, was the work of Messrs. Bemrose and Sons.

THE FRIENDLY SOCIETIES OF DERBY.

The following address from the Derby Friendly Societies was presented by Mr. John Cook and Mr. Henry Mee :—

To Her Most Gracious Majesty the Queen.
May it please your Majesty,—
We, the representatives of the Friendly Societies in the borough, beg to approach your Majesty with the most profound respect for your throne and person.

We hail with the utmost pleasure and interest your visit to Derby, on an occasion of such supreme importance to the industrial population of the town and county as the laying of the foundation-stone of the building of one of our noblest institutions, which confers such great benefits on the class to which we belong.

Our societies especially appreciate your Majesty's gracious purpose in being here to-day, inasmuch as it is in entire consonance with the work in which we are engaged, namely, by mutual association to relieve distress, aid the sick, to comfort the mourner, and to promote habits of thrift and forethought.

We remember with pride and gratitude the foresight and noble efforts of the late Prince Consort in regard to works of beneficence and humanity, and the well-being of the industrial classes and the poor.

We deem it to be one of the glories of your Majesty's reign that the spirit which prompts to such objects has so largely grown in this Kingdom and resulted in conferring incalculable benefits on your Majesty's subjects.

Praying that your Majesty may long be spared to reign in peace and happiness over a contented and prosperous people,

We remain, your Majesty's humble servants,

JOHN COOK, D.C.R., Ancient Order of Foresters.
WILLIAM WOODWARD, P.G.M., Order of Druids.
JOHN VERE, P.G.M., Independent Order of Odd Fellows (Manchester Unity).
DANIEL DE SOIZA, P.D.G.M., Independent Order of Odd Fellows (London Unity).
H. C. WOODWARD, Order of Loyal Caledonians.
E. A. ARNOLD, P.G.M., Grand United Order of Odd Fellows.
HENRY MEE, G.C S., Derby Midland United Order of Odd Fellows.

This address was in book form, and was executed by Messrs. Bemrose and Sons. Each page was adorned by a floral border, delicately painted on vellum. At the end were the emblems, painted in miniature, of the various societies, in the following order :—Ancient Order of Foresters, John Cook, D.C R. ; Order of Druids, William Woodward, P.G.M.; Independent Order of Odd Fellows, John Vere, Prov. G.M. (Manchester Unity); Independent Order of Odd Fellows, Daniel de Soiza, P.D.G.M. (London Unity); Order of Loyal Caledonians, H. C. Woodward ; Grand United Order of Odd Fellows, E. A. Arnold, P.C.M. ; Derby Midland United Order of Odd Fellows, Henry Mee, G.C.S. The binding was of maroon morocco, delicately tooled, the designs being taken from books bound *temp.* Elizabeth.

THE TEACHERS OF DERBY AND DISTRICT.

Mr. Thomas Newton and Mr. Benjamin Toft next presented an address from the Teachers of the Elementary Schools, which was as follows :—

To the Queen's Most Excellent Majesty.

May it please your Majesty,—

On behalf of the Teachers of the Derby and District Association of Teachers, we humbly desire to offer your Most Gracious and Imperial Majesty our sincere and hearty thanks for your condescension in honouring the inhabitants of this ancient borough with your royal presence.

We cannot fail to appreciate deeply the great kindness of heart which has influenced you to pay this visit in the interest and for the benefit of the poorer and more unfortunate of your Majesty's subjects, nor can we doubt but that your gracious act this day will deepen and strengthen the affectionate regard and devotion of your subjects generally, and will further bind you to their hearts as the " Mother of your people."

We would desire to offer to your Majesty our felicitations upon the surpassing brilliance of your reign, during which strides so marvellous have been taken in science, the arts, commerce, and universal progress.

Your Majesty must contemplate with pleasure and satisfaction the great progress that education has made under your rule and governance, and especially the education of those who earn their bread by manual labour. It is our high privilege to bear our part of this work ; and we beg to assure your Majesty that, as it has been in the past, so in the future it shall be our aim and earnest endeavour, as far as in us lies, to train up a God-fearing, loyal, and devoted people. We are,

Your Majesty's most loyal and devoted subjects,

THOMAS NEWTON,

BENJAMIN TOFT, Secretary.   President of the Derby and District Teachers' Association.

The ceremony of presenting addresses concluded, the children sang two verses of "Auld Lang Syne," again accompanied by the band of the Grenadier Guards, and as soon as this was over the Royal procession left the square in the same order as it entered, amidst the enthusiastic cheers of the immense assembly, and these were continued as it made its way round the Market Place; along St. James' Street, the Strand, the Wardwick, and Victoria Street, the crowd giving Her Majesty a hearty welcome. After the Royal procession had passed the top of Victoria Street, the crowd broke through the barriers, but were kept back by the police and soldiers. Along St. Peter's Street and the London Road, the crowd, on seeing the Queen a second time, did not fail to cheer heartily, and up to the Infirmary gates, where the children sang sweetly, Her Majesty frequently and gracefully bowed her acknowledgments.

THE CEREMONY AT THE INFIRMARY.

At the Infirmary site, where spectators began to assemble before three o'clock, the tedium of waiting was relieved very pleasantly by the excellent performance of a selection of music by the band of the 1st Battalion of the Derbyshire Regiment (the 45th) from Plymouth, which was stationed upon a platform situated under a spreading birch tree, and further sheltered from untoward elements by a canvas awning. A constant stream of visitors continued to arrive, admission to the grounds being at the entrance in Osmaston Road. The spacious tent enclosing the foundation-stone was guarded by a detachment of the Metropolitan police, under the charge of Chief Inspector Wren, of the A Division, and Inspector Shannon, C Division. These were stationed round the tent and in the enclosure, and did good service in directing the spectators to their allotted places. An incident of interest was the arrival, about 8.30, of the guard of honour, consisting of two companies of the Cheshire Regiment, which, bearing its colours, was formed up in line in front of the entrance to the tent. These gallant fellows, it was observed, bore in their helmets sprigs of oak leaves, in commemoration of the battle of Dettingen, in which the regiment bore an active part. As time passed on, the school children began to arrive, trooping down the paths leading to their prescribed seats in regular order, and exciting a good deal of interest. Some of them were made to utilise the time by singing, presumably by way of practice, the National Anthem; and the youngsters were further put through their paces in the matter of cheering, a call to which they responded with shrill alacrity and unanimity. All this time the seats in the grounds facing the London Road were filling up, and when, about 4.30, the squadron of the 6th Dragoon Guards passed at a smart trot on their way to the Station to meet the Queen, there lacked not a considerable body of spectators upon whom the erect and martial bearing of the detachment made its due impression. To the spectators in the street, wedged tightly in as they now were between the barriers, the passing of the Dragoons was a positive godsend. It aroused the spirits which persistent dull and damp weather had caused to flag; and the genius of the crowd being thus set in motion, any trivial incident which subsequently happened was greeted with an outburst of merriment, altogether in disproportion to its importance. When, however, incidents that lend themselves to humorous suggestion do not of themselves arise, it perhaps is necessary to invent them. Rapturous applause, for example, was caused, when at five o'clock the outriders, clad in their scarlet coats, hove in sight on their way to the railway station, followed by a couple of carriages, and the excitement rose to fever heat on the appearance, shortly afterwards, of the corporate procession, which was considerate enough to pass at a walking pace.

At 5.15 a corps of the 2nd Volunteer Battalion of the Derbyshire Regiment was marched up and deployed into the Infirmary grounds, lining the route of the Queen's approach, but this evolution seemed to be akin to the famous and traditional exploit of the Duke of York, for very shortly afterwards the men were marched out again, and became, so far as the Infirmary spectators were concerned, "lost to sight," though, doubtless, "to memory dear."

The return of the corporate cavalcade from the station about a quarter to six, was hailed gladly as tangible evidence that now the Queen would very shortly pass on her way to the Town Hall. The hope was well founded. Shortly before six o'clock the heralding members of the Dragoon Guards came up on their horses, which, at the sound of the tumultuous cheering that broke from the Infirmary grounds, curvetted and pranced in surprise. The first half of the troops quickly followed, and then the Royal carriage came *en pleine vue*. "There she is," was the cry that went up from a few of the spectators whose activity had led them to the ascent of poles, gate posts, tree branches, and other excellent but physically inconvenient points of vantage ; and straightway the cheering broke out again with fresh vociferousness. Her Majesty, despite a slight sprinkling of rain, did not find it necessary to use an umbrella, a fact very much to the satisfaction, of course, of the whole assembly. The Princess Beatrice was at once recognised, but the identity of Prince Henry of Battenberg was largely a matter of inference, since His Royal Highness, wearing a full beard and looking older and more bronzed, is very different in appearance from the photographs through which he was first made familiar to the public.

The rear guard of Dragoons having passed, a general move on the part of those duly qualified by ticket was made to the large Pavilion, within which the foundation-stone was enclosed. Up to that moment it had remained practically deserted, but speedily the throng of visitors besieging the entrances served to fill the seats to their full capacity. The nurses of the institution were here rightfully accorded the place of honour, and to the number of about a score occupied the front seats, attired in their ordinary uniform of light mauve dresses with white caps and aprons, with the addition of a hooded cloak of rough woollen material, of an agreeable shade of terra-cotta. The gathering within the Pavilion included many persons of distinction in the town and county of Derby, as well as a number of visitors from neighbouring counties. Amongst those present were :—The Right Hon. Lord Scarsdale, the Right Hon. the Earl of Harrington, the Hon. W. M. Jervis, the Hon. F. Strutt, Sir Francis Burdett, Bart., Sir John and Lady Smith, the Hon. Lady Walker, the Hon. Mrs. Newdigate, Sir Wm. Harcourt, M.P., Mr. Alderman Roe, M.P., Mr. Walter Evans, J.P., Mr. G. Herbert Strutt, J.P., Mr. H. Boden, J.P., Mr. J. B. E. Blackwall, J.P., Lieut.-General Thomson, J.P., Mr. Rowland Smith, J.P., Mr. R. W. M. Nesfield, J.P., Mr. N. C. Curzon, J.P.,

Mr. W. Cox, J.P. (Brailsford), Mr. G. F. Meynell, J.P., Mr. A. P. Heywood, J.P., Mr. H. J. Wood, J.P., Mr. G. M. Dixon, J.P., Mr. F. C. Arkwright, J.P., Mr. E. S. Milnes, J.P., Mr. W. T. E. Cox, J.P., Mr. F. W. Bagshawe, J.P., Mr. J. Shaw, J.P., Mr. T. O. Farmer, J.P., Mr. T. P. Copestake, J.P., Mr. H. Swingler, J.P., Mr. J. H. Gascoyne, J.P., Mr. J. Williams, J.P., Mr. Alderman Higginbottom, J.P., Col. Buchanan, J.P., Mr. Bailey, J.P., Mr. Alderman Bemrose, J.P., Mr. Alderman Hobson, J.P., Mr. Alderman Sowter, J.P., Mr. Alderman Woodiwiss, J.P., Mr. J. Wright Baker, J.P., Mr. W. Turpie, J.P., Mr. Lewis Harcourt, Mr. H. F. Gadsby (Town Clerk of Derby), Mr. W. Harvey Whiston (Clerk to the Borough Magistrates), the Mayor of Lincoln (Mr. E. Pratt), the Mayor of Ilkeston (Mr. Alderman Tatham), the Mayor of Leicester (Mr. Alderman Kempson), the Mayor of Burton-on-Trent (Mr. R. Wilkinson), Col. John Evans, Mr. Henry Evans, Mr. H. Sands (Mayor of Nottingham), the Ven. Archdeacon of Derby (Dr. Freer), the Rev. Canon Knight, the Rev. Canon Hamilton (Doveridge), the Rev. Canon Olivier, the Rev. A. H. Prior, the Rev. R. Fawkes (Spondon), Mr. F. W. Cox, Rev. Harcourt Anson (Littleover), Rev. W. Martin, Rev. C. Boden (Morley), Rev. H. Price (Normanton), Rev. F. J. Adams, Rev. W. Chandos-Pole (Radbourne), Rev. G. H. Sing, Rev. E. Hacking, Rev. F. Utterson, Rev. F. Hoare, Rev. J. S. Holden (Aston), Rev. C. E. Crellin, Dr. Ogle, Dr. Curgenven, Dr. Greaves, Dr. Collier Green, Dr. Southern, Dr. Benthall, Dr. J. A. Sharpe, Dr. O'Callaghan, Dr. Hough, Mr. Evans Broad, Mr. J. F. Thirlby, Major Holmes, Mr. George Wheeldon, Mr. Robotham, Mr. Blews Robotham, Mr. Burbidge-Hambly, Mr. A. B. Hamilton, Mr. G. Sutherland, Mr. J. C. Barnes, Mr. J. Walker, Mr. R. Slater, Surgeon-Major Gentles, Colonel Pedder, Mr. F. Ball, Mr. Arthur Longdon, Mr. H. Monkhouse, Mr. Humphreys, Mr. Arthur Cox, Mr. W. Legge, Mr. N. J. Hughes-Hallett, Mr. W. R. Holland (Ashbourne), Mr. Councillor F. E. Leech, Captain Reid (Secretary to the Infirmary Building Committee), Mr. F. L. Sowter (Secretary to the Infirmary), Mr. Councillor J. Hill, Mr. Alderman Waite (Duffield), Mr. Alderman Hart (Leicester), Mr. H. J. Bell, Mr. W. Peat, Mr. A. Smith, Mr. W. Goudie, Mr. W. Johnson, Mr. Councillor T. L. Riley, etc., besides which there was a large attendance of ladies.

At twenty minutes to seven a fanfare of trumpets, followed by the National Anthem, announced to the expectant throng that Her Majesty's arrival was imminent. All rose to their feet, and in a few moments the stalwart form of Lord Lathom was descried ushering Her Majesty from the reception-room to the platform. The Queen walked easily with the aid of a stick, and accompanied by the Princess Beatrice and Prince Henry of Battenberg, passed to the seat which had been provided behind the foundation-stone. Her Majesty, who looked exceedingly well, was attired as usual in black, with the sole relief of some coloured flowers upon the summit of her bonnet. A number of privileged persons took up their positions, standing behind and on each side of Her Majesty.

Amongst these were the High Sheriff of Derbyshire (Mr. E. M. Mundy), the Under Sheriff (Mr. A. Grimwood Taylor), the Sheriff's Chaplain (the Rev. E. M. Robinson), the Mayor and Mayoress of Derby (Mr. and Mrs. A. Seale Haslam), the Bishop of Southwell (Dr. Ridding), the Bishop of Derby (Dr. Were), the Recorder of Derby (Mr. M. C. Buszard, Q.C.),

Mr. H. Boden, J.P., Mr. Buchanan, J.P., Mr. H. Swingler, J.P., Mr. Alderman Bemrose, J.P., the Rev. Canon Olivier, Mr. Burbidge-Hambly, Mr. G. Sutherland, Capt. Reid, Mr. J. C. Barnes, Mr. W. G. Norman, Dr. Ogle, Dr. Curgenven, Dr. C. H. Taylor, and Miss Pratt, matron of the Infirmary.

Lord Scarsdale, in the regrettable absence of Sir William Evans, was charged with the duty of reading the Address from the Governors of the Infirmary. The Address was in the following terms :—

May it please Your Majesty,—

We, the President and Governors of the Derbyshire General Infirmary, beg to approach your Gracious Majesty with feelings of profound respect on this occasion of your Majesty's first State visit to our ancient Borough of Derby.

We tender to your Majesty our heartfelt gratitude for having consented to honour us with your presence, and to mark with your illustrious sanction the important formality of laying the foundation-stone of a new and much-needed General Infirmary in our midst. For more than half a century the beneficent work of ministering to the relief of the sick and injured artisans and poor of the thickly populated district embraced within the Borough and County has been successfully carried on within the walls of our Infirmary; but circumstances beyond the control of those responsible for the proper administration of the charity have cast upon them the immediate and arduous duty of providing an effectual remedy for admitted evils in the existing building.

After mature deliberation, and with the advice and assistance of experts in Infirmary construction, the Governing body came to the decision that they had no alternative but to sanction the removal of the old structure, and to undertake the substitution of an entirely new building, on an enlarged scale, and with means and appliances more in accordance with the requirements of modern sanitary and medical science.

We, whose privilege and happiness it is to number ourselves amongst your Majesty's loyal subjects in this the very centre of the United Kingdom, are deeply conscious of the distinction conferred upon us by your Majesty's presence on such an auspicious occasion; and we entertain a strong conviction that the countenance given to the good work in which we are engaged will not only be a great encouragement to us, but that it will exercise an all-potent influence in enabling us to carry it to a complete and successful issue.

With the heartfelt prayer that your Majesty may long be spared to preside over the destinies of this nation, and a renewed expression of our grateful feelings for the signal service rendered to the Borough and County of Derby on this occasion by your Majesty,

We have the honour to be

Your Majesty's loyal, dutiful, and obedient subjects and servants.

(Signed) T. W. EVANS, President.

Derby, May 21st, 1891.

The Address was on vellum, and in scroll form, backed and fringed with red silk and white fringe and bands. It was written in old English text, with illuminated heading and capitals. At the top was the County Badge, the Tudor rose and crown, on a blue ground. The borders had in the corners shields, on which were the lions, harp, lion of the Royal Arms, and also the Borough Arms. The borders were devices of emblems of the United

Kingdom, the rose, shamrock, and the thistle, treated heraldically. The designs were entirely new, and were made expressly for this address, as was the case with the other three executed by the artist, Mr. George Bailey, of Derby.

After a moment's pause, the Queen proceeded to read her reply, doing so in a clear, steady voice. Her Majesty said :—

"It is with sincere pleasure that I receive your address and lay the foundation-stone of the new building which you propose to erect. I earnestly hope that this undertaking, in which I take a deep and personal interest, may effectually contribute to the relief of human suffering and to the health of those whose career of honourable labour has been interrupted by accident or by sickness. I am glad to testify, by my presence here to-day, my appreciation of the generous efforts that have been made on behalf of this noble Charity."

A slight outburst of cheering from the spectators followed the delivery of this reply.

The Lord Bishop of Southwell offered up the following prayers :—

O Almighty God, of Whose manifold gifts it cometh that Thy servants bring any work to a good end, look down, we pray Thee, on this Thy people here gathered together to ask Thy blessing upon this Hospital, of which the foundation-stone is now purposed to be laid in Thy Name ; grant wisdom to the designers of its plans, and to those who shall build it grant safety from bodily risk and accident, and that they may by loving and faithful labour share the Christian spirit of this work of charity ; guide the doctors, nurses, and officers who shall hereafter minister in the noble service of this house, and may Thy Spirit ever be their spirit in all their counsels and ministrations, that this house may be ever Thine ; and to all those who shall seek help and healing here from sickness and suffering, do Thou of Thy loving mercy grant, in Thy infinite wisdom, comfort and relief of body and soul, according to their several necessities. This we beg for Jesus Christ's name. Amen.

O God, Who has put it into the heart of Thy servant, our gracious Sovereign Lady and Queen, to aid and encourage by her personal presence and sympathy this charitable work in which we are united here before Thee ; we pray Thee to bless and reward this her loving thought for the poor and suffering among her people, that the hearts of all may be ever more and more knit to her in loyalty and affection, in Thee and for Thee, Who dost live and govern all things, world without end. Amen.

Our Father, which art in heaven, Hallowed be Thy Name. Thy kingdom come. Thy will be done in earth, As it is in heaven. Give us this day our daily bread. And forgive us our trespasses, As we forgive them that trespass against us. And lead us not into temptation ; but deliver us from evil : For Thine is the kingdom, the power, and the glory, For ever and ever. Amen.

The audience joined heartily in the responses.

Then came the actual stone-laying ceremony. Messrs. Hall and Young, the architects of the new buildings, were largely in evidence ; and to their credit let it be stated that each discharged his duty with commendable neatness and *savoir faire*. It fell to the lot of the latter gentleman to place in the cavity prepared there the usual bottle containing coin and other mementoes. The articles deposited were a set of the last silver coinage, a copy of the last Report of the Infirmary, and the appeal for the New Building, a programme of these proceedings, with a copy of each of the newspapers following, viz. :—*The Times, The Derby Mercury, The Derby and Chesterfield Reporter, The Derbyshire Advertiser, The Derby and Derbyshire Gazette, The Derbyshire Times, The Derby Daily Telegraph,* and *The Derby Daily Express.*

THE QUEEN LAYING THE FOUNDATION STONE.

Taking an ordinary working trowel, Mr. Young then deftly laid some mortar upon the stone, and handed to Her Majesty a gold trowel wherewith to perform the necessary act. Her Majesty, smiling the while in a very pleasant and gracious way, took the instrument and spread the mortar out, whereupon, by means of some hidden machinery, the stone above began slowly to descend, being guided into its place by the architects jointly. Mr. Hall next handed to the Queen an ivory mallet, and Her Majesty, after administering three fairly vigorous taps to the stone, declared it, in a low voice, to be "well and truly laid." An outburst of applause greeted the announcement, and the ceremony of the day was over. Acknowledging the cheers of the spectators, Her Majesty bowed low three times, and retired from the platform into the ante-chamber. The Royal party shortly afterwards entered the carriage, and the Dragoons having fallen into position, the signal was given, and the procession moved away, passing down the central entrance from the Infirmary grounds, and turning to the right for the station. Immediately afterwards the long maintained restraint which spectators in the streets had endured behind the barriers was relaxed, and presently the London Road was crowded by a surging mass of persons, all eager in the recital of their experiences, and agreeing with a common accord that the visit of Her Majesty was a gracious and kindly act, and that the proceedings of the day, despite considerations of weather, had passed off with unequivocal success.

THE DEPARTURE.—THE MAYOR KNIGHTED.

After the conclusion of the ceremony at the Infirmary, the Queen and the royal party re-entered their carriages, and were accompanied to the Midland Station by His Worship the Mayor and the Mayoress, Major-General Wilkinson, C.B., Col. Kelly-Kenny, Col. Hooke, and Captain Birkbeck, proceeding viâ London Road and Midland Road, where Her Majesty again received a most enthusiastic and loyal welcome from the assembled onlookers. On arriving at the Station Her Majesty immediately left the carriage and proceeded to the Reception Room. The Mayor was then summoned to the Royal Presence, and received from Her Majesty her sincere thanks for the splendid reception accorded to her. She also expressed her hearty appreciation of the loyalty of "her people of Derby," and the good order of the town, and said it had afforded her the greatest possible pleasure to visit Derby, and to assist in promoting so worthy and excellent an object as the re-construction of the Infirmary. The Mayor then retired, but a few moments afterwards the Secretary of State (Mr. Henry Matthews) appeared, and said he had been instructed by the Queen to convey a Royal message to His Worship. This gracious message was an intimation that it would afford the Queen great pleasure to confer the honour of knighthood upon the Mayor of Derby if he would accept it. His Worship replied that it would give him sincere pleasure to receive this mark of Royal favour from Her Most Gracious Majesty. This answer having been conveyed to the Queen, the Mayor was immediately re-introduced into the Royal presence, and in the Retiring Room a very pleasing event took place, which effectually set the seal of Her Majesty's approval on the proceedings of the day, and conferred an honour on the town, in the person of its chief magistrate, which was received on all hands with the greatest possible acceptance and appreciation. The Queen having announced to the Mayor that it would give her very great pleasure to bestow upon him the honour of knighthood before leaving the town, His Worship thanked Her Majesty for this mark of her condescension and Royal favour. He was told to kneel, and Her Majesty, with the sword of the Equerry-in-Waiting (Major-General Sir Hy. Ewart), went through the ceremony of knighting him—which included the kissing of the Queen's hand, and then said, " Rise, Sir Alfred." The Mayor again conveyed his thanks to the Queen for this distinction, and retired from her presence. A most gratifying incident in connection with this auspicious ceremony was that it was performed under

THE QUEEN KNIGHTING THE MAYOR.

the personal observation of the Mayoress and her four children, who were standing opposite the doorway leading to the Reception Room, and were thus witnesses of this gracious and condescending mark of Royal favour. Several other pleasing incidents subsequently occurred. The Mayoress had the honour, on behalf of Mr. Richard Keene, of Iron Gate, of presenting to the Queen as a *souvenir* of her visit, an album containing some splendid platinotype photographs of the interior of Hardwick Hall, the renowned Derbyshire seat of the Marquis of Hartington. The album was in the form of an oblong book, handsomely bound in morocco, and contained views of the entrance hall of the mansion, as well as the dining-room, the drawing-room, picture gallery, etc. All of them were exquisite specimens of the photographer's art, and had gained medals—including the gold medal at Calcutta. Inside the cover there was a handsome label, bearing the following words—" Presented to Her Majesty the Queen, on her State Visit to Derby, May 21st, 1891, by the Mayoress of Derby, on behalf of the Photographer." The Queen appeared very pleased with the gift, and expressed her thanks to the Mayoress, to whom she gave her hand to kiss a second time before leaving. Her Majesty's thanks have also been conveyed to Mr. Keene for his gift. The Mayor had the further honour of presenting to Her Majesty a basket of choice apples which had just arrived by the Peninsula and Oriental Co.'s steamship *Ballarat* from Tasmania. These apples formed a part of the first large cargo of apples brought from the Antipodes by means of the machinery which has made the name of Haslam of world-wide celebrity, and conferred great benefit upon the producer in the colonies and the consumer at home. Her Majesty graciously received the offering of fruit from the Antipodes, spoke of the apples as beautiful specimens, and said it had given her great pleasure to accept the present. At the close of this part of the proceedings, which Her Majesty had graciously authorised previous to her arrival, the Queen left the Reception Room, and proceeded to the Royal train, repeatedly acknowledging her thanks by bowing to the Mayor and Mayoress and their children, the Reception Committee, and the gentlemen who had the honour and privilege of grouping themselves in front of the Royal carriage prior to its departure. A lovely basket of flowers and fruit was presented to Her Majesty by Miss Hylda Paget, daughter of Colonel Paget, the Chairman of the Midland Railway Company, and then farewells were exchanged. As the Queen was leaving the station three hearty cheers were raised by the ladies and gentlemen present, and the band played the National Anthem. Thus concluded one of the most eventful days which has ever been known in the good old town of Derby—a day to be long remembered as Derby's "Derby Day." The auspicious circumstance of the Mayor's knighthood, thus bestowed only a short time before the Queen entered the train to resume her journey north, was known only to a very limited number of persons, and it was not until the pointed allusions to "Sir Alfred" were made in the course of the subsequent banquet, that the facts of the case became known, and then the new knight was warmly congratulated on the deserved honour which he had obtained.

Another correspondent describes the same events as follows :—The station was reached at exactly seven o'clock. It quickly became known that Her Majesty would leave for Scotland a few minutes earlier than was originally fixed, and it soon became apparent that this was the case by the attendants removing the presentation addresses and the other gifts, and by the arrangements that were being made for tea. The Queen was assisted from her carriage by her two Scotch attendants, and walked briskly to the Reception Room. Here the visit was brought to a fitting, though certainly unexpected, climax, by Her Majesty conferring a knighthood on the Mayor of Derby. A few minutes after this interesting ceremony the Queen walked to the train, which was in waiting, and in the State saloon took up a seat next the platform, appearing exceedingly interested in all that was taking place. A lovely basket of flowers was presented to Her Majesty by Miss Hylda Paget, and then farewells were exchanged. Three cheers were given by the soldiers and others assembled on the platform, and the train steamed away exactly at 7.10.

THE QUEEN'S COSTUME.

The Queen was attired in a black silk dress and black cape, and the customary white feather was noticeable in her bonnet. Princess Henry of Battenberg wore a cloak covered with fur, and blue bonnet with gold and pink.

THE QUEEN'S BOUQUET.

The bouquet presented to the Queen by the Mayoress was composed of the choicest and most exquisite flowers—orchids: cattleyas, lelia purpurata, and odontoglossums, being the principal varieties used in its composition. The bouquet was in the "Standish," or flat, style, which Her Majesty likes, as it can be put down at any moment without injuring the flowers. In explanation of this, we may state that the bouquet was supplied by Messrs. John Standish & Co., Court Florists, of 52, St. George's Place, Knightsbridge, London, S.W., who have made several for the Queen at different times of this shape, with which Her Majesty has expressed her great satisfaction and pleasure.

THE OTHER BOUQUETS.

The Princess Henry of Battenberg's bouquet (presented by Miss Hilda Haslam) was made up of Katherine Mermet roses. The bouquet of the Countess of Erroll (Lady-in-Waiting) was composed of white roses and lilies, and that of the Hon. Ethel Cadogan (Maid-of-Honour) consisted of white roses and lilies also. The Mayoress' bouquet was composed of La France and Souvenir d'une Ami roses, whilst her daughters carried posy bouquets of yellow roses and Marguerites. All the above most tasteful compositions were supplied (to the order of the Mayor) by Messrs. John Standish & Co., of London, and were tied with large silk bows to match the flowers.

THE MAYOR'S RECEPTION ROBE.

His Worship the Mayor of Derby (Sir Alfred Haslam) wore a reception robe of the richest crimson Genoa velvet, lined throughout with white corded silk, with minever cape and edgings, and massive gold cords and tassels, also satin rosettes, etc. This was worn over a Court suit of black silk velvet, with cut steel buttons. The hat was three-cornered, and of black silk velvet, with real ostrich feather trimmings, and steel loop. It may be added that it was a special robe such as is only used on occasions when a Mayor receives Her Majesty. It was supplied by Messrs. Ede & Son, of Chancery Lane, makers to Her Majesty and the Corporation of London.

THE DRESSES OF THE MAYORESS AND THE MISSES HASLAM.

The Mayoress (Lady Haslam) wore a very handsome gown of serpent *damas broché*, trimmed with black chiffon and *old point de Venise lace*, embroidered with jet *carbochons*; Louis XV. cloak to match, trimmed with jet, bordered with feather trimming; and small bonnet, composed of pink roses and jetted tulle. The Misses Haslam wore charming little frocks of crême bengaline, trimmed with embroidery, tied with baby ribbon; picturesque hats of crême chip, trimmed with broad satin ribbon and feathers to match, and cloaks of tan colour Amazon cloth.

THE OFFICIAL ACCOUNT OF THE QUEEN'S VISIT.
(From the Court Circular.)

BALMORAL CASTLE, May 22.

The Queen yesterday laid the foundation-stone of the new Infirmary at Derby.

Her Majesty, accompanied by Their Royal Highnesses Prince and Princess Henry of Battenberg, and attended by the Ladies and Gentlemen-in-Waiting, arrived at the Midland Railway Station, Derby, at 5.35 p.m., where Her Majesty was received by the Mayor and Mayoress (Mr. and Mrs. A. Seale Haslam); the High Sheriff (Edward Miller Mundy, Esq., J.P.); Major-General Wilkinson, C.B., commanding N.E. District; Colonel Kelly-Kenny, Assistant Adjutant-General N.E. District; Colonel Hooke, commanding the troops at Derby; Captain Birkbeck, aide-de-camp to the Major-General; and the Reception Committee.

The Mayoress had the honour of presenting a bouquet to the Queen.

On the platform at the station a guard of honour of the Volunteer Battalion the Sherwood Foresters (Derbyshire Regiment) received Her Majesty with the usual salute.

The following had the honour of being presented to Her Majesty in the reception room at the railway station by the Earl of Lathom, Lord Chamberlain :—The Mayor and Mayoress (Mr. and Mrs. A. Seale Haslam), the Recorder (M. C. Buszard, Esq., Q.C.), the Town Clerk (H. F. Gadsby, Esq.), the Chairman of the Midland Railway Company (G. E. Paget, Esq.), and the General Manager of the Midland Railway Company (Lieut.-Colonel J. Noble, J.P.).

Outside the railway station a guard of honour of the Derbyshire Yeomanry Cavalry was drawn up in line.

The Queen then entered her carriage, the Royal procession being formed in the following order :—

Lieutenant-Colonel Delacombe, Chief Constable.

Escort of the 6th Dragoon Guards (Carabineers), accompanied by Major Porter, Captain Massey, and Lieutenant Francis.

An Officer of Carabineers.

FIRST CARRIAGE.

THE QUEEN.

Their Royal Highnesses Prince and Princess Henry of Battenberg.

An Officer of Carabineers.

Major-General Sir Henry Ewart, Equerry.

Major-General H. C. Wilkinson, C.B., commanding N.E. District; Captain Birkbeck, aide-de-camp; Colonel T. Kelly-Kenny, Assistant Adjutant-General N.E. District; and 16 men of the 6th Dragoon Guards (Carabineers).

Second Carriage.—The Countess of Erroll, the Hon. Ethel Cadogan, the Right Hon. H. H. Matthews, and the Earl of Lathom.

Colonel H. H. Hooke (commanding troops at Derby) on horseback.

Third Carriage.—Miss McNeill and Miss M. Cochrane, in waiting on Princess Beatrice, General the Right Hon. Sir Henry Ponsonby (Private Secretary to Her Majesty), and Lieut.-Colonel Sir Fleetwood Edwards (Assistant Private Secretary to Her Majesty).

Fourth Carriage.—Lieut.-Colonel Lord Edward Pelham Clinton, the Hon. A. Yorke, Dr. James Reid, C.B., and Mr. Muther.

Fifth Carriage.—The Munshi Abdul Kerim.

The Procession proceeded by the Midland Road and London Road to the Town Hall, in the Market Place, where Her Majesty was received by a guard of honour of the 1st Volunteer Battalion the Sherwood Foresters (Derbyshire Regiment).

The school children, accompanied by the Grenadier Guards' Band, sang "God save the Queen."

An Address from the Corporation of Derby was read by the Recorder and presented to Her Majesty by the Mayor in a gold casket.

The Queen from her carriage graciously replied to the Address as follows:—

"I have received with much pleasure your loyal and dutiful address, and I highly appreciate the cordial welcome which has been accorded to me by my faithful people at Derby.

"It is with sincere satisfaction that I observe how largely your ancient borough has shared in the great prosperity and progress of my kingdom, and I feel encouraged in meeting the responsibilities that devolve on me when I know that I have the hearty support of my faithful subjects, and I am glad to be here to-day.

"I cannot but feel the greatest sorrow, which I am sure is shared by you all, at the death of Lord Edward Cavendish, who was so universally loved. I condole sincerely with his father and family, and I regret that this sad event should have deprived us of the presence of Lord Hartington on this occasion."

The following Addresses were also presented to Her Majesty:—

The Justices of the Peace for the Borough, the Derbyshire County Council, the Justices of the Peace for the County, the Derby Board of Guardians, the Derby School Board, the Clergy, the Medical Profession, the Nonconformist Ministers, the Nurses of the Derby and Derbyshire Nursing Association, the Repton School, the Derby School, the Trent College, the Members of the Derbyshire Provincial Grand Lodge of Freemasons, the Chamber of Commerce, the Derby Friendly Societies, the Elementary Schools, the Temperance Society.

The school children, accompanied by the Guards' Band, then sang "Auld Lang Syne."

The procession then proceeded round the Market Place, by the Corn Market, Victoria Street, St. Peter's Street, and the London Road, and entered the Infirmary grounds.

On arrival at the Infirmary, where a guard of honour of the 1st Battalion the Sherwood Foresters (late 45th Regiment) was drawn up, Her Majesty was received by the High Sheriff of the county, the Mayor of Derby, and Lord Scarsdale, in the absence of the President of the Infirmary.

Lord Scarsdale read an address, to which the Queen made the following reply:—

"It is with sincere pleasure that I receive your address and lay the foundation-stone of the new building which you propose to erect.

"I earnestly hope that this undertaking, in which I take a deep and personal interest, may effectively contribute to the relief of human suffering, and to the help of those whose career of honourable labour has been interrupted by accident or sickness.

"I am glad to testify by my presence here to-day my appreciation of the generous efforts that have been made on behalf of this noble charity."

The Lord Bishop of Southwell offered prayers.

Upon the trowel and level being handed to Her Majesty by Mr. Young and Mr. Hall, architects, the Queen laid the foundation-stone, after which the following presentations were made to Her Majesty by the Earl of Lathom:—

The Lord Bishop of Southwell.
The Lord Bishop of Derby.
The High Sheriff of the County.
Lord Scarsdale, Vice-President.
The Architects.
The Senior Physician, Dr. W. Ogle.
The Senior Surgeon, Dr. W. G. Curgenven.
The House Surgeon, Dr. C. H. Taylor.
The Matron, Miss Pratt.

Her Majesty re-entered her carriage, and the Royal party returned to the Midland Railway Station by the London Road.

Before leaving, Her Majesty conferred the honour of knighthood upon the Mayor (Mr. Alfred Seale Haslam).

Miss Hylda Paget, daughter of the Chairman of the Midland Railway, had the honour of presenting Her Majesty with a basket of orchids and fruit.

On leaving Derby at 7.10 p.m., the Queen, accompanied by Prince and Princess Henry of Battenberg and Their Royal Highnesses' children, and attended by the Countess of Erroll, Miss M'Neill, the Hon. Ethel Cadogan, Col. Lord Edward Pelham Clinton, Lieut.-Colonel Sir Fleetwood Edwards, the Hon. A. Yorke, Mr. Muther, and Dr. Reid, left for Balmoral, which was reached this morning at 10 o'clock.

A Guard of Honour of the 1st Royal Scots Fusiliers under the command of Major R. F. Willoughby, was mounted at Ballater on Her Majesty's arrival.

GRAND MAYORAL BANQUET.

At eight o'clock on Thursday evening, a grand invitation banquet was given by the Mayor of Derby in commemoration of the Queen's visit to the town earlier in the day. The function—alike from its completeness and splendour—was well worthy of the occasion, and it is not too much to say that it was one of the most successful and brilliant entertainments of the kind ever held in Derby. In fact the experienced representative of a metropolitan newspaper aptly observed that "it could not have been better done at the Hotel Métropole, London." This will be at once understood when we state that the Mayor, with his customary enterprise and hospitality, had practically given *carte blanche* to that prince of caterers, Mr. William Towle, who—backed by the great resources of the company of which he is the chief *restaurateur*—fairly excelled himself (if that was possible) in the production of the repast. The magnificent decorations of the marquee, which had been specially erected alongside the Midland Hotel for the purposes of the banquet, are graphically described in detail on another page, and there is no need to repeat them. It only need be added that when the fairy-like structure was lit up with the electric light—the incandescent rays of which, though brilliant, were softly subdued with opaque ground glass—and the magnificent plate (of which there was £3,000 worth in the room), the rich cut glass, and the exquisite flowers of the dinner tables were set off by their refulgence to the best advantage, the scene, in the local history of prandial festivities, may be fairly said to have been unsurpassed. No less elaborate and *récherché* was the gastronomic aspect of the entertainment, as will be gathered from the following:—

MENU.

Hors d'œuvre variés.
Milk Punch. Tortu claire. Crême Princesse. Madeira.
Saumon. Sauce Hollandaise.
Hochheimer, 1874. Homards en caisses à la Bagration.
Poulardes braisées à la Cumberland.
Max Soutaine, 1884. Filet de bœuf a la Vernon. Giesler, 1884.
Aspic d'œufs de Pluviers en Bellevue.
Selle d'Agneau a l'Anglaise.
Pommes nouvelles. Petits Pois Frais.
Sorbets Beatrice.
Cailles sur Croustades.
Salade.
Asperges en Branche Sauce Mousseline.
Bordure de Pêches a la Monte Carlo.
Mousse aux fraises.
Petits fours.
Canapés Marseillais.
Port, 1863. Dessert. Chateau
East India Sherry. Café. Liqueurs. Montrose, 1869.

The serving up of the dinner and the attendance by the numerous and experienced staff of waiters left nothing to be desired, and the wines and liqueurs, which were freely served with the different courses, were of the choicest possible character. The company present to support the Mayor—in response to His Worship's invitation—was, notwithstanding many unavoidable and regrettable absences, of a most influential and representative character, and the bright uniforms of the notabilities lent an added air of splendour and gaiety to the festive scene.

The Mayor of Derby (Sir Alfred Seale Haslam, Knight, J.P.) presided, and to His Worship's right at the cross-table were seated the Right Hon. the Earl of Harrington; the Right Rev. the Lord Bishop of Derby; Sir Vauncey Harpur Crewe, Bart., D.L.; the Hon. W. M. Jervis, J.P. D.L.; the Hon. F. Strutt, J.P.; Sir James Allport, Knight, J.P.; Mr. Alderman Roe, M.P.; the Mayor of Ilkeston; the Mayor of Burton; Mr. Hy. Boden, J.P.; Mr. Alderman Worthington, J.P.; Mr. J. Bailey, J.P.; Mr. W. Turpie, J.P.; Mr. L. R. Starkey, J.P. (High Sheriff of Nottinghamshire); Mr. Fitzherbert Wright, J.P., D.L.; and Mr. H. T. Hodgson (a director of the Midland Railway Co.) To the left of the Mayor were seated the Right Hon. Sir William Vernon Harcourt, Q.C., M.P.; Alderman Sir John Smith, Knight, J.P.; the Recorder of Derby (Mr. M. C. Buszard, Q.C.); Sir Frederick Bramwell, Knight; Mr. E. S. Norris, M.P., D.L.; the Mayor of Leicester (Mr. Alderman Kempson); the Mayor of Lincoln (Mr. Edwin Pratt); Mr. Charles Thomas (Vice-Chairman, M.R.); Mr. J. W. Cropper; Mr. Gustave Behrens (Directors of the Midland Railway Co.); Mr. Alderman Hobson, J.P.; Major-General Wilkinson, C.B.; Lieut.-General Thomson, J.P.; Colonel Kelly-Kenny; Rev. Canon Knight; and Rev. John Haslam (his Worship's brother).

Mr. George Gilbert, of the Town Hall, acted as toastmaster most efficiently, and, at his request, the guests to the right and left of the Mayor successively took wine with His Worship. Mr. Gilbert also, in the course of the proceedings, announced that letters of apology, regretting their inability to be present, had been received from the Duke of Portland; the Marquis of Hartington; Lord Vernon; Lord Burton; Sir William Evans; Sir Henry Wilmot; Sir John Monckton; Colonel Martindale; Mr. Barnes, M.P.; Mr. T. D. Bolton, M.P.; Mr. H. Wardle, M.P.; and many others.

The following are the names of those who received invitations :—

Sir James Allport; Rev. Canon Abney; Mr. R. J. Allison, M.P.; Mr. Councillor E. T. Ann; Mr. F. C. Arkwright, J.P.; Mr. A. G. Anderson; Mr. W. E. Adie; Mr. W. R. Anderson ; Editor of *Derbyshire Advertiser*; Mr. H. Arnold-Bemrose.
Mr. Alderman H. H. Bemrose, J.P.; Right Hon. Lord Burton; Sir F. Bramwell; Mr. Councillor S Bennett; Mr. Councillor T. H. Bennett; Mr. Councillor H. Boam; Mr. Councillor G. Bottomley, J.P.; Mr. Councillor C. C. Bowring, J.P.; Mr. Councillor A. Butterworth; Mr. J. C. Barnes; Mr. H. Boden, J.P.; Mr. J. Wright Baker, J.P.; Dr. Benthall; Mr. W. Boden, J.P.; Mr. A. Buchanan, J.P.; Mr. M. C. Buszard, Q.C.; Mr. John Bailey, J.P.; Mr. W. L. Beale; Mr. Gustav Behrens; Mr. H. T. L. Bewley; Mr. W. Bemrose, J.P.; Mr. George Bailey; the Mayor of Birmingham; His Honour Judge Barber; Mr. H. Buckley, Mr. George Brigden; Mr. J. R. Sterndale Bennett, M.A.; the Mayor of Burton; Mr. S. B. Barnes; Mr. C. S. B. Busby; Major Blaxland; Mr. John Bell; Mr. T. D. Bolton, M.P.; Mr. A. Barnes, M.P.; Editor of *Black and White*; Mr. W. B. Blunt; Mr. F. O. F. Bateman, J.P.; Mr. C. Brentnall; Mr. E. Bradbury; Mr. H. W. Butler; Mr. Sharpley Bainbridge, J.P.; Editor of *Birmingham Daily Post*.

Sir D. Currie, M.P.; Sir C. Clifford; Sir Vauncey H. Crewe; Mr. Alderman J. G. Crompton; Mr. Councillor G. Cholerton; Mr. Councillor W. Clemson; Mr. Councillor T. Cox; Mr. W. Cox, J.P.; Colonel J. C. Cavendish, J.P.; Dr. W. G. Curgenven; Mr. N. C. Curzon; Mr. J. W. Cropper; Mr. W. Coddington, M.P.; Mr. T. G. Clayton; Mr. J. Close; Mr. W. Cooper; Mr. W. Crowther; the Mayor of Chesterfield; Mr. W. T. E. Cox, J.P.; Mr. F. Clifton; Mr. S. Court; Mr. T. Clarke; Mr. P. B. Chadfield; Mr. E. Cayford; Mr. R. Carr; Rev. Dr. Cox; Mr. A. L. Charles; Mr. T. W. Coxon; Mr. George Corbett; Mr. W. G. Copestake; Mr. C. H. Coulson; Mr. E. Clulow; Captain Gordon Cumming; the Editor of *Central News*.

His Grace the Duke of Devonshire; Right Hon. Lord Denman; Right Rev. Bishop-Suffragan of Derby; Mr. Councillor G. Dean; Mr. Councillor J. P. Doherty; Mr. Councillor F. Duesbury; Lieut.-Colonel Delacombe; Mr. W. Dawes; Mr. E. S. Dawes; Colonel Dawes; Mr. T. L. Devitt; Professor Dewar; Mr. George Drabble; Editor of *Daily News*; Mr. W. D. N. Drury-Lowe; Mr. W. B. Delacombe.

Alderman Sir T. W. Evans, Bart.; Mr. Councillor E. C. Ellis; Mr. Councillor S. Evans; Mr. Walter Evans, J.P.; Mr. W. P. Edwards; Mr. Henry Evans; Mr. C. K. Eddowes; Mr. A. M. Edlin; Mr. James Eadie.

Sir B. W. Foster, M.P.; Mr. Councillor Fletcher; Mr. Councillor Foster; Mr. Councillor Foulds, Rev. Canon W. M. Furneaux; Rev. A. F. E. Forman; Dr. A. O. Francis; Mr. G. Frost; Capt. Farquharson; Mr. R. J. Fittall; Lieutenant O. Francis; Mr. G. Findlay.

Sir J. Gorst, M.P.; Mr. Councillor T. L. Gentles; Mr. Councillor J. Grundy; Dr. C. A. Greaves; Dr. E. C. Green; Mr. H. F. Gadsby; Mr. G. Gascoyne, sen., J.P.; Mr. J. H. Gascoyne, J.P.; Lieut.-Colonel Gascoyne; Mr. Alfred Giles, M.P.; Lieutenant Dan Godfrey; Mr. F. W. Greaves; Mr. E. Gellatly; Editor of *Graphic*; Mr. H. E. Gooch; Editor of *Derby Gazette*; Sir Douglas Galton, K.C.B.

The Earl of Harrington; Right Hon. Lord Hartington; Right Hon. Sir W. V. Harcourt, M.P.; Mr. Alderman Higginbottom, J.P.; Mr. Alderman W. Hobson, J.P.; Mr. Alderman G. Holme, J.P.; Mr. Councillor T. H. Harrison; Mr. Councillor W. Hart; Mr. Councillor E. Haslam; Mr. Councillor Heathcote, J.P.; Mr. Councillor J. Hill; Mr. C. H. Burbidge Hambly; Rev. G. Hunsworth, M.A.; Mr. A. C. Percival Heywood, J.P.; Major A. W. Holmes; Dr. C. H. Hough; Mr. A. F. Hurt, J.P.; Colonel Hooke; Mr. W. U. Heygate; Mr. H. T. Hodgson; Mr. W. H. Hodges; Mr. R. J. Harrison; Mr. H. M. Haywood; Mr. H. M. Holmes; Mr. W. G. Haslam; Rev. J. Haslam; Mr. Arthur B. Hamilton; Mr. H. G. Harris; Mr. E. S. Houlder; Mr. Henry Hall; Major Hudson; Mr. W. E. Hubbard; Mr. A. Howden; Mr. R. A. Hankey; Mr. Thos. Hall; Mr. R. Hodder; Mr. G. Holme, jun.; Mr. H. M. Hobson; Mr. Alfred Hobson; Major H. Hall; Mr. N. J. Hughes-Hallett; Mr. Robert Harvey; Rev. W. F. Harris.

Mayor of Ilkeston; Mr. W. Iliffe; Mr. I. H. Ismay; Editor of *Illustrated London News*.

Hon. W. M. Jervis, J.P.; Mr. Councillor Jackson; Mr. S. W. Johnson; Rev. W. Johnson; Mr. Thos. Johnson; Mr. Felix Joseph; Mr. W. F. Jackson; Mr. J. A. Jacoby, M.P.; Mr. E. S. Johnson.

Rev. Canon Knight; Mr. R. Keene; Mr. F. R. Kendall; Mr. J. F. King; Mr. J. Keys.

Mayor of Leicester; Mayor of Lincoln; Mr. Alderman C. Leech, J.P.; Mr. Alderman F. Longden, J.P.; Mr. Councillor Laurie; Mr. Councillor F. E. Leech; Mr. Councillor W. Lowe; Mr. F. Ley; Mr. W. E. Langdon; Captain Leslie; Mr. S. Lothe, jun.; Mr. H. Litherland.

Sir Fred. T. Mappin, M.P.; Sir John Monckton; Sir W. Mackinnon; Monsignor McKenna; Mr. Councillor W. H. Marsden; Mr. E. M. Mundy, J.P.; Colonel P. P. Mosley; Mr. W. L. Mugliston; Dr. MacPhail; the Mayor of Manchester; Mr. W. Milburn, jun.; Mr. G. W. Manuel; Mr. D. Mackinnon; Mr. A. MacIlwraith; Mr. J. Maxey; Mr. J. A. McDonald; Mr. George Morrall; Mr. H. J. Morgan; Colonel Martindale; Mr. H. Monkhouse; Capt. P. H. Massey; the Editor of *Derby Mercury*; the Editor of *Manchester Examiner*; Rev. A. Mills; Mr. E. McInnes.

The Mayor of Nottingham; Mr. Alderman J. W. Newbold, J.P.; Mr. John Noble, J.P.; Mr. W. G. Norman; Mr. C. E. Newton, J.P.; Mr. E. M. Nelson; Mr. F. Nelson; Mr. E. S.

Norris, M.P.; Mr. G. P. Neele; the Editor of *Nottingham Express;* the Editor of *Nottingham Guardian.*
The Rev. Canon Olivier; Dr. W. Ogle; the Rev. J. Stanley Owen; Mr. T. P. Osborne; Mr. D. Ottewell.
His Grace the Duke of Portland; Mr. G. E. Paget, J.P.; Mr. W. J. Piper; Mr. E. H. Pares, J.P.; Mr. C. H. Plevins; Mr. J. Pettifor; Mr. J. Park; Mr. E. Pembroke; Mr. T. D. Parker; Captain Parry; Mr. C. A. Peters; Major T. C. Porter; Major R. W. Chandos-Pole. Mr. Alderman T. Roe, M.P.; Mr. Alderman R. Russell, J.P.; Mr. Councillor T. L. Riley; Mr. Councillor I. Roome; Mr. Councillor J. E. Russell; Mr. Robert Rankin; Capt. W. J. Reid; Mr. F. J. Robinson; Mr. C. T. Ritchie, M.P.; Mr. J. R. Ragdale; the Editor of *Derby Reporter.*
Right Hon. Lord Scarsdale; Sir T. Sutherland; Sir John Smith; Right Rev. the Lord Bishop of Southwell; Mayor of Sheffield; Mr. Alderman W. B. Sherwin; Mr. Alderman U. Sowter, J.P.; Mr. Councillor T. Sims; Mr. Councillor R. W. Spriggs; Mr. Councillor F. Stone; Mr. Councillor C. J. Storer; Hon. F. Strutt, J.P.; Mr. Councillor G. Sutherland; Dr. J. A. Sharpe; Mr. Rowland Smith, J.P.; Mr. Herbert Strutt, J.P.; Mr. H. Swingler, J.P.; Mr. L. R. Starkey; Mr. F. L. Sowter; Mr. W. Turner Shaw, J.P.; Mr. Francis N. Smith, J.P.; Mr. A. H. Stokes; Mr. T. C. Simmonds; Mr. W. Savill; Mr. Jno. Smith; Mr. John Shaw, J.P.; Mr. O. R. Strickland; Mr. C. J. C. Scott; Mr. W. Sidebottom, M.P.; Mr. B. Stretton; Editor of *Standard;* Editor of *Sheffield Telegraph;* Editor of *Sheffield Independent;* Captain Shaw; Mr. W. Cecil Salt; Mr. W. Antill Spencer.
Mr. W. Gladwin Turbutt, J.P.; Mr. W. Turpie, J.P.; Lieut.-General J. Sinclair Thomson, J.P.; Mr. C. Thomas; Sir M. W. Thompson, Bart.; Mr. C. Trubshaw; Mr. G. H. Turner; Mr. W. Towle; Dr. C. H. Taylor; Mr. Frank Tatam; Mr. John Tatam; Mr. G. Turner; Mr. A. Tait; Mr. A. G. Taylor; Mr. J. H. Todd; Colonel Du Plat Taylor; Editor of *Daily Telegraph;* Editor of *The Times;* Dr. F. E. Taylor.
Mr. Councillor G. B. Unsworth.
Right Hon. Lord Vernon.
Sir A. Walker, Bart.; Sir R. Webster, M.P.; Sir H. Wilmot, Bart.; Mr. Alderman S. Whitaker; Mr. Alderman A. Woodiwiss, J.P.; Mr. Councillor J. Walley; Mr. Councillor C. Wallis; Mr. Councillor P. Wallis; Mr. Councillor F. Ward; Mr. Councillor W. Williamson; Mr. Councillor W. W. Winter; Mr. Councillor J. Wright; Mr. H. J. Wood, J.P.; Mr. W. Woodward; Mr. W. H. Worthington, J.P.; Mr. H. Wiggin, M.P.; Mr. Jas. Williams, J.P.; Mr. W. H. Whiston; Mr. W. G. Wheeldon; Mr. H. Wardle, M.P.; Mr. FitzHerbert Wright, J.P.; Mr. W. Wilkinson; Mr. J. Wills; Mr. J. B. Westray; Mr. J. J. Wallis; Mr. H. W. Williams; Mr. W. B. Woodforde; Mr. G. Wheeldon; Mr. J. Wells; Mr. L. W. Wilshire; Mr. R. Wilson; Major-General Wilkinson; Mr. Alderman Richard Waite.
Mr. Keith Young; the Editor of *Yorkshire Post.*

Grace after meat having been said by the Bishop of Derby,

THE MAYOR rose to propose the first toast, and was loudly cheered. He said he had very great pleasure in submitting for their acceptance " The Health of Her Most Gracious Majesty the Queen." (Applause.) It was well known to all of them that the Queen during her life had endeavoured to the best of her ability and strength to discharge her duty, and he must say that day she had set an example to the rulers of the earth. (Cheers.) After living more than threescore years and ten, and at a time when people were inclined to take their repose, the Queen of England had yielded to the invitation of the people of Derby, and performed a duty which she said she had experienced great pleasure in doing. (Cheers.) It was made known to Her Majesty some weeks ago that it had been found absolutely necessary to rebuild the hospital, and that, in all probability, if she set her seal to the work, those who were undertaking it would be able to accomplish it more speedily than without her gracious assistance. At that time the subscription list amounted to about £8,000, but that day it exceeded £45,000. (Applause.) He thought they might fairly say that they owed a large amount of that success to Her Majesty. (Cheers.) She had come to Derby, and had performed her duty, and the inhabitants of both the borough and county felt indebted to the Queen for having condescended to visit them. (Applause.) When Her Majesty was leaving she expressed more than once or twice her great satisfaction at the loyalty of the people, and the excellence with which the whole of the arrangements had been carried out. (Cheers.) Indeed, the words the Queen had used were most flattering, and reflected the highest credit upon his native town for the way they had endeavoured to rally round and help him (the Mayor) in that great undertaking. (Applause.) He did not desire to detain them longer, but he would say that the Queen had set a noble example to all classes of the people. She had shown to parents how they ought to discharge their duties—(applause)—she had shown the women of England what they ought to be, and she had always shown to the rulers of the world what they ought to be. (Applause.) The Queen lived in the hearts of her people, and it was their earnest wish and prayer that Providence might spare her life for many years to come. (Loud cheers.)

THE MAYOR was again loudly cheered on rising to propose the toast of the "Prince and Princess of Wales and Members of the Royal Family." He said they would all agree with him in observing that the Prince of Wales was perhaps one of the hardest-worked men in the Kingdom. He was called upon to perform many important and onerous duties, and he invariably endeavoured to meet all the demands upon his time. There was a great deal of talk in these days about a reduction of the hours of labour, but he was convinced that unless the Prince of Wales was unsparing in the discharge of his important duties, many interests would suffer, and that he worked longer hours than most gentlemen occupying a high position in life in the British Empire. (Applause.) The Princess of Wales had endeared herself to the hearts of the people of this realm—(applause)—and he did not know that any more popular lady lived in this country, with the exception of the Queen, than Her Royal Highness the Princess of Wales. If ever the time came, and probably it would arrive, when the Prince and Princess of Wales were called to take upon themselves the arduous and important affairs of the State, he was quite sure they would prove themselves fully equal to the occasion, for the excellent example set before them by the Queen could not have failed to impress itself upon their minds. (Applause.) The other members of the Royal Family endeavoured to do their duty, and the inhabitants of this realm were proud of them. (Applause.)

THE RECORDER OF DERBY, who was cordially greeted, said he was fortunate that night in having, next to the loyal sentiments so well expressed by the Mayor, the first toast to propose —by virtue, he supposed, of the position he occupied in relation to this borough. He was fortunate in that respect, because his mind was at once relieved of anxiety. (Laughter.) He was fortunate also in being restricted to time by one who was a "past master" in the art of post-prandial speaking, and he was fortunate also in that he knew very little about the subject of his toast. (Renewed laughter.) Having closely examined his pedigree with reference to the duty allotted to him of proposing this toast—that of "The Army, Navy, and Reserve Forces"—he could discover no further family connection with the forces therein mentioned than the fact that his grandfather possessed a yeomanry sword. (Much laughter.) He was unfortunate, however, in the comparison which might ensue from his own in competition with more practised efforts, for three paces to his right was one of the great orators of the time (Sir William Harcourt), whilst his next door neighbour (Sir F. Bramwell) was one of the most successful after-dinner speakers of the day. Too long would it take him to recite the history and to recount the heroic deeds of our Army and Navy—they were not there to hear a history of their country, and that was what the history of those forces meant. The Army and the Navy had a glorious past, and he had no doubt they would have an equally glorious future. (Hear, hear.) The Reserve Forces had not at present had any practical opportunity of displaying their powers, but those of them who lived in London, at all events, saw, Saturday by Saturday, the ability they displayed in manœuvring, and the good promise they gave of maintaining, should the necessity arise, the traditionary prowess of the forces with which they were allied. (Hear, hear.) Before he sat down, he should like, as the first speaker of the evening, to congratulate—as he thought he had a right to congratulate—the town on the extreme success of the reception of Her Majesty the Queen. (Applause.) With some little experience of these pageants—of which he confessed, for the most part, he was not over fond—he never saw a town more beautifully decorated, nor the populace of a town —Radical as he knew it to be—(laughter and hear, hear)—and as he was glad it was— conduct itself in a more loyal manner. (Hear, hear.) He thought he might say, moreover, that there had been a thorough and hearty recognition of this fact by Her Majesty the Queen —who, with her successors, he prayed might long reign over them—a recognition that was alike gratifying to the Mayor and to the people of this town. (Loud applause.)

MAJOR-GENERAL WILKINSON (commanding the North-east District), in returning thanks, said he need hardly remind them that, whilst conscription—compulsory service—prevailed on the Continent, in England they were all volunteers. (Hear, hear.) Some of them volunteered to serve their Queen and country for the whole, or, at all events, for the greater part of their lives, whilst others, out of their busy lives, found time to undergo the training of the reserve forces, with the successful results that they had seen that day; for the Militia, the Yeomanry, and the Volunteers, in the arduous tasks assigned to them that day, had done their duty in a singularly efficient manner. (Applause.) He returned his special and heartfelt thanks for the kind words which had been used by the Recorder, and for the cordial reception which had been accorded to the toast of "The Army and Navy." He knew that when serving the Queen in distant lands—and he had no doubt on distant seas also—the members of those forces read accounts of such gatherings as these with peculiar interest, and when they saw that they were kindly spoken of it was the very greatest pleasure to them. (Hear, hear.) They, as regulars, admired more than he could tell them the willingness and the efficiency of the auxiliary forces, and were fully persuaded that, if the necessity should arise, every man in those forces would take his share in the defence of the British nation and of the glorious Empire to which they belonged. (Cheers.)

COLONEL BUCHANAN, J.P. (in the regrettable absence of Colonel Lord Burton), also returned thanks, and said he should like, as Colonel of the Volunteers, to say how greatly they appreciated the Mayor's kindness in arranging for them to assemble in such large numbers to do honour to the Queen, whom they all loved and honoured so much. (Hear, hear.) The senior force, the Yeomanry Cavalry, had been present in the streets that day, and he regretted the unavoidable absence of their colonel. They, as Volunteers, were anxious to do what honour they could to Her Majesty the Queen, and he ventured to say that the words just spoken by the commanding officer of this division (General Wilkinson) would not be forgotten by those to whom they referred. (Hear, hear.) There was no praise they liked so much as that which was bestowed by experienced officers of the regular army, who knew so well what they ought to be, and their hearty commendation was the greatest acknowledgment they could possibly have. (Hear, hear.) On behalf of the Volunteers, he heartily congratulated the Mayor upon the great success of everything that had taken place that day, knowing, as they did, that His Worship had set his mind upon what was best for the people of this town, and had right nobly accomplished it. (Applause.)

MR. ALDERMAN BEMROSE, J.P.—whose opening words, "*Sir Alfred Haslam*, my lords, and gentlemen," was received with loud cheers (this being the first public intimation of the title which the Queen had conferred on the Mayor)—said that, fitly following the other great institutions which had been toasted, he had the honour to propose "The Bishops and Clergy, and Ministers of all Denominations"—a recognition of the great principle that religion must be the foundation of the constitution of an ideal State, and the source alike of the government and of the greatness of their country. (Hear, hear.) To the sanctity of their office, to the extent of their labours, and to the Christ-like character of their work he paid a cordial tribute, remarking that, in these respects, they set a noble example, which we should do well to follow. The presence of the Queen that day, the remembrance of the life Her Majesty had lived, and the principles she had maintained, as well also as the exalted position which she held, under God, in relation to this country, forced on them the conviction that religion was the very essence of their constitution and of their being, and that no State could prosper which did not recognise, in religion, a power superior to its own. (Hear, hear.) From this recognition sprung the stability of their constitution and the blessings which, as Englishmen, they enjoyed. By this had the greatness of their country been established, and it would be continued by the same means. (Cheers.)

THE BISHOP OF DERBY, who was received with applause, said he wished to follow His Worship's orders, and to be exceedingly brief. He must first say, however, how sorry he was that the Bishop of Southwell was unable to be present that night, and how sincerely his lordship regretted that he was compelled to return home by engagements which he could not possibly put off. With reference to the eloquently expressed sentiments of Mr. Bemrose, he trusted that they might take them as true, and as felt by all. (Hear, hear.) There was no body of men who worked harder to promote the great principles to which that gentleman had referred—religion as the foundation of the nation's constitution, and of the sanctity of home life—than the bishops, clergy, and ministers of all denominations. (Hear, hear.) That day they had met to express their loyalty and to express the highest instinct of Christian people—that of charity—and he was sure both were happily knit together in the presence of Her Majesty the Queen. (Hear, hear.) In conclusion, he felt he should be doing no more than expressing their general feeling, when he said how heartily he thanked Almighty God that they had been spared any serious accident—(hear, hear)—for His Worship's anxiety on that point must have been necessarily great—(hear, hear)—and that the memorable proceedings of that day had passed off without any use of the Infirmary at all. (Laughter and applause.)

THE REV. JOHN HASLAM said he had much pleasure in responding on behalf of the ministers of the Free Churches. The form in which the toast was printed and the language of the mover of the toast, showed that the Free Churches were recognised as Churches of Christ, and their pastors as ministers as truly as the clergy were. There was a distinction, and he did not desire to minimise it. All that he claimed for his brethren was that their conscientiousness should be conceded, and that whilst the position of a clergyman had great advantages, their position as the chosen pastors of free communities had its advantages also. It was well to meet, as they were met, on neutral ground. If they only knew each other better, they would respect each other the more, and an intimate knowledge could not be gained except by personal contact. (Cheers.) Differences would then be welcomed as signs of health. Any way, as the Bishop of Ripon once said, "Hollow and insincere agreement was infinitely worse than honest differences of judgment." (Cheers.) Where men were free to think there would be diversity, and he claimed that freedom without apology. The man who had to apologise for his trade, or his politics, or his religion, depend upon it had not much that was worth apologising for. (Cheers.) No man could ever speak with power unless he uttered his convictions, and no man could ever accomplish much in the world unless he had love for his work, and confidence in its ultimate success. (Cheers.) As a native of Derby, he regarded it as a great honour to speak on that occasion, but he should feel humiliated if he did not acknowledge his indebtedness for all he was, and for the influence he had exerted, to the home in which he was reared, and the principles in which he was trained. Nothing during his life had affected him so much as the references made by all the speakers when the Mayor was installed, to his honoured father. It showed how good men influenced society after they were dead, and he was sure his brother would also say that he owed his character and his success largely to the sacrifices of an honoured father, who lived for his children, and whose memory is blessed. (Loud applause.) Turning again to the toast, he said there was no nobler name than minister. This he illustrated by a reference to the minister in "Jessica's First Prayer." The most Christ-like man was the man who served, who ministered, who craved the deepest wisdom, the clearest knowledge, the firmest faith, the brightest hope, the most intense love, not for himself, but that thereby he might render the most effective service, that he might be perfected to minister. (Cheers.) It would be a dark day for England when any other type of life was exalted above this. Religion bound men to God, and therefore to each other. Faith in God led to faith in man. Where there was no faith there must be disintegration. (Cheers.) Some of them had seen this illustrated in France. Voltaire's teaching led to the Reign of Terror, the Bloody Revolution, and they could read now on the blackened ruins, ghastly monuments of anarchy, *liberty*—which meant license, *equality*—which meant degradation at its lowest level, *fraternity*—the fraternity of rampant passion. We heard the same words in England, but the revolution was a peaceful one. The claims of God had been honoured—man had been elevated as God's children, and therefore brothers, precious because for them Christ died. We owe the difference largely to the influence of a pure and self-denying Christianity, to ministers of religion. In closing he pleaded for more of this spirit of ministry—large-hearted philanthropy—mutual help, brotherly service ; for infinite is the help that man can give to man. (Applause).

MR. CHARLES THOMAS, the deputy-chairman of the Midland Railway Co., proposed the " Houses of Lords and Commons." He expressed his deep regret that the sad event which had deprived the Cavendish family of one of its members, had prevented the Marquis of Hartington from taking the prominent part which had been allotted to him in the day's proceedings. He next alluded to the important position which the House of Lords took with regard to the legislative enactments of this country, and said that the representative assembly which gathered in the House of Commons devoted a vast amount of time and attention to the interests of this country. He hoped that Parliament would continue to act in the same constitutional way that it hitherto had done for many centuries to come. (Applause.)

THE EARL OF HARRINGTON, whose name had been coupled with the toast, was applauded on rising to respond. He said much had been said by a previous speaker about his fortune and also his misfortune in replying to the toast allotted to him. He (Lord Harrington) was in a peculiarly unfortunate position, because he felt that every word he spoke would be a word too many. (" No, no," and laughter.) He knew that they would like him to be as brief as possible, because an illustrious statesman was to follow him ; and he could not enter into politics, because he had a friend on his left with whom he should not like to cross swords. (Laughter.) He would, therefore, content himself by thanking the company, on behalf of the House of Lords, for the heartiness with which they had drunk the toast, and would leave the remainder of it to his friend on the left. (Laughter.)

SIR WILLIAM HARCOURT, M.P., also responded to the toast. He said that if he had any claim by the favour of that town to call himself a representative of Derby, in that capacity he begged leave to offer his congratulations and those of the people to the Mayor on the events of that day. That day would be a memorable epoch in the history of Derby. He (Sir William) had occasion to know how rarely it was, that with all the great duties that devolved upon the Queen, she was able to favour any town as she had favoured Derby. (Cheers.) It was due in no small degree to the Mayor's unwearied exertions that Derby had been able to receive the Sovereign in the manner in which it had done on that occasion. (Cheers.) His friend the Recorder had spoken of the political sentiments of the people of the town, and he said " though they were what they were that the demonstration had been loyal." The Recorder made one mistake—he ought to have said it was *because* the people were what they were that the demonstration had been so loyal. (Applause and laughter.) The party to which he belonged claimed an historical and traditional interest in the history of the House of Hanover, and he could not forget, as the representative of Derby, that it was in that town the Pretender to the throne turned his back and fled. And therefore Derby had claim to a peculiar position in respect to its loyalty to the House of Hanover. (Cheers.) Lord Harrington had spoken for the House of Lords. He (Sir William) always recognised that that House had superior qualifications to the House to which he belonged. (Laughter, and hear, hear.) It consisted of superior beings—(laughter)—who were able to transact the affairs of the nation in an extremely brief space of time—in a time which never interfered with their repose, and seldom interrupted their digestion. (Laughter.) Therefore he (Sir William) spoke as one belonging to an inferior order of beings, and what he had to say and what he was called upon to say was for the House of Commons. He could not, however, speak of the House of Commons except under a sense of the calamity which had befallen them all in the death of one of his colleagues. It was to all a public loss, and to many in that room, as it was to him, (Sir William) the loss of a dear personal friend. Those who knew Lord Edward Cavendish, and there were many present who both knew and loved him, were aware that he was a man of a singularly simple and single-minded character. If he (Sir William) had to describe him he should say he was one of the best and truest of friends, and was one of the kindest and most lovable human beings he (the speaker) had ever known. They all felt in Derby and in Derbyshire that they had sustained a great loss, and they felt the deepest sympathy with that family which for so many generations had been of great distinction in the county. They felt for the Duke of Devonshire and for Lord Hartington. (Hear, hear.) It had seldom happened to a father to lose two such sons, and it was a heavy burden to any brother who had lost two such brothers in such a space of time. He had too much respect for that assembly, and too much feeling on the subject to which he had alluded to detain them long. The House of Lords which he had spoken of had one advantage in transacting its affairs, because that body—all of them or most of them—were all of the same mind on the same subject. (Laughter.) That, unfortunately, or fortunately, was not the case with the Commons. They knew that the history of the country had been made and fashioned by party government. He would not then discuss whether that was a good system, but it was the system at least under which the history of England had been made. He claimed that the House of Commons was the first representative institution in the world. (Cheers.) Whatever might be thought and said about that assembly, they had a right to say it was the House of Commons in past ages and in present times that had made and moulded the English nation. It was a body which, whatever might be its defects, had solved the problem of reconciling liberty with order; it was a body which had known how to maintain loyalty to the Throne, and at the same time to vindicate the freedom of the people. (Cheers.) That was a difficult task to perform, and it was a task which for generations past—and he hoped for generations yet to come—the British House of Commons would continue to accomplish. The House of Commons was a body, whatever might be said of it, that remained, and would always remain, the mainspring of the Constitution—which was being the support of the Throne and the vindicator of the rights of the people. In that light and in that respect it had been a great force, and would for all time, he believed, be an example and a hope to mankind. (Cheers.)

THE MAYOR at this point announced that he had just received a telegram from Normanton, saying that Her Majesty had arrived there, and that all had passed off well. (Loud cheers.) He then said that the next toast on the list was that of "The Health of the Duke of Devonshire, Lord Lieutenant of the County and Lord High Steward of the Corporation." He, however, thought that in view of the general loss experienced in the death of Lord Edward, it would be the truest compliment to the Duke of Devonshire to drink the toast in silence.

The toast was drunk with great reverence and in perfect silence.

SIR FREDERICK BRAMWELL submitted the toast of "The Mayor, Corporation, and Borough Magistrates." He said he had known Derby for fifty years, and had watched its growth with a very great amount of interest. He could not help feeling that this growth and its accompanying prosperity were due in no small degree to the good government of the town, and he thought that at that present moment it was as well governed as it ever had been during any previous period of its history. (Applause.) As the hour was growing late he would not detain them with any further remarks, but would ask them to drink to the health of Sir Alfred Haslam and the Corporation and Magistrates of Derby. (Applause.)

The toast was drunk with enthusiasm, and followed by musical honours.

THE MAYOR, who was received with applause, again and again renewed, said he rose with very mingled feelings to respond to the toast. They had just told him that he was "a hearty good fellow." Well, he could only say that he had endeavoured to faithfully perform his duty. When they elected him to the high position of Mayor and Chief Magistrate on the previous 9th of November, he promised to do the best he could to promote the interest and prosperity of this good old borough. He had been guided by the desire conveyed in that promise, and if he had given satisfaction to the town at large that was a reward that he was proud to receive. (Applause.) He had before him the example of many worthy men who had filled the office of Mayor and Chief Magistrate of Derby in past years, and when he glanced at the past history of the borough he considered that the inhabitants had been exceedingly fortunate in having had many excellent mayors at the head of its municipal affairs. (Applause.) There were present,gentlemen to whom his remarks aptly applied, and he could mention families, such as the Strutts, who had taken a very deep interest in the affairs of the Infirmary and the town in the past years. (Applause.) He had also in his memory the admirable example set by their late revered friend—Mr. Bass—(cheers)—while the whole country had before it the glorious example set by the House of Cavendish. (Applause.) There were numerous instances of the deep interest taken in the county by members of that illustrious House for many generations—an interest which was still as vigorous as ever. (Applause.) Therefore, if he and those who succeeded him in the civic chair only looked back upon past history, they had plenty to inspire them to follow in the glorious steps of their predecessors, and in doing so they would deserve well of their town and county. (Applause.) He was proud to see around him so representative a body of his fellow-townsmen, who had rallied round him most earnestly, and he was quite convinced that, unless they had given him their most cordial co-operation and support, he could not have brought the ceremonial of that day to a successful issue. (Applause.) He thanked one and all present, as well as those absent, for the assistance they had rendered him, and was proud to say that the Corporation had maintained their well-earned reputation. (Applause.) He could not allow that occasion to pass without a reference to the Midland Railway Company. From the very first time that he approached them with regard to this auspicious occasion he had received from them the greatest consideration and the most valuable help. From Mr. Paget, the Chairman, and Mr. Noble, the General Manager, down to the lowest official, he had received great courtesy and most efficient help, and desired to return his hearty thanks to those gentlemen. (Applause.) One other compliment he had to bestow, and that was to the able manager of the catering department of that excellent railway system—he meant Mr. William Towle—whose arrangements certainly could not be surpassed. (Applause.) Mr. Towle had made his way in the past, and had not only achieved a position of distinction, but had also maintained it. (Applause.) With regard to the observations of Sir F. Bramwell, he (the Mayor) could only say that if he had done anything to merit the approval of his colleagues and the town, he was quite satisfied, although he did not feel that he had done more than his duty to the Queen, to his country, and to his native town. (Applause.) No man, however, could possibly have a greater reward than the inner consciousness of having done his duty. (Applause.) He concluded by saying the Corporation did their best to promote the welfare of the town, and he believed they would always be actuated by the same motive. (Applause.)

Mr. ALDERMAN ROE, M.P., submitted the toast of "The Visitors." He said the Mayor could not fail to be highly delighted at seeing so many visitors amongst his guests, and the number would have been greater had not the prevailing epidemic of influenza made such ravages among his numerous friends and well-wishers. (Applause.) He coupled with the toast the names of Mr. E. S. Norris, M.P., and the Mayor of Lincoln (Mr. Edwin Pratt). (Applause.) Nobody was more pleased than himself to see their old townsman and friend, Mr. Edwin Pratt, in their midst. (Applause.) All who knew him would sincerely congratulate him upon serving the office of Mayor of Lincoln for a second term, knowing that in the future, as well as in the past, he would perform the duties with dignity, ability, and efficiency. (Applause.)

Mr. E. S. NORRIS, M.P., in responding, said the visitors had been most warmly received and hospitably entertained. He congratulated the Mayor—the chief Magistrate of this great town—upon the dignity and success of the day's ceremonial, and thanked the Corporation for their hospitality. It was a great honour and compliment to have received a visit from Her

Majesty the Queen, especially in connection with one of those movements in which she was so deeply interested. (Applause.) The re-establishment of the Infirmary was a work of great importance, and would doubtless be supported by all who valued such noble institutions. (Applause.) The event of that day would form a memorable period in the borough of Derby, and the visitors would return to their respective homes impressed with the loyalty and hospitality of Derby, and anxious for its continued growth and prosperity. (Applause.)

The Mayor of Lincoln, who was very cordially received, also responded. He said it was very difficult for him, as a native of Derby, to realise that he was now only a visitor. He could not, however, help remembering that in the town of his birth he was for more than a quarter of a century actively connected with its municipal life and government. As a visitor he desired to offer to the Mayor his sincere and hearty congratulations upon the honour that day bestowed upon him—(applause)—and he could truthfully say that no one had more fully deserved such a recognition from his Sovereign. (Applause.) He remembered that he (Mr. Pratt) had been identified with two previous Royal visits to Derby, and on both those occasions the town had the good fortune to have at the head of its municipal affairs gentlemen whose princely liberality and great energy produced such successful issues to those important events. (Applause.)

This concluded the toast list, and the gathering then dispersed.

THE DECORATIONS AND ILLUMINATIONS.
THE APPEARANCE OF THE STREETS AT NIGHT.

We remember to have read a description of a great Italian Carnival, in which the writer's store of adjectives was somewhat restricted, for he could get no further in the matter of terms than gorgeous pageant, gorgeous ceremonial, and gorgeous equipages. The effect of the illuminations after the veil of night had fallen over Derby, on Thursday night, May 21st, may be epitomised as "gorgeous," but even that is vexing in its completeness, and one would rather be inclined to adopt the ejaculation of our old friend Dominie Sampson, and exclaim "Prodigious!" At any rate the display which the Corporation, the Midland Railway Company, and the citizens of Derby generally, had for several days been preparing, could not truthfully be alluded to in any other but the superlative degree. The arrangements in many cases included novelties, and in no single instance could the effort to add lustre to the scene be considered in any way to have approached failure. From at least three positions on the Royal route the spectacle would bear comparison with all we have read, or heard, or seen of the great festivals abroad, or even the much-vaunted Jubilee illuminations of the Metropolis: the effects being marvels of magnificence, revels of brilliancy, feasts of lanterns. Some judges might be inclined to aver that, if you put the Town Hall and Free Library together, the efforts of the Corporation would (in the young-man-of-the-period phraseology) "take the Huntley and Palmer;" but we imagine that not a few discriminating spectators mentally inscribed their verdict, *facile princeps*, across the Midland Railway Station front. One of the finest effects at the Station might be said to consist of the huge revolving wheel in the centre of the grand front, in which the hub thereof, which remained stationary, was surrounded by two huge glittering circles revolving in opposite directions. Flanked and surmounted and supported as this was by fifteen or sixteen large devices in scintillating crystals, and surrounded by string-courses of Bengal lamps, with green connective festoons of the latter looped up by ruby tassels, a *tout ensemble* was achieved, which was in every way unique. If to this be added the large designs and lamp lines on the Midland Hotel, and the griffins, and stars, and crowns on the other Midland property in Station Street, we may be considered to have committed to paper only an inadequate notion of a spectacle to which might very well be applied the hackneyed phrase, "better imagined than described." The various hotels in Midland Road seemed in friendly rivalry to vie with each other in the effectiveness or novelty of their contributions to the blaze of luminosity in which the struggling masses of humanity, during Thursday evening, May 21st, spent many hours in wandering up and down. It rested with Mr. W. W. Winter to introduce a feature in photographic illumination, which attracted a very numerous company—viz., the projection, on a transparency, of a number of views by the aid of a large camera. London Road, by reason of the sparsity of habitations, was in comparative darkness, nevertheless some very pretty effects were accomplished by means of Chinese lanterns, crystal devices, and Bengal lamps, while near Trinity Church a large spreading tree was charmingly delineated by means of fairy lamps hung among the tender leaflets. Passing down London and St. Peter's Streets,

and the Corn Market, the illuminations increased in volume and brilliancy; one or
two items were none the less meritorious because they were old friends, while in at least a
single case there was exhibited a dual desire to do honour to the great occasion and to
advertise the business. The narrowness of the Wardwick to a certain extent prevented an
adequate appreciation of the marvellous results of the treatment of the Free Library, which
was admirably seconded by the Gas Company a little further on. No prettier object could be
imagined than the former building with every outline, angle, quoin, and string course picked
out in lamps of different hues—green, white, yellow, ruby, and violet. Here, too, electricity
came in, and the combined effect was decidedly dazzling. In the Market Place the principal
feature was of course the Town Hall, which, though of a diametrically opposite style of
architecture, was treated similarly to the Free Library; and with at least rivalling success.
So far we have endeavoured to give an epitomised general idea of the illuminations themselves; but they constituted only half the scene, which was considerably heightened by the
waving of flags and banners, the perpetually changing and swinging and wriggling festoons
of greenery and artificial flowers, which were ever and anon brought out in sharp relief
against the dark sky and comparative gloom of some side streets. Add to this the roadway
and sidewalks densely packed with a struggling sea of humanity, whose pale faces were
always turned towards the light, and the continuous streams of carriages, cabs, and vehicles
of all kinds requisitioned for the special service, and some notion may be gathered of the
scene in the streets from the time daylight went out up to midnight. Not the least congratulatory part of the business of the day was the absolute refusal of the populace to allow
their ardour to be damped by the rain, which spat with spiteful persistency upon them
during the proceedings. Fun and good humour were the order of the day and night,
throughout which the hilarity of the good old town of Derby rose higher until, like
Sir Middlesex Mashem on his wedding morn, it attained a condition of "delirious delight,"
of "rollicking rapture," which refused to be modified until the advent of heavy rain about
midnight sent most folk home and to bed.

The illuminations in the town—those of the Town Hall, Free Library, and Midland
Railway Station and Hotel, being the chief centres of attraction—were continued on the
following Friday and Saturday evenings, and, notwithstanding the damp and cold, were
visited, until midnight, by large crowds of appreciative and orderly people. The
illuminations at the Mayor's residence on the Duffield Road were continued during
the following week. Notwithstanding the extension of the hours of licensed houses, in
order to enable the people inspecting the illuminations to obtain refreshments, on both
Thursday and Friday nights, the streets were singularly quiet, and almost entirely free
from drunkenness and disorderly behaviour.

THE INTERIOR OF THE RAILWAY STATION.

The only part of the railway station in regard to which there was any attempt at decoration consisted of the particular portion of the down platform at which the Royal train was arranged to arrive. The remainder of the station was left severely alone. Though few surfaces permit of more effective or more elaborate decoration than a large railway station with its multitudinous girders, and bars, and rods, each of which serve as an additional point from which to add something to the general display, yet in this case the mere fact that so large a portion of the station remained unadorned by a solitary banner served to show up the effect of that particular section to which the hand of the decorator had been applied. As already stated, this portion was only of limited extent. It stretched from the Directors' Room either way for a distance more or less of twenty-five yards, and, under the directions of Mr. Pettifor, the chief of the Stores Department, this individual part of the platform had been made to assume an appearance of considerable gaiety and picturesqueness. The first building entered by Her Majesty the Queen after leaving the Royal train was the Directors' Room at the station, through which she passed in order to reach the Royal Reception and Retiring Rooms. The entrance, therefore, was decorated so as to hide the sombre appearance of an ordinary brick wall and doorway. The doorway was draped very effectively in a light material of red and blue. The window by which it is flanked on the right, and the entrance to the stationmaster's office on the left, were each draped with a crimson cloth, and had on the whole a very bright effect. Along the gallery above a more elaborate decoration extended, formed of a draping of crimson cloth with blue and white festooned reliefs, and extending over the whole distance of about fifty yards. Immediately over the doorway leading through the Directors' Room to the floral corridor was the Royal Standard, emblazoned on a large and beautiful shield, whilst throughout the decorations, shields and trophies of flags had been fixed at short intervals, some of the shields bearing in small figures the emblazonments of the Royal Standard, others the motto of the Order of the Garter, and others conventional designs of a very chaste and harmonious character, whilst from the ironwork of the roof, within the section selected for decorative treatment, hung banners and bannerets, which imparted a very pleasing *tout ensemble*. Of course the station officials had to bear in mind the convenience of the ordinary passenger traffic. In order, therefore, to create as little crushing and impediment as possible on the stairways leading to and from the various platforms, it had been decided to board up the bridges and so cover up the various staircases as to prevent any person seeing Her Majesty from that point of vantage. This arrangement minimised the danger of passengers waiting upon the bridges and the stairs to the lowest degree, and most effectually carried out the object for which it was designed.

THE FLORAL CORRIDOR.

Somewhat resembling an arbour, in which the imagination of the gardener, the painter, and the decorator combined to produce a light and beautiful retreat, was the Floral Corridor through which Her Majesty passed from the station to the Royal Reception Room, and from the Royal Reception Room to the Royal carriage. The corridor was a light and beautiful retreat, formed in the shape of a palm house or aviary, and, as we have said, leading from the station buildings outwards. It consisted of light bays or spans of equal proportions, and at the junction of each was an arrangement of lattice work, among and about which , roses, interspersed with rose leaves, springing out of the supports, were intertwined with all the art of the landscape gardener's craft. The architect of the corridor had certainly succeeded in producing a most pleasing and graceful effect by the use of the most commonplace materials of poles and laths, which is in truth no empty compliment, for on such occasions as these the man who with small materials can build up a temporary superstructure of beauty is the man who is wanted. The lattice work at the intersections of the bays gave a most pleasing effect to the corridor itself, and afforded the means of the most graceful display, while it formed a support to the canvas roof with which the corridor was covered in. The sides of the awning were formed of canvas, arranged in alternate panels of white and sage green, the white being box pleated with green stripes, and the effect being in entire harmony with the flesh-tinted roses growing from the supports and the vari-coloured flowers which were lavishly used in the decorations. Through the centre of the corridor ran a raised wooden platform some eight feet in width, and leading away to the right was the approach to the reception-room. Right and left of this raised way, and springing from the sides, were flower boxes filled with hot-house flowers and plants and shrubs, the boxes striking out at each one of the supports into octagonal form round the base, so as to provide additional and ample room for covering the pillars with floral wealth of green and colour as required. Between the raised way and the flower boxes were gravel beds, in the which at short intervals, so as to fill in the intervening spaces between the supports, had been planted various varieties of evergreen shrubs, which certainly had the effect of imparting a life-like and natural air to the whole place. The centre way was covered with crimson cloth, reaching close up to the decorated sides; and from the centre of each bay was suspended an electric light in the form of a bronze bell. The corridor was designed by Mr. Trubshaw, the architect to the Midland Railway Company, and the floral decorations were provided by Mr. Cooling, of the Mile Ash Nurseries, who found himself much embarrassed by the lateness and coldness of the season in finding a sufficiency of excellent shrubs and plants to enable him adequately to carry out these decorations; but no one who saw the almost wonderful wealth of bloom which was displayed all over the corridor could deny that he had been able, with all his difficulties, to furnish a most effective and beautiful display. It would be almost impossible to enumerate the many rich and rare specimens of floriculture which he brought together. In one bay there was a profusion of geranium flowers, varying in shade and differing in hue, but displaying all the depth and richness of colouring of these species. In the next bay were the *cupressus aurea*, interspersed with margueritas, and magnificent specimens of the *spirea japonica* and the *spirea palmata*; while in other bays were fine plants of the order of the *pelargonium*, the *cineraria*, the *hydrangea portensus*, with the commoner rhododendron, the fuchsias, and the forget-me-not, interspersed with fine examples of the bamboo and beautiful plants of the Chinese maple. The whole provided a floral display which was much and deservedly admired.

INTERIOR OF THE ROYAL RECEPTION ROOM.

[*T. Scotton, Derby*

THE ROYAL RECEPTION ROOM.

The Reading Room ordinarily used by the clerks at the station had undergone a metamorphosis so complete as to render it one of the most beautiful and airy apartments one could conceive. It is no exaggeration to say that the art of the upholsterer and the decorator had done wonders. From a somewhat sombre apartment, surrounded with equally sombre adjuncts, we found the place transformed into an apartment light in character, with a gossamer sort of air about it, and possessing all the charm and attraction of a modern drawing room. Every particle of the old had given place to the new, and a more effectual hiding away of all that could offend the sight was surely never accomplished. The room itself in dimensions extends for about forty-five feet in length, and about twenty-four feet in width. To begin with, it stands on the right-hand side of the open space lying between the station buildings and the hotel, and is immediately contiguous to and adjoining the directors' rooms. In order to connect the clerks' room, that is the Royal Reception Room, with the directors' room, through which Her Majesty passed from the station, had been constructed the floral corridor already described. On entering the Reception Room one was immediately struck with the air of richness with which everything about it was invested. As you walked through the doorway you were directed right or left by a semi-circular handrailing, branching out in both directions in the form of the two outer feathers in the Prince of Wales' plume, behind which the Queen's attendants stood as Her Majesty passed through the entrance way. The upholstery of the place was rich and beautiful in the extreme. The doorway leading from the corridor stood out in the richness of its draperies among the floral decorations of the wall. The entrance was placed about half-way along the corridor between the station buildings and the Midland Hotel, and was hung with a pair of rich and handsome chenille *portière* curtains, and draped with satin, terra-cotta in shade, arranged in small festoons. On either side of the short path leading from the central way to the Reception Room, the most beautiful of the floral decorations were massed, and gave the corner an appearance which stood out in contrast almost even with the general beauty of the enclosure. The entire appearance of the room, when viewed from the outside, was one of ease and comfort, united to richness and taste. The walls were covered with pleated draperies in cream-coloured satin, relieved with old gold satin decorations. Along the side of the wall, opposite the entrance, were ten panels, each of which was filled in with pleated draperies, arranged to fall in perpendicular folds, the division between the panels being formed by handsome cretonne draperies. The end walls were in like manner divided into three panels, the centre one being double the width of the others, so as to allow for the fire-grate at the one end, and the entrance to the Royal Retiring Room in the corresponding panel at the other end of the room. The ceiling was also draped with similarly coloured satin material, intersected with old gold ornamentation; and the room was lighted by two windows, which were draped with cretonne and festooned draperies. Artificial light was provided by two electric lamps hanging from the ceiling. The glass pendants were of a colour to match the decorations of the room, and were richly and beautifully chased, so as to diminish as far as possible any glare from the light.

Turning to the furniture of the apartment, it was difficult to select for special commendation a particular object where all was uniformly excellent. As we have already said, though richness and taste have without doubt been the dominant idea in the mind of Messrs. Gillow in furnishing the room, yet they had not altogether overlooked the comfort which is always an important element, however much the eye may be turned to the general effect. And so the various articles of furniture had been chosen with a due regard as well to their usefulness as their beauty in design and workmanship. There were chairs in the Queen Anne, the Chippendale, and the French styles of make, all of them beautiful, and all of them costly. Some of the ladies who were permitted to view the apartment, and to receive some account of the various objects of interest contained therein, seemed to be as much impressed with the costliness of the things as with their merits as works of the cabinet maker's art ; but all were

THE QUEEN'S CHAIR.

united in the opinion that the particular chair set apart for Her Majesty's use after her long journey was a model of comfort as of elegance. This chair, known as one of Gillow's Worthing chairs, was constructed in the form of a gentleman's ordinary easy chair, upholstered in silk tapestry with rolls of plush and borders, trimmed with heavy tassel fringe and cord to match the general decoration of the room, and was the embodiment of comfort and ease. The room contained, in addition, all the beautiful objects which of late years especially have come to be regarded as essentials to a well-appointed drawing-room. Handsome Japanese cabinets, rich in the quality of wood of which they were made, as in the inlaying work and the brass mountings, were placed here and there along the wall ; while cabinets in rosewood with ivory inlays, of ebony inlaid with lighter woods, of rosewood inlaid with satinwood, and various other designs stood in convenient corners, and added immensely to the general appearance of comfort and luxury. Over the mantelpiece was a magnificent bevelled mirror, enclosed in a frame of inlaid ebony surmounted by a velvet-plush bordering in crimson. The remainder of the chairs, of which there were at least a dozen, were heavily gilt in the French style, covered with rich silk upholstery. The floor was covered with blue felting overlaid with Persian rugs of beautiful design and richest materials; and the recesses of the room were rich in beautiful Japanese urns and screens, and various articles of bijouterie and vertu gave a finish and a charm to a beautiful apartment.

It will no doubt interest our readers to know that though the celebrated firm of Messrs. Gillow and Co. came to fit up the rooms for Her Majesty's reception, yet the stoves and all that belong to them were made in our town, and for correctness of design and quality of workmanship they could not be surpassed. It is certainly agreeable to find that in these days of cheap goods we have still amongst us those who are both willing and able to do such good and genuine work, which, while it reflects the highest credit on those who do it, still also adds to the credit of our town. The makers were The Derwent Foundry Co. (Messrs. Jobson), whose productions are to be found in all quarters of the world wherever the English fireplace is used, and who even in the most depressed times have always produced sound, substantial work which shall be lasting, rather than those cheap goods which are a credit to no one.

The Stove in the Reception Room was an "Abbotsford," and made entirely of cast brass, polished and chased in the most elaborate way in the style adopted by the Brothers Adam, who built Kedleston Hall, and other noble houses round about us. The tiles in the cheeks were painted by hand specially to match, and formed a panel complete of itself, relieved with festoons and scroll work. All the tiles in the hearth were also painted by hand, so that no expense had been spared to produce the finest effect obtainable. The fender was polished steel and brass. The *tout ensemble* was most elaborate and rich in effect without being overdone, and perfectly harmonised with all the rest of the fittings of the room without appearing too gorgeous or out of place.

THE ROYAL RETIRING ROOM.

The Royal Retiring Room was reached from the Reception Room by a doorway which was fitted with a heavy brass *portière* pole and a pair of beautiful Chinese curtains which separated the one apartment from the other and secured privacy. Inside the Retiring Room the furniture was of much the same character in construction as that in the Reception Room. The floor was covered with a rich Axminster square of a dark blue ground. The walls of the apartment were draped with a light cretonne of beautiful design, festooned with blue satin decorations, and the ceiling was hung with similar material as was used in the Reception Room, but a different style was adopted, the pleating here being from a central rose, and radiating to the wall so as to form a sun-ray. The window was draped in blue satin, the decorations again taking the form of festooned hangings of the same material. The furniture in this room was partly Queen Anne in style and partly of a modern description, but was equally rich in the material and the workmanship, as was that in the Reception Room. It consisted of two very handsome washstands of the style of Queen Anne period and other articles of furniture to match, with several occasional tables of various design and character. The whole of the furniture and decorations were supplied by Messrs. Gillow and Co., of London, Liverpool, and Manchester.

The stove in Her Majesty's Retiring Room was also one of the celebrated "Abbotsfords," and was made of wrought brass, and by the old *repousse* process. The design is in the style of Louis XV., which at present is so much in vogue. The tiles, both in the sides and in the hearth, are laid in panels worked up in Portland cement, a kind of work which this firm have made a speciality for some years past. The side tiles were designed specially for this occasion, showing a promptitude and enterprise we are glad to notice. The fender in this case was also of polished steel, and relieved with brass, to match the grate; and while the whole suite was just as elaborate as the one in the larger room, yet it was so entirely different in design that, were it not for the excellence of the work, it would hardly be supposed to have been produced by the same firm.

The Queen's magnificent apartments were thrown open to the public, at a charge of 1s. a head, on Friday and Saturday, May 22nd and 23rd, the result being that a substantial sum (amounting on the first day to about £25) was realised, and generously handed over to the Building Fund of the Infirmary. Altogether 1,200 people visited the rooms on the two days, and the handsome sum of £60, for the excellent object above mentioned, was realised.

THE STATION EXTERIOR.

The decorations of the exterior of the Midland Railway Station buildings and the Midland Hotel had been entrusted to the care of Messrs. Defries and Sons, of Houndsditch, London; and when it is mentioned that probably no other firm in existence has an equal experience in decorative work of this description, not only in this country but in almost every city of any magnitude throughout Europe, it will be unnecessary to go further, and to say that the work was most satisfactory. Yet such was the case. The Midland Railway Company seem to have desired to do their best to make their buildings attractive, and the decorators well seconded their efforts, the result being a mass of colour in the day time and a blaze of light in the evening, which formed an attraction and a delight to thousands. As would be seen at once by the observer, the general idea in the mind of Messrs. Defries and Sons was to cover the whole of the building as far as possible with trophies, crystals, devices, flags, and banners, and this was accomplished so as to carry out a tasteful design. Dealing first with the front of the station buildings, it would be seen that the columns forming the entrance were enriched with numerous trophies of flags, each trophy supported by a shield bearing a device. This style of ornamentation was carried straight across the lower wall; but at each of the windows of the centre portion, and at each of the pillars forming the archways, a similar treatment was brought in, and so the ordinary brick frontage was greatly relieved and brightened. Over the cornice of the entrance to the station, and continued along from end to end of the outer wall, was a broad band of crimson cloth, bordered with heavy gold fringe, and festooned in design, each of the festoons being gathered in the centre with a golden rose. This design was warm and cheerful, and did a great deal to relieve the eye. Surmounting the central or main archway was a large crystal shield bearing the device of the Royal Standard. This shield was formed of decorated glass, and was surmounted with a large crown, and encompassed with laurel leaves set in green crystal on each side, and containing in addition the letters V.R. in crystal. In the sunlight these crystal devices shone with ever changing colour, while in the evening they lent an additional lustre and brilliancy to the illumination which enhanced in a great degree the general effulgence. On the left of this device was affixed a medallion under a crown bearing the words, "God Save the Queen," and on the right was a similar medallion and crown, in the centre of which was a continuation and completion of the loyal wish expressed in its counterpart by the words, "Long may she reign." At the extreme right and left were two brilliant stars bearing the well-known motto of the order of the Garter, *Honi soit qui mal y pense*, while across and over the entrance were arranged festoons or garlands of green and ruby illumination lamps. The design of the arrangement of these lamps was to so place them that at the right and left extremities were the *fleur de lis* in appropriate colours (red, amber, and green). Proceeding to the main *façade* and still going upwards, the treatment increased in richness and elaboration. Underneath the row of windows which extend across the high portion of the building, was a garland formed of evergreens, so as to make the decoration in keeping with the archway and turrets on the right. This evergreen decoration was relieved with trophies and festoons of crimson draperies. The clock in the centre of the building was balanced on either side with trophies and shields and crystals, six in number, three of which bore the letters "V.R.," while one on the left and one on the right was enriched with the arms of the Borough of Derby, and on the remaining shield was a device of the Royal Standard. Over the clock came a crimson cloth adornment, and in the centre a magnificent and brilliant transparent star of coloured glass, 12 feet in diameter, formed of three separate circles, each revolving independently so as to produce a fine kaleidoscopic effect; and over the head of this transparency was the word "Welcome" in Roman capitals, four feet long, also in brilliants edged with green; this being in turn surmounted with a large and beautifully decorated medallion surrounding the coat of arms of the Midland Railway Company, and through this ran up the flag-staff. Arrangements were made by the electrician to the Midland Railway Company for a special electrical connection between the platform and this flag-staff, whereby on the arrival of the Queen the Royal Standard was immediately floating in the air, and formed a fitting triumph to the blaze of decorations with which the whole frontage of the station was adorned.

THE MIDLAND HOTEL.

Turning our attention to the Midland Hotel for a moment, the decorations at this spot were no less tasteful than were those on the station itself. Of course the open space between the two buildings named was well and completely occupied by the fine arch and supports afterwards described; but when the hotel building was reached we again found evidence of careful design and skilful workmanship. The entrance to the building, and right across both wings, was covered with navy blue cloth tapestry, which, as in the case of the similar adornment of the station, was bordered with a heavy border of gold, and gathered into festoons surmounted by golden rosettes. This design formed the decoration over each of the two tiers of windows. Over the chief entrance was a large medallion surmounted with a crown, and bearing the words, "God Bless the Queen," with the monogram "V.R." interlaced in the centre, and resting upon a frame work of laurel leaves similar to that used in the decoration of the station buildings. Right and left were two trophies of flags, one of which was supported by a shield bearing the coat of arms of the Borough of Derby, and the other by a similar shield containing another device. The principal part of the building was outlined in amber lights for illumination purposes, and in the framework so created were represented in crystal the letters "V.R." at either end of the two wings of the hotel buildings, with a crystal star containing the motto of the Order of the Garter in the centre. The stars were connected to the central letters by garlands formed of green lamps terminating in *fleur de lis*. It will probably have been observed with respect to the decorations of the Station Buildings and the Free Library, that Messrs. Defries had adopted at these two places the very opposite modes of treatment employed in the illuminations. At the Free Library the most chaste style was selected, and not a line was out of place. At the Railway Station, consequent upon the very small space at disposal, every device that could be crowded into the illumination was adopted; and again at the Town Hall a combination of the two styles was employed, so as to obtain a full benefit of the *façade*. It was generally conceded that the display at the station and hotel was superior to any design on a similar scale executed in London on Jubilee Day.

The whole of the designs were settled and the arrangements carried out by Messrs. Defries, under the personal direction of Mr. G. H. Turner, the assistant general manager of the Midland Railway Company.

THE EVERGREEN ARCH AT THE MIDLAND STATION.

Surrounding the Royal enclosure, which really was the open space lying between the entrance to the directors' room in the station buildings and the side of the Midland Hotel, was erected a spacious gallery for the accommodation of visitors, and this was allotted to the principal officials of the Midland Railway, of whom a great number were present. This gallery extended on both sides of the enclosure, joining on each side to the magnificent archway which spanned the entrance from the hotel to the station buildings. A great deal of taste and an equal amount of labour had been lavished upon this magnificent archway, with its supporting towers and splendid workmanship. It was through this archway that Her Majesty passed on leaving the Reception Room to obtain access to the public street, and it was here that a grand welcome was accorded to her as she first emerged to the view of the enthusiastic inhabitants of the ancient town. To describe the archway itself in detail would be a matter of considerable difficulty, but we may give our readers a general idea of its features, and they by that means will be able to judge for themselves of the imposing addition it made to the decorations of the town. The archway itself, then, had a span of about 20 feet, and was semi-circular, not Gothic, in form, the rise to its summit being about 10 feet. It was flanked on each side by octagonal towers covered with domes, and, so far as one could allocate it to any distinctive style, it was Italian in feeling. The thought that

Record of the Queen's State Visit to Derby. 77

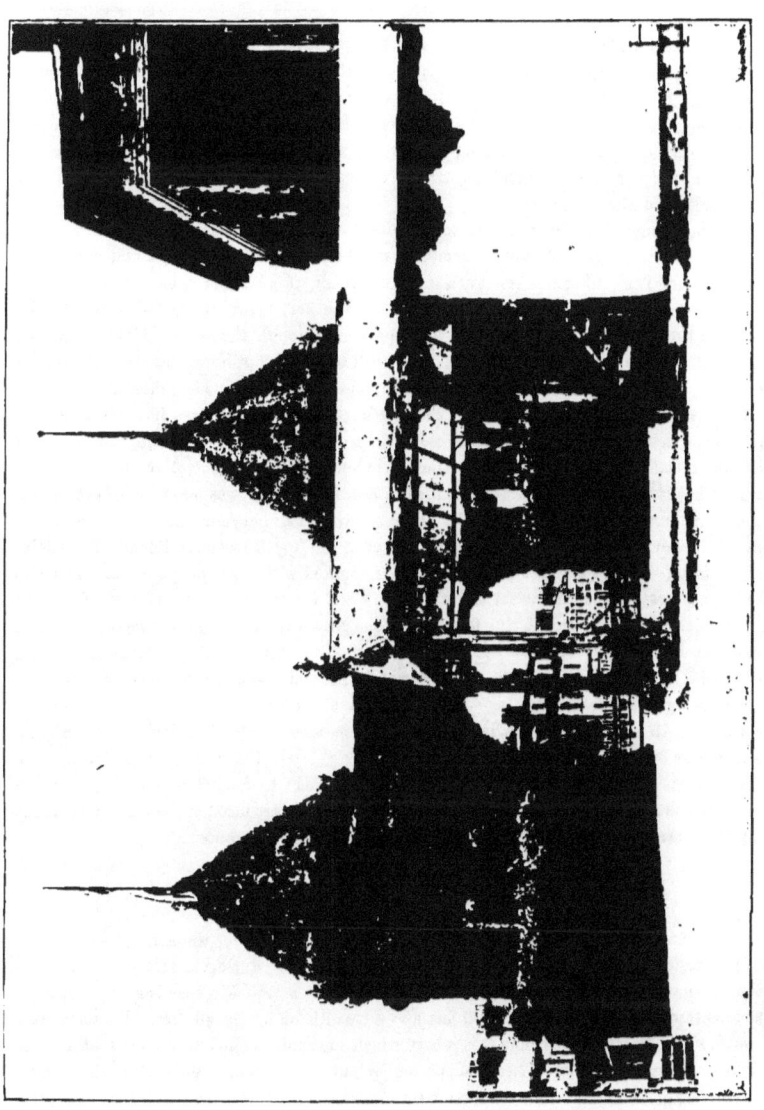

The Evergreen Arch, Midland Station.

Photo. by] [F. E. Renrose.

struck the spectator in viewing it was that it had been mainly designed to represent an old tower, over which evergreens and ivy had spread with advancing years until they covered it altogether. The sides were octagonal in form, and rose to a total height of about 42 feet, or an altitude of 20 feet more than the arch itself. Each turret was surmounted with a flag staff. The construction of the flanking towers was of a nature to afford ample means for decorations, and to give the general appearance of the archway and its accessories an air of great dignity and attractiveness.

To enter somewhat into details as to the construction of these flanking towers, we may say that the interior of each tower formed a stand a few feet from the ground capable of accommodating from fifteen to twenty people, and within this shaded enclosure some privileged spectators were stationed, and enjoyed one of the best views of Her Majesty and the procession that was obtained during the Royal progress through the town. Underneath the window sills in the tower were balconies filled with beautiful hot-house plants, supplied by Mr. Lewis, of The Leylands, Derby, who also supplied the flowers which filled the vases on the top of the pilasters of this edifice. The towers were solid at the base in order to form a platform for the visitors as already described. Then came the space containing seven arched windows in each of the turrets. In these windows, which were Gothic in form, were beautiful hot-house flowers, so that from base to top the structure was one mass of evergreens and flowers, varied and intermingled with the same art which had characterised the arrangement of the floral display in the Royal corridor and in the Royal Reception Room. The angles of the octagon were emphasized with pilasters surmounted with vases of giant size, filled also with the choicest hot-house flowers and shrubs. Each tower was domed upwards from the main cornice to the bottom of the flag-pole. The archway itself was surmounted with a balustrade, immediately over the centre of the arch being a pedestal also surmounted by a vase filled with exotics. The effect obtained was varied and grand, and formed a magnificent relief to what would otherwise have been rather a blank space in the general scheme of decoration. As it was, Mr. Trubshaw seized upon an appropriate site, designed a building which was in every way in harmony with it, and carried it out in a manner which left nothing to be desired. The great aim was to secure a grand effect by a combination of greens and the various shades of shrubbery, which, when intermingled, produced in the whole a harmony of blending that was one of the most pleasing features of the decorations.

THE MAYOR'S DINING MARQUEE.

The whole of the garden attached to the Midland Hotel had, for the nonce, been changed into a series of marquees, designed to serve various purposes during the Royal visit. The principal chamber, so constructed, was the Mayor's dining marquee, a spacious and handsome apartment, extending to a length of 90 feet and a breadth of nearly 50 feet. Its sides were of wood, rising to a height of nine feet, above which the roof was led to an apex at a great height from the boarded floor, being supported by substantial poles, themselves the subject of decoration. The sides of the marquee were draped in breadths of the well-known Liberty art fabrics of various colours, dark and light terra cotta, and amber and cream being tastefully alternated, and the surface being relieved by numerous Madras muslin-draped mirrors. Running along the top of these side walls was an orange-coloured valance, gracefully arranged in festoons. The roof was lined with red and white bands of cloth, and of the marquee as a whole, it may be said that it was lofty, well ventilated, well constructed, and comfortable; whilst its appearance, especially as illuminated by the electric light, had a singularly brilliant Oriental effect. The lighting was, indeed, a feature upon which great care had been expended. Suspended from the roof were two large clusters of lights hanging free, and, again, the supporting roof columns were pressed into the service to support additional globes, whilst brass brackets around the sides contributed their quota to the general brilliance. The floor of the marquee was carpeted in red baize. As to the tables, the principal guest table ran along the whole length of the apartment, whilst at right angles eight shorter tables served well nigh to cover the floor, and to provide accommodation for a large number of participants in the feast. The entrance to this scene of picturesqueness and beauty was from the Midland Hotel corridor, which was continued by means of a specially constructed covered way, 52 feet in length, giving direct access to the dining tent. Off this avenue, however, were intermediately two minor marquees, the one on the right being devoted to the purposes of a cloak-room, whilst on the left a larger one, plainly but effectively draped with alternate red and white cloth, and with a roof similarly treated, served the purpose of a reception chamber. The floor of this was covered with a figured carpet, and as in the dining-room, the electric light was employed for illumination. It should be stated that the construction and decoration of these marquees, and the erection of the kitchens and serving room in connection with the dining chamber, were in the capable hands of Messrs. Womersley, St. James's Street, Leeds. The electric light, which formed so significant a feature in the arrangement, was supplied from a large number of storage batteries near at hand, under the control of Mr. Langdon, of the Electrical Department of the Midland Railway Company, and it is also to be stated that many of the fittings employed were kindly lent by Messrs. Verity and Son, of London, who stepped forward and generously offered the advantages of their plant and appliances.

THE ELECTRIC ILLUMINATIONS.

The electric lighting arrangements were under the control and direction of Mr. Langdon, electrician to the Midland Railway Company, and it is almost superfluous to say that they were well devised and carried out. No expense and labour were spared to render this part of the decorative programme as complete as possible, and it formed no small part of the whole. The introduction of electricity to the general purposes of illumination adds one more instrument of utility to the armoury of the decorative artist, and enables him to dare effects of which only a few years ago he never dreamed. So it proved on this occasion. In the Reception Room, in the Floral Chamber, in the Banquetting Hall, on the Midland Hotel, on the Station Buildings, in fact wherever the electric illuminant was brought into force, the effect was superb. The softened radiance seemed almost to steal unobserved through the

Royal apartments, and as the perfume of a flower sometimes seems to be an insinuation of a presence rather than an actuality, and yet to bathe the whole atmosphere in fragrance, so the little globes of light which decked the apartments, like so many living glow-worms suffused all around in a subdued luminance which formed an additional charm. The batteries which were used to create the electric light were the same which supply the passenger trains on the Midland system, and were brought to the various spots required, and arranged in sufficient numbers to generate the power necessary to supply the requisite current of electricity.

THE ROYAL PAVILION.

As the Infirmary was the *raison d'être* of the visit of the Queen so it was only to be anticipated that on and about the old Infirmary buildings and the site of the new institution great efforts should be put forth to give *éclat* to the ceremonies and rejoicings of the day. We had therefore a lavish display of bunting, and the approaches to the pavilion, which covered the site of the foundation-stone and afforded probably the very best position for obtaining a view of the Sovereign and Royal and distinguished party, were gay with colours and alive with waving decorations. At the extreme end of the site a wide entrance had been opened out, opposite Canal Street, and as this was supposed to be the point at which Her Majesty would enter the grounds, unusual efforts had been made to give it an attractive appearance. The entrance itself was about fifty feet in width, and at either side had been erected a quartette of poles, surmounted with a crown, and bearing beautiful floral and artistic designs and devices, in keeping with the general idea which seemed to have prevailed in regard to the street adornments all along the route. Stretching across the wide opening ran a sort of gallery, decorated with crimson cloth, and offering, in large letters, a "Welcome to Derby." Evergreens and bunting covered the gallery, and, in contrast with the brighter colours, added to the effect by giving to it a brightness which otherwise would have been wanting. Along the whole of the roadway leading up to and ending in the Royal marquee, massive stands, rising tier above tier like the old Roman circus, occupied the space on either side. The scene which was presented to the eye when these immense semi-circular galleries were fully occupied, was one of intense beauty and animation. From the entrance to the grounds to the very doors of the pavilion stretched a sea of human life, animated with one desire, and dominated with one impulse—to see and to do honour to their Sovereign. The roadway between was also a scene of great beauty. Venetian masts were erected at short intervals along this portion of the route, trophies of flags, and a profusion of banners and shields adorned the supports, and across the roadway long bands of streamers formed a sort of roof to the approach, and these temporary adornments being backed by the radiant faces of the visitors and the green of the trees, the whole presented a picture in which there was nothing lacking to give it the attraction of beauty and the action of a living power. Turning to the front approach to the old Infirmary buildings, the efforts of the decorator had not been forgotten, but as compared with the extraordinary results on the road from the temporary approach, but little had been done. The iron gates had for the day given up their old solidity of appearance, and, under the softening influences of evergreen decorations, presented a much more welcome and inviting aspect. Masts, shields, and trophies, as elsewhere, formed the line of approach to the Infirmary building, and banners and bannerets, waving in the cold easterly breeze, gave motion and animation to the scene. The façade of the old building was enlivened with designs similar to those used elsewhere in the grounds, but with all that had been done it appeared to wear an aspect of sombre sadness that seemed to presage the end. It may be but the imagining of a mind conscious of its condemnation, but there was an air of dejection about the old place, and about all that encompassed it, that was in strange contrast with the life and buoyancy of its immediate surroundings.

The principal object in the Infirmary grounds was, of course, the Royal Pavilion, in which the main ceremony connected with the visit of the Queen took place, and the object of Her Majesty's sojourn in Derby consummated. This was in fact a noble and beautiful structure, and justified in every way the wisdom of the committee when they entrusted the work to Messrs. Pigott Bros. and Co., of London. The particular site was on the left of the old Infirmary as you approached it from the London Road, and the exact locality of the foundation-stone was in the centre of the raised platform at the front of the building. The pavilion itself was probably one of the largest and most beautiful canvas structures ever erected in Derby. Facing to the main road was a façade extending probably a hundred feet, along which ran a canopy, and at the base of which was a raised platform sheltering a profusion of foliage and shrubbery, which gave it the appearance of a long floral corridor. There were two entrances leading by a wide wooden staircase to the Queen's rooms. The vestibule nearest to the town formed the approach to the Royal Retiring Room ; the one on the station side led by a corresponding staircase to the Royal Reception Room. In these approaches was again a rich display of palms and flowering shrubs and plants, rising gradually with the stairs and flanking the footway on either side with a magnificent profusion of colour, and filling the air with the fragrance of flowers. The Reception Room was rather larger than the Retiring Room, but both of them were apartments arranged and furnished with great taste and effect. Beautiful tapestry hangings covered the walls; the floor was spread with a rich Axminster square, and here and there about the apartment were choice drawings, including a capital sketch of the new Infirmary, which may be said to have received its birth on May 21st. The decorations of the Retiring Room were equally chaste though somewhat less ornate, and the furniture in each apartment was in perfect keeping with the accessories of the place. The work in connection with the arrangement of these two rooms was in the hands of Mr. John Topham, of St. Peter's Street, and they bore good comparison with the similar apartments at the station. The plants were supplied and arranged by Mr. Cooling.

The entrance to the Royal Pavilion or marquee was on to the platform from an opening in the Reception Room, and standing at this point the spectator was able to obtain a fine view of the Pavilion, and to see and appreciate its extent and general beauty. It was a structure capable of seating 1,500 people, and yet its construction was on such lines that only three small wooden poles intervened to obstruct the sight of any person seated in the vast expanse. Gothic in shape, the centre of the canvas roof rose to a height of 48 feet from side supports of about 12 feet in height. Over the platform, and for about half the distance towards the rear, this Gothic form was continued, after which the canvas covering sloped downwards until at the extreme back it came to a level with the sides. The whole of the floor space was available for seating the visitors, and as the floor rose by easy steps from the front to the back, there was provided an uninterrupted and splendid view of the platform and of the ceremonies performed upon it. Here, again, we had a magnificent floral display. In fact, it was a matter of common observation among the visitors that the abundance of the foliage and the wealth of the flowers formed one of the sights in regard to the decorations, considering the unpropitiousness of the season. The floor of the pavilion was covered with red baize, which gave the apartment a warmth it would otherwise have lacked, and the roof and sides were made Oriental in appearance by the wide bands of red and white into which the canvas covering was divided. The foundation-stone itself was in position early in the day, awaiting but the Royal hand to fix it in its place as the corner-stone of what it is hoped and believed will prove to be an institution of wide and lasting benefit to the suffering poor. The inscription approved by Her Majesty and carved upon the stone was as follows :—

VICTORIA,

QUEEN OF GREAT BRITAIN AND IRELAND,

EMPRESS OF INDIA,

LAID WITH HER OWN HAND

THIS FOUNDATION-STONE,

MAY 21st, 1891.

The DUKE of DEVONSHIRE - - - - - Lord Lieutenant.
EDWARD MILLER MUNDY - - - - - High Sheriff.
ALFRED SEALE HASLAM - - - - - - Mayor of Derby.
Sir THOMAS WILLIAM EVANS, Bart. - - President of the Infirmary.

MIDLAND ROAD.

There cannot be a shadow of doubt that this thoroughfare formed one of the most attractive and artistic points on the whole line of procession. The extensive and magnificent decorations undertaken by the Midland Railway Company alone would fully warrant this assertion, even if no further embellishment of the buildings and thoroughfare had been undertaken. But the town authorities and the owners and occupiers of property therein had done their utmost to produce a bright, pleasing, and effective display of ornamentation, and by their united efforts a charming picture was obtained. The view from either end of the street was imposing, but the scene which presented itself to the spectator who placed himself in front of the Tudor Arch and looked towards the Midland Station, was one of great beauty and magnificence. Leaving the splendid decorations at the Midland Station and Hotel (elsewhere described), we find that the town authorities had placed the public decorations in the hands of Messrs. Womersley and Co., public decorators, of Leeds, whose local agent was Mr. John Jones, of the Market Place. Each side of the street was lined with Venetian masts, covered with crimson cloth, and surmounted with gilded spear-heads, but the first two near the station were surmounted by crowns. From the top of each mast there was an arrangement of shields and trophies of flags. From mast to mast, and running longitudinally along the street were lines of pretty streamers, while across the road were canopies of roses, from the centre of which were suspended baskets of flowers. Near the top of the Midland Road, and spanning the thoroughfare near Mr. Winter's shop, a Gothic Arch (Tudor period) was erected, and formed a very imposing and remarkable feature. It was composed of material which adequately represented the "time-weathered stone" of ancient mansions like Haddon Hall. The structure consisted of a centre opening of 20 feet, through which the Royal procession passed to and from the station, and two smaller openings spanning the pathway on either side of the road. There was a portcullis over the large opening or gateway. The fabric was surmounted by battlements, in accordance with ancient custom, and from the large turrets hung streamers, the Royal Standard, and other national flags. The idea was to represent the ancient gateway of a town, with which the situation of the arch greatly coincided, and by their admirable treatment of the material used—the crumbling walls and other appearances of the decaying influences of the hand of time—the decorators succeeded in giving a very faithful picture of such a structure. The numerous platforms in this street were also decorated with due care and taste.

The private decorations were extensive, and many of them very tasteful, and there was not a building in the street on which some token of loyalty was not displayed.

The York Hotel was most effectively decorated. The balcony over the doorway was draped with blue cloth, bordered with yellow fringe; on most of the window sills scarlet cloth with yellow-fringed borders was tastefully disposed, and the front of the building was literally covered with shields and trophies of flags. The illumination consisted of a large transparency, with an admirable portrait of the Queen in the centre of it.

The office of the Midland Railway Company's architects was enriched with shields and trophies of flags. One shield represented the shamrock, rose, and thistle ; on another three stags' heads were vividly depicted; a third shield was surmounted by a crown and painted with national devices; and another bore round it the motto *Honi soit qui mal y pense*. The illuminations were made to represent a star and the Midland Railway arms.

Mr. T. E. Yeomans, tobacconist, had an illuminated representation of the Queen and the Yeomen of the Guard.

From the upper windows of the Portland Hotel, recently opened by Mrs. Edwards, depended decorations consisting of scarlet and yellow cloth, ornamented with flags, whilst over the doorway there was a handsome arrangement of scarlet cloth, the centre being occupied by a portrait of the Queen surmounted by royal shields.

Sturgess's Caledonian Hotel was embellished by well-arranged trophies of different coloured flags.

Miss Riley, manageress of the Clarendon Hotel, made a most effective display. Conspicuous amongst her decorations stood out the word "Welcome," formed in large white letters on a scarlet ground, bordered by yellow fringe. The upper windows of the hotel were draped with crimson cloth, adorned with yellow fringe. Dark blue cloth with a similar border adorned the window sills, and the whole was completed with a capital arrangement on each side of the windows of shields and trophies of flags. The illumination consisted of a large plain star.

Messrs. F. Sanderson and Son's coach-making establishment had been decorated upon a scale combining beauty of design and effective colouring. Streamers floated over the top of the premises from one end to the other. Occupying a central position over the Midland Road entrance were the Prince of Wales' feathers flanked by flags, and above the Union Jack floated gracefully. Along the front of the building were the words "A hearty welcome greets you," in white letters, which showed up conspicuously on the crimson ground. Underneath this device there was a tasteful arrangement of navy blue cloth, enriched with gold lace and fringe, while at each end there were trophies of flags, the shields bearing the Royal Arms and Prince's feathers. Underneath these there was also a tasteful arrangement of scarlet cloth.

The Carrington Street part of the works was decorated with a double line of coloured streamers, and coloured figured cloth. Different flags, consisting of Union Jacks, Royal Standards, &c., floated from each window of the workshops, which occupy a building three storeys high. The illuminations consisted of a five-feet star, with the letters "V.R." on each side. The carriage showyard on the opposite side of the Midland Road was also tastefully decorated, the motto, "God Save the Queen," in gold letters being a conspicuous feature of the arrangement.

The Mineral Offices of the Midland Railway Company on the opposite side of the street to Messrs. Sanderson's works were ornamented with scarlet cloth, surmounted by an arrangement for illuminations, showing a crown and the Prince of Wales' feathers.

The George Hotel, kept by Mrs. Warrington, was illuminated with a large crystal transparent device of the Garter, in the centre of which were the letters "V.R.," and round it were the words "Long live the Queen."

Mr. Borrey, undertaker, Midland Road, decorated the front of his premises with crimson cloth, in the centre of which were a crown and the Prince of Wales' feathers. Over the gateway there was a splendid arrangement of trophies and flags. The centre one was very large and pretty. The Royal Arms were admirably represented, and above them were the words "God Save the Queen." Running along the bottom of the shield was the wish, repeated many times on Thursday by thousands of her loyal subjects, "Long May She Reign." From the windows of the Station Inn the Union Jack and a number of small flags proudly floated.

Mrs. Annie Edwards' eating house was tastefully embellished with flags and streamers.

The Midland Coffee Tavern was surmounted by streamers, and the front of the building was literally covered with a similar species of ornamentation.

Flags proudly floated from the shop of Mr. Calvert and the Midland Arms; and Mr. Sanders, tobacconist, ornamented his shop front with coloured cloth, &c.

Mr. Winter, photographer, had several flags floating from the summit of his premises. On the wall, also, there was a magnificent representation of the Royal Arms, flanked by flags.

Mrs. Holmes, milliner, had a tasteful arrangement of red, white, and blue cloth round the frames of her upper windows.

LONDON ROAD.

On entering this thoroughfare from the Midland Road, a very pretty and effective scene met the view. On every hand there were extensive decorations, and the profuse ornamentation of the Infirmary Grounds also caught the eye of the spectator. Venetian masts lined each side of this wide and pleasant street, the masts being adorned with flags and shields. Along each side of the road, and suspended from the masts, ran a double line of evergreens, some distance apart, their sombre hues beautifully contrasting with the bright crimson and yellow cloths and banners which everywhere formed part of the decorations. Extending nearly the whole length of the thoroughfare, from Midland Road to Castle Street, canopies of beautiful roses, adorned with floral baskets, or lines of streamers, stretched across the road, and imparted a most graceful and beautiful finish to the design. This part of the public decorations of the road, and as far as Castle Street, had been entrusted to Messrs. Paine and Co., of London; their local agents were Messrs. J. and G. Haywood and Co., of the Market Place, Derby, whose execution of the work gave general satisfaction. Venetian masts were used as far as Castle Street, where the conventionality of treatment was pleasantly relieved by a small but effective arch, erected by Mr. Harris, of Liverpool. The main arch was about thirty feet high, but the arches over the pavement were considerably lower. The top of the central arch was surmounted by palisades, and on each side were the letters V.R., arranged in red squares, and mixed with evergreens; along the top of the arch were the conspicuous words "Welcome to Derby," a little above this and at each end being a crown and cushion. Baskets of flowers, garlands, and other decorations, completed the superstructure, from which flags floated, while plants and flowers beautified the lower portion of this pretty and artistic design. Passing from this arch towards St. Peter's Street, there were no masts, but the thoroughfare was most effectively adorned with lines of flags, streamers, and flowers. Every available spot in this thoroughfare was occupied by a platform, each of which had received a considerable amount of adornment.

Regent Terrace was beautifully decorated with trophies of flags and shields.

The shop front of Mr. Councillor Butterworth, at the corner of London Road and Regent Street, was most successfully adorned. A conspicuous feature of the design consisted of the Prince of Wales' feathers and a line of streamers.

Curling's grocery stores, at the opposite corner of London Road and Regent Street, were one tastefully-arranged mass of flags and bunting.

The Nottingham Arms and the Leviathan Inn, as well as the premises of Mr. George, butcher, were suitably adorned. On the front of Mr. George's premises the words " Welcome to Victoria " stood out in bold relief.

Dr. Gentles, of Wellington House, had tastefully decorated the front of his residence with coloured bunting and pretty trophies of flags.

From the upper windows of the Crown and Cushion Hotel Mr. Baldock had suspended flags and banners, while the whole face of the building was one mass of flags and shields.

Mr. Marshall, chemist, had draped his upper windows with red, white, and blue cloth, tastefully trimmed, whilst Mr. Domleo, butcher, also made a brave show.

Streamers and flags gracefully floated in the air in front of the London Road Wesleyan Chapel and the adjoining house of the Superintendent Minister.

Messrs. Brooks and Co., tea merchants, had a nice arrangement of flags, &c.

Trinity Parsonage, the residence of the Rev. F. Hoare, presented a beautiful appearance. A line of streamers stretched along the front garden, while a series of flags, &c., embellished the *façade* of the building, on which there were also some coloured lamps formed into the letters V.R.

The authorities of the Royal Derbyshire Nurses' Home had selected as their mottoes the very appropriate Biblical words, " Blessed is he that considereth the poor ; " and, " I was sick and ye visited Me." There were two other inscriptions below these, viz., " God bless our Royal Patroness," and " God Save the Queen." These were printed in large white letters on a red ground, and extended along three sides of the building over the third storey window. So prominent, indeed, were they that a person of good sight could read them directly after leaving the Midland Road, and the whole arrangement undoubtedly attracted the attention of thousands to an institution which has [done a vast amount of good in our town and county for many years past.

At Chetwynd House, the residence of Mrs. Leech, the decorations and illuminations were upon an extensive scale. Flags and bunting were used freely and tastefully disposed. Two large inscriptions read thus:—" Loyal Hearts Greet you," and " A Thousand Welcomes." Conspicuous amongst the illuminations was a large crystal transparency forming the letters " V.R."

From Trinity Church a national flag gracefully floated.

The Terrace between Trinity Church and Liversage Street presented a charming appearance. Flags, shields, and coloured cloth adorned the house fronts and windows, and on a portion of the verandah there was an arrangement of scarlet cloth, while from the verandah were suspended a number of Chinese lanterns and coloured glasses, which looked very pretty at night.

There was a very graceful arrangement in front of the house of Mr. Henry Morley, surgeon dentist, red, white, and blue cloth, with appropriate trimmings, being brought into requisition, and the whole was completed with trophies of flags and shields, the latter having upon them representations of the shamrock, rose, and thistle, and the Prince of Wales' feathers, and being surmounted by crowns, &c.

Mr. Wilkins, ironmonger, decorated with bunting; Mr. Hutchinson, taxidermist, with flags; and there was an effective arrangement of bunting around the platform at the corner of London Road and Bradshaw Street.

The premises occupied by Messrs. Taylor, photographers, and the Young Men's Christian Association were very prettily adorned. Red and blue cloth, with suitable trimmings were used, and between the windows of the second and third storey stood out in conspicuous white letters the inscription "God Bless our Gracious Queen."

Messrs. Holmes, coachmakers to the Royal Family, had superbly decorated the large and exceedingly handsome front of their extensive works. Cloth of different shades of green and yellow was gracefully looped about the large windows of the show-rooms, and also ran halfway down to the ground at each end of the building. The Union Jack also floated from the top of the building. Over the wide gateway entrance to the premises there were illuminations, the device being a crown between the letters "V. R." The front of Mr. Holmes' residence, which is directly opposite the works, had been treated in a similar beautiful and artistic manner, and altogether the design was unconventional as well as artistic.

The premises of the Midland Furnishing Company, Mr. Poyser (hair dresser), and the *Nottingham Guardian* Branch Office were adorned with bunting, &c.

Mr. John Clulow, of the Crown Vaults, had arranged a most artistically decorated platform over the front part of his premises. This was ornamented with scarlet cloth, enriched with orange-coloured bunting and white lace, and there was a very pretty awning over it.

Messrs. Walker & Co., tailors and hosiers, ornamented the front of their shop with blue cloth and trophies of flags.

Mr. Maltman, confectioner, displayed flags and streamers.

The Reading Room connected with the Castle Fields Works, belonging to Messrs. Boden & Co., had been treated with flags, and in addition to the red cloth which stretched across the front of the building, excellent arrangements had been made for illuminating the premises, the device being a star, with 1837 to the left of it and 1891 on the right. There was also a nice arrangement of coloured lamps.

The Midland Furnishing Stores surmounted their premises with lines of streamers, and embellished the front with coloured cloth and trophies of flags.

Mr. Thomas Lloyd, undertaker, had a very pretty and elaborate system of ornamentation. Running in a line with the spouting was the inscription, "God bless our Queen." Immediately below this were capitally executed portraits of the Queen, Sir William Evans (President of the Infirmary), and the Mayor (Sir A. S. Haslam, Kt.). Just above the door and window, but below the portraits, there was another inscription, "Long may she reign!" in white letters on a blue ground. There was also a cluster of flags and emblematic devices.

Mr. Slater, smallware dealer, had a pretty arrangement of bunting intermixed with flowers and surmounted by flags.

The Public Benefit Boot and Shoe Company exhibited a large Union Jack and numerous trophies of flags, and their illumination advertised the name of their firm.

The Derwent Hotel was prettily clothed with bunting and flags. Mr. Hummel, watchmaker, had tastefully blended coloured cloth in front of his premises. Mr. Brewer (gas fitter), the occupier of the Prince of Wales Inn, Mr. Saxton (tobacconist), and the occupier of the Granville Hotel, all showed their loyalty by nicely decorating their windows and houses.

The premises of Mr. George Kitchen were adorned with trophies of flags, and standing out prominently was a portrait of the Prince of Wales, the Prince of Wales' feathers, and other articles of an ornamental description.

Messrs. Frank Earp & Co., auctioneers, displayed much taste in connection with the decoration of their mart. The upper storeys were clothed with cloth of bright scarlet and gold, and over and above the sign there was a similar tasteful arrangement.

The Mutual Benefit Boot Company liberally displayed trophies of flags, and running along the side of the building there was a device containing the words "Queen of England and Empress of India."

Mr. Frank Murray, bookseller, had decorations of a novel character. They consisted of exact fac-similes of the covers of the Queen's own books: "Leaves from our Life in the Highlands," and "More Leaves from our Life in the Highlands"; also the words "Welcome to our Author Queen," the Royal Arms, an excellent portrait of Her Majesty, and the *Fleur-de-lis*.

ST. PETER'S STREET.

Viewed from any point this street presented a brilliant appearance. Flags and banners waved from most of the buildings, whilst the decorations of the house and business premises combined beauty with elegance. At the junction of this street with London Road and Osmaston Road, locally known as "The Spot," there was a triple arch which formed a conspicuous feature in the route followed by the Royal procession. The fabric was constructed so as to span both thoroughfares, the buttresses and the whole material being coloured so as to represent stone work. Between the two principal arches a band stand was provided, this being about ten or twelve feet from the ground. Balustrades covered with evergreens surmounted the top, and over the minor arches were raised platforms, each bearing a gold crown on a crimson cushion. Over the centre arch the words "God Save the

Queen," were worked in red letters on a white ground, and surmounting the whole fabric was a figure of Britannia, with the Royal Arms underneath, and flags to form a trophy. Underneath the band stand there was a mass of ferns and other plants, in the centre of which stood a fountain throwing up silvery sprays of water. The buttresses of the arch were adorned with paintings done on panels at the Derby Crown Porcelain Works. These represented various ancient industries, such as the potter at his wheel, the weaver at his loom, and other modes of industry which, happily for the workman as well as the public, have disappeared with the introduction of steam, and the advance of scientific knowledge

From a Photo. by)　　　TRIUMPHAL ARCH, TOP OF ST. PETER'S STREET.　　(*W. W. Winter, Derby.*

Festoons of flowers, evergreens, and baskets of flowers were also employed to embellish the arch and beautify the scene. This arch, it may be added, was the work of Mr. William Harris, of Liverpool, whose local representatives were Messrs. George and Dean, of the Strand and Sadler Gate, Derby.

The public decorations were upon a most extensive and elaborate scale, and formed a remarkably pretty feature in the midst of artistic surroundings. There were no Venetian masts, but the street was crossed by lovely festoons of flowers, enriched with floral baskets or wreaths, with a liberal sprinkling of flags, banners, and bannerets. These last-named aids to effectiveness somewhat impeded the view from the

Corn Market end of the thoroughfare, but from the Spot the whole arrangement was imposingly grand. On some of the flags there were heraldic devices, whilst others bore inscriptions at once hearty, appropriate, loyal, and enthusiastic. Amongst them were the words "God Save our Queen," "A Loyal Greeting," and the words which found an echo in many hearts: "Come again," an invitation which, however loyally given and as readily received, can scarcely be expected to be realised in the reign of our present Most Gracious Majesty the Queen.

Across the end of Albert Street, and passing from the Birmingham and Midland Bank, there was a line of flags and roses, with the conspicuous word "Welcome," which met the eye of the processionists as they were returning from the centre of the town.

At the Green Dragon Inn the front of the building was decorated with shields and trophies of flags, and navy blue cloth, with yellow fringe.

Page's umbrella warehouse was adorned with trophies of flags and streamers, and the illuminations consisted of large coloured lamps.

Along the front of the three old-fashioned houses occupied by Messrs. Fowkes, butcher; Parkins, tobacconist; and Kirby, basket maker; there was a pretty line of streamers, and a series of trophies and flags.

Mr. J. H. Hirst, draper, decorated his premises with cloth of bright colour, and a striking part of the arrangement was the inscription "God save the Queen." Mr. Embery, carver and gilder, and the Educational Company also had pretty decorations at the front of their establishments.

Messrs. Staincliffe and Son, woollen drapers, and Mr. A. F. Pemberton, tobacconist, each had wreaths of red and white roses round the upper windows of their premises, and pretty coloured bunting below them, and flags were suspended from the roof.

The decorative display of Messrs. Bennett Brothers, provision merchants, was very beautiful. Green and yellow valances were arranged along the front of the building, where there were also trophies of flags. Their illuminations were also most effective, numerous different coloured glasses being admirably arranged round the frames of the upper windows.

At Babington House streamers were suspended from flag poles placed at intervals on the roofs, and there was also an interesting display of shields and trophies of flags, as well as the inscriptions, "God save the Queen" and "God bless the Queen."

The handsome line of buildings at the corner of Babington Lane and St. Peter's Street, occupied by Messrs. Thompson and Son, tailors, and by Messrs. Orme, of the Babington Music Warehouse, looked very pretty. Garlands of evergreens were stretched over the shop windows. From the upper storey windows crimson cloth was suspended, and on each side of the windows on the second and third storeys there was a tasteful display of shields and flags.

At the adjoining shops occupied by Mr. Archer and Mr. Smith, jeweller, the display of coloured cloth and flags was very striking.

A conspicuous part of the ornamentation on the front of Mr. J. Newton's shop consisted of representations of the Royal arms, surrounded by national flags, one containing the words "Welcome to our Queen," and the other "Long live our Queen." The shops of

Messrs. Squirrel, bookseller; Charles Smith, hosier; and W. H. Fletcher, draper; were prettily adorned with trophies of flags.

Mr. Charles Clarke, hairdresser, exhibited trophies of flags.

Mr. Councillor Spriggs, grocer, had a good deal of decoration. From the top of his premises flags floated. The front of the building was adorned with trophies of flags and shields, and along the whole width of the upper storey red, white, and blue cloth, bordered with yellow fringe, was stretched.

Mrs. Edwards, glass and china dealer, had some elaborate decorations. The four windows of the second and third floor were adorned with coloured cloth; below the sign there was an arrangement of bunting; whilst the face of the building was also embellished with the Prince of Wales' feathers and the Royal arms.

Mr. J. Topham, upholsterer, had one of the most charming displays in the street. Above the top windows ran a line of blue cloth, enriched by gold fringe. Below this, and on the sides of the windows, were trophies of flags. The sign was bordered with red cloth, and below this were other trophies, all placed with great care and taste.

Mr. Swan displayed a flag and bunting, and Messrs. King and Co., provision merchants, had a nice arrangement of decorative material.

The front of Messrs. John Wells and Co.'s café was ornamented with trophies of flags and bunting.

Mr. D. Hackney, china dealer, had some coloured glasses for illumination.

Messrs. John Progress and Co., fancy drapers, decorated with bunting.

Mr. Rose, draper, had elaborately decorated his premises. The front was almost entirely covered with different coloured cloth, crowns, and emblematic devices, and conspicuous amongst the design were the words " God save the Queen."

The Green Man Inn, although off St. Peter's Street, could be seen therefrom, and the landlord had consequently made a capital display of ornamentation, the word " Welcome " being distinctly visible from the main thoroughfare.

Mr. John Dean, draper, showed his loyalty by tastefully adorning his premises with flags and the letters " V.R."

The Midland Drapery Company had a grand display of bannerets and other species of decorations, and the illuminations were also pretty.

Messrs. Shackleton, drapers, had a very effective display of crimson cloth, with gold cord and fringe tastefully disposed on the upper part of the premises, which were further embellished with artistic festoons, bannerets, and shields. A large flag also floated from their upper windows, and lines of streamers passed from the top to the bottom of the building.

Messrs. Wilkins & Ellis had a quantity of blue and white bunting round their upper windows, and over the shop window there was the word " Welcome " in white letters on a red ground.

The Grand Clothing Hall Company did not arrange for any decorations beyond displaying a flag, but their splendid front was extensively illuminated, the chief feature of this department being a crown, the letters " V.R.," and three plain stars.

The stone-fronted buildings occupied by Mr. Déqué and Mr. Dicks were ornamented with a nice arrangement of evergreens and flags.

Mr. Goddard decorated his premises with an effective design formed by dark blue cloth, with yellow fringe border, and numerous banners.

Mr. D. W. Bardill's shop was treated with a line of coloured cloth, and banners tastefully interspersed along the front.

Along the frontage of the shops of Mr. Hoare, chemist, and Mr. Buckley, hosier, stretched a line of coloured cloth, in which white and blue colours were tastefully blended, and there was also a capital display of shields.

Mr. Clarke's dining-rooms were beautifully decorated with flags, banners, and other species of ornamentation.

Mr. Cholerton, boot maker, and Mr. Sangster, grocer, whose premises adjoin each other, had a line of red, white, and blue cloth running across the front of them, and at the side of the windows there was a series of handsome flags of similar colour.

Messrs. Thurman and Malin, drapers, introduced into their handsome decorations the large inscription "Welcome to Derby," which showed up wonderfully well.

Mr. Walker, draper, covered a portion of his front premises with scarlet cloth, and added to the festive appearance of the thoroughfare by also displaying flags and banners.

Mr. Sharratt, painter, and Mr. Fisher, tobacconist, had a nice arrangement of coloured cloth to the front of their establishments.

Mr. L. W. Brookes, printer and stationer, effectively decorated his premises with bunting, flowers, trophies, &c.

THE CORN MARKET.

In the Corn Market, the prevailing type of street decoration—we mean the public part of it, undertaken by the Decoration Committee—was of a somewhat conventional, but, on the whole, of a very effective character. Tall Venetian masts, covered with crimson cloth, with spiral gilt terminals, and relieved half way up by shields of arms, surrounded with trophies of parti-coloured banners, were the prevailing order of the day. Much fault was found by some people with the masts aforesaid. Enveloped in scarlet cloth, these elevated " scaffold poles "—as with some contumely they were designated—are said by the critics in quarters to have been veritable " wolves in sheep's clothing "—making terrible havoc with the streets which were dug up for their reception, being (it is said) personally objectionable to the Prince of Wales, who is sick of their ever-recurring conventionality, and having the unfortunate effect of narrowing (in appearance) the vista of the thoroughfares which they lined. But " destructive criticism " is an easy task, and it would be difficult, if not impossible, to suggest any publicly undertaken form of street decoration which would at all adequately supply their place. Like the much-abused bazaars, we cannot—theories and criticism to the contrary—do without them, and their absence (to employ a phrase which is used of departed worthies) would leave a blank which it would be difficult to fill. The decoration of this thoroughfare—and, indeed of most of the central thoroughfares we are about to describe—was in the very capable hands of Messrs. Pigott and Co., of London (locally represented by Messrs. Topham and Co., St. Peter's Street), who also erected at the Royal Hotel corner a handsome double arch of evergreens, &c., and a band stand round the "Five Lamps," the base being of crimson cloth, relieved with handsomely painted coats of arms, and surmounted with Venetian masts, trophies, and bannerets, the whole relieved, like the adjacent arch, with an effective arrangement of greenery. At the corner of the Corn Market and St. James's Street was suspended a

THE ROYAL HOTEL.

magnificent floral canopy, of dome-like shape, surmounted in the centre by a royal crown, whilst dependent from it was a beautiful basket of flowers. This also was the effective handiwork of Messrs. Pigott and Co. The private decorations of this thoroughfare were of an extensive character, though some of them were so very late in being put up as to run great perils of omission from our record. The occurrence of the Whitsuntide holiday in the very midst of the undertaking impeded to some extent the operations of the private decorators, though they did their best to make up for the loss of time thus involved by working all night on Tuesday and Wednesday. The "Royal" Hotel—as became its name and fame—was a centre of demonstrative loyalty aptly embodied in type and symbol. There was a large coloured (illuminated) transparency of the Queen—or rather what we might more precisely term a "Jubilee" profile of Her Majesty—flanked on either side of the central stone arcading with crystal devices containing the initials of the Queen and Prince of Wales. There was also an effective drapery of red and amber to the window sills, and the whole building was set off with shields and trophies of bannerets, and surmounted with the Royal Standard and other appropriate flags. Messrs. Jefferson, drapers, of Albert House, had similar arrangements of shields and trophies, the effective novelty in this instance being an over-hanging drapery of blue and amber, which had a very pretty effect. The central window was flanked by the initials "V.R." in illuminated gas jets. The strong point of the Derby and Derbyshire Banking Co's. premises was its splendid series of crystal illuminations, in Messrs. Defries and Co's. best style, embracing a magnificent device of blue and white, with Royal initials in the centre, and surmounted with a ruby and amber crown. On either side were the letters "V.R." in huge white crystals, and above them were stars with red cross centres, encircled with the motto of the Order of the Garter, *Honi soit qui mal y pense*. Here, also, in addition to a noble shield of the Royal arms, was a most effective drapery of brown material, with a heavy fringing and tassels of amber—quite the prettiest thing in this part of the thoroughfare. On the other side of the road Messrs. John Wells and Co., provision merchants, and Mr. Pinder, mantle maker, had notable displays, whilst the Derby Brewery Company (Mr. Hugh Scott), at the "Old Angel" Inn, showed a most effective gas jet illumination representing a winged figure of Fame, blowing a trumpet, with the inscription on a scroll, "The world greets thee, Queen and Empress!" Mr. Moore, jeweller, the *Mercury* Office, and Messrs. Ratcliff and Co., ironmongers, furnished an almost continuous line of drapery in crimson and amber, relieved with shields and trophies of banners, and surmounted with flags. The premises of Mr. Richardson, hatter and hosier, furnished an effective contrast, the draperies consisting of a striking tricolored arrangement of red, white, and blue, with bright red flags, relieved with many coloured crosses. Mr. Clifton, chemist, took up the red and amber arrangement, whilst Mr. Hurd, pork butcher, displayed, in white letters on a red ground, the motto, "God bless our Queen." The Conservative Club —though not by any means so tastefully adorned as on the occasion of the Jubilee commemoration—was, nevertheless, gay with the conventional shields and drapery of the professional decorators, much improved by the additional touches of Mr. Edwin Haslam, who prettily picked out the windows with pink and white rosettes, and connected the blue and amber window hangings with festoons of evergreens and flowers. The doorway was surmounted by the Royal arms, and on a large crystal device at the corner, emblazoned with the initials "V.R.I." and surmounted by a crown, was the superscription in blue letters, "Conservative Club." The *Reporter* Office had a pretty arrangement of yellow and red, and Messrs. Orme, Renals, and Co., in addition to a handsome crystal device, flanked by large crystal crowns, had the orthodox display of flags, banners, and shields. Mr. J. Cholerton, bootmaker, displayed a loyal motto, banners, and "V.R." in coloured lamps; and

Messrs. Ward, boot and shoe manufacturer, had a singularly effective display, consisting of draperies of bright colours, coloured lamps, Royal arms, and motto, "Loyal hearts greet thee, India's Empress and England's Queen." The premises of Messrs. Hurd and Bentley, drapers, were tastefully adorned, and Messrs. Bourne and Hussey, tailors, and Messrs. Poole and Co., tobacconists, besides flags and shields, showed pretty devices in coloured lamps. The corner premises of Mr. Eaton, tobacconist, were brightly decked, and bunting was displayed by Mr. Gilbert, draper. To sum up, the whole thoroughfare, with its bright garlands of artificial flowers running between the Venetian masts, presented a particularly bright and pleasing appearance.

THE MARKET PLACE.

The Market Place, as was fitting for the civic centre of the town, was pre-eminently successful in its decorative adornments, and the Town Hall, as the home of the municipality, was the object of a large amount of appreciative attraction. Round the barricades of the Market Place, Mr. Wm. Harris, of Liverpool, had placed, at intervals, Venetian masts and other decorations of an effective character. The Bass' statue stand and the band stand were richly decorated by Messrs. James Pain and Sons, of London, whose managing representative was Mr. F. C. Womersley, their local agents being Messrs. J. and G. Haywood, of the Market Place. These stands were covered in with red material, surrounded by handsome masts in green satin, with base of crimson plush pedestals. The whole of the masts were entwined with floral festooning, and around the centre of each mast also was a handsome floral bracket. These masts were connected by floral festooning in canopy style, with elegant floral baskets suspended from the centre of each. The Town Hall, apart from its liberal display of bunting and decorative adjuncts, presented a veritable *chef d'œuvre* of the illuminator's art. There is no need to enlarge on this point when we say that it was entrusted to the celebrated firm of Messrs. Defries and Co., of London, valuably supplemented by their local agents, Messrs. W. T. Crump and Co., of Friar Gate. From the base of the building to the summit of the tower, the whole *façade* of this handsome classic structure—which is singularly adapted for treatment of this character—was encompassed with a frame, effectively marking its architectural outline, of many-coloured lamps and rows of naked gas jets. In this way, every moulding and window frame and canopied niche was lit up and displayed to the best possible advantage, and several handsome devices in crystal were used to fill in the design. The lower portion of the building was set off with a balcony-like drapery of crimson and gold, lit up with festoons of many-coloured lamps. The walls higher up were adorned with shields and banners, and from the tower, which was connected with the building beneath by streams of bannerets, flags floated gaily in the spring-like breeze. The Queen's Reception Stand—the stand immediately in front of the Town Hall, where the Corporation and other addresses were presented—was entrusted to the eminent firm of Messrs. Liberty, of London. The stand, which was reserved for the Corporation and their officials and for the Mayor's friends, was of semi-circular form, in height somewhat unnecessarily top heavy, and capable of accommodating 500 persons. It was decorated in a very tasteful manner, being sumptuously covered and hung with claret-coloured material —which had a very rich and at the same time a very warm and comfortable appearance — and surmounted with gilt-topped crimson poles, carrying parti-coloured bannerets, emblazoned with the various arms and insignia of Royalty, the whole heightened in effect by an unstinted use of artistic adjuncts and a liberal display of evergreens and flowers. In front, and well within view of the large and influential company here assembled, was a pavilion or canopy of Indian character—very correctly designed by Messrs. Liberty and Co., of London—under which the royal carriage was drawn whilst the Queen received the various addresses which were presented to Her Majesty, that of the Corporation by the Mayor from a raised daïs. The four corner supports of this very pretty structure were adorned with curtains drawn in towards the bottom, and the eaves of the roof were surmounted by stencil work forming a kind of Moresque palisade round the roof, which tapered gradually upward, a miniature banner being placed at each corner, whilst the summit was crowned with a flagstaff carrying the Royal Standard. The large stand adjoining it was covered with a canvas awning, and it was wisely determined to remove the whole structure as soon as possible after the completion of the ceremonies aforesaid, in order not to obstruct the Town Hall illuminations, and magnificent crystal device erected by Messrs. Defries in front of the clock tower, and the splendid illuminated sentiments of loyalty—such as "God bless our Queen," and "There are none like her"—with which they had adorned the front of the municipal buildings. Though not quite germain to the subject of decorations, we ought whilst on the subject of stands, to notice the capital stands, all more or less brightly draped and adorned, which were put up in various parts of the Market Place. These comprised the grand pyramidal stand for 3,000 children in the centre of the square, the Bass' statue stand, capable of accommodating 500 people, the stand in front of the Assembly Rooms (which held 500) for the boys of Repton School, and the stand for the Grenadier Guards' Band. The character of the decorations employed in the adornment of these structures— greatly enhanced by the numbers of well-dressed people who occupied them—has already been indicated. If the public decorations of the civic authorities were good, those of the private residents and shopkeepers were proportionately no less spirited in their character. The extensive block of buildings occupied by Messrs. Moult, tailors; Mr. Frost, chemist; and Messrs. Pike and Co., baby linen sellers; with the offices of Messrs. Watson, Sowter, and Co., accountants—were effectively adorned with a drapery of blue material, edged with amber fringe. Above were shields and trophies of flags, and in the centre, in gold letters on a white ground, surrounded with a border of pink and white rosettes, was the motto, "God save our gracious Queen." The premises of Messrs. Austin and Co. (late Storer's), grocers, and Mr. A. J. Emery, hatter, were cheerfully bright with draperies of crimson and amber, shields and banners, and the Royal arms flanked with the inscription, in white letters on a bright red ground, "God bless our Queen." The classic front of Messrs. Smith's Bank was suitably decorated with an æsthetic drapery of olive-coloured material, festooned with yellow silk, and, in addition to several bold and effective shields of arms and trophies of bannerets, it had a large ruby crystal star of great beauty in the centre of the building. Mr. Yeomans, tobacconist ; Messrs. Barlow and Taylor, drapers ; and Mr. J. R. Taylor, furrier, continued the line of loyalty; and Messrs. Bakewell and Wilson, grocers, besides the customary conventionalities, had a nice show of evergreens and white flowers, pleasantly relieved by the warm red draperies of Mr. Rosson, gunmaker, on the adjacent premises. Passing the very tasteful adornments of Messrs. Bemrose's premises, which were visible from the corner of Irongate, and noticing the shields of Mr. Steer, jeweller, we come to the premises of Mr. Carter, glass and china dealer, on which were inscribed, in yellow letters on blue boards, "Long may Victoria reign." Messrs. Haywood, ironmongers, effectively displayed, in white letters on a broad red cloth band, the superscription, "Victoria, Regina, Imperatrix." The Bible Society's Depôt (Mr. Ward) was rendered conspicuous by a singularly appropriate design, which was admirably executed, of a Holy Bible (open at St. John iii. 13), with a halo of glory and a crown above, and the motto, on a foundation-stone, "The foundation of England's greatness," with a coloured representation of roses, shamrocks, and thistles intertwined beneath. Mr. Stanesby, cooper, displayed flags, and Mrs. Hall's premises were tastefully adorned. The same remark applies to those of Mr. Jones, upholsterer, who showed a fine cast of the Royal Arms ; Mr. Slack, refreshment house keeper ; and Messrs. Girardot, Forman, and Pountain, Limited. The usually dingy Assembly Rooms showed signs of festivity, and the premises of Mr. Edgar Horne, music seller, were gaily adorned. Very bright was the colouring of the canopied balcony of Messrs. Peters, Bartsch, and Co., which was surmounted by a crystal star. The newly-erected premises of the Royal Oak (Mr. Eadie) were tastefully decked with a festoon of pale blue and white, surmounted by the Royal Arms, and the Police Office was decorated in harmony with the adjacent Town Hall. The *Advertiser* Office was suitably adorned, the draperies of red and amber—embodying the motto, " God Save the Queen "—being relieved by an illuminated crystal star. The premises of Mr. Ernest Brindley, provision dealer ; Messrs. Scales and Son, boot makers ; and Messrs. Smith and Son, clock makers and jewellers, were also gay with bunting and flags. Before leaving the Market Place, we ought to emphasize the fact that the æsthetically arranged draperies of the Queen's Reception Stand —in most exquisitely blended art shades, the curtains being of Japanese manufacture—were the subjects of special admiration. Plants and flowers—in vases and on floral brackets round the Venetian masts and in other points of vantage—were introduced with excellent effect. The *tout ensemble* was admitted, on all hands, to be singularly effective.

ST. JAMES'S STREET.

Venetian masts were absent from this thoroughfare, but the street was gaily garlanded from side to side with bright artificial flowers, in canopy style, baskets of flowers being suspended from the centre, the whole presenting a most effective appearance. The St. James's Hotel (Mr. Wagstaff's) was draped with prettily shaded "Liberty" silks, and,

7

besides a large cast of the Royal Arms, a crystal star, and floral devices, displayed the motto in bold red letters on a white ground, "*Salve Regina Imperatrix.*" Mr. Riches, milliner, showed a pretty drapery of crimson and amber, and Mr. Fletcher, confectioner, displayed an effective motto, "God Bless our Queen." Messrs. Simpson and Rickard, tailors; Messrs. Morgan Bros., boot and shoemakers; Mr. Husband, tailor; Mrs. Lowe, milliner; Mr. Morris, tailor; and Mr. Lineham, hairdresser, also displayed emblems of loyalty; whilst Mr. Wheldon's umbrella depôt exhibited a magnificent "Mrs. Gamp," which he had manufactured for an African chieftain.

THE STRAND.

The imposing *façade* of the Town Club, at the corner of the Strand, presented a very brilliant appearance. The cornice at the top of the building was draped with blue and amber, surmounted with large shields of the Royal arms, set off with trophies of many-coloured banners, the towers at the top of the building being gay with a multitude of flags. The Strand Boot Co.'s shop beneath was adorned with shields of the Royal arms, a prettily devised drapery of red and amber, and a motto, in the same colours, "God Bless our gracious Queen." The Birmingham District and Counties Bank, on the other side of the street, was similarly bedecked—its window-sills in red and amber, and its stone wall relieved with shields and trophies of flags—whilst the whole range of Mr. Woodiwiss' buildings on the same side of the road was brightened by a liberal display of flags and bannerets. The blank wall at the back of the Mechanics' Institute was relieved by an effective motto, in white letters on a red ground, the whole surmounted by a very pretty border—" Welcome to Derby." The rear of the Free Library was decked with shields and trophies of banners, with an overhanging device of red cloth, inscribed with the appropriate sentiment, in amber letters, "Touched with human gentleness and love." The Corporation Art Gallery took advantage of the opportunity to set up their image and superscription on a vacant panel—*i.e.*, to paint the borough arms in gold, and beneath them the words, "Derby Corporation Art Gallery." This will be a useful intimation to visitors long after the Queen's visit has passed by. The front of the Art Gallery was suitably set off with banners and shields. Messrs. George and Dean, upholsterers, and Mr. Atherstone, hatter, displayed signs of gaiety, and the premises of the Liberal Club were brightly adorned. The whole thoroughfare was prettily embowered with garlands of bright flowers.

CHEAPSIDE.

The short neck of thoroughfare known as Cheapside, through which the procession passed on its way to the Wardwick, was principally given up to stands. There was one for the public in front of the shop of Mr. Watt, draper, and a much larger one, running the whole length of St. Werburgh's churchyard, for the use of the children. The cross of St. Werburgh floated bravely from the church tower, and that of St. George depended from the window beneath. Here, again, too, our old friends, the Venetian masts, made their appearance, whilst in the distance the gaieties of Friar Gate were visible. The " Buck in the

Park," as became its designation, displayed a banner, on which was painted the arms of the borough; and Messrs. Geo. Bottomley and Co., in addition to a plaster cast of the Queen, surmounted by a crown and cushion, had a pretty balcony-like drapery of red and amber, with a goodly show of shields and flags. Mr. Wallace, ironmonger, displayed several devices, whilst the premises of his neighbour, Mr. Ashley, chemist, had a bright tri-colour arrangement; and the premises of Mrs. Sinclair, hosier, were effectively adorned. Festoons of evergreens and banners connected the Venetian masts on either side of the road.

From a Photo. by) THE FREE LIBRARY. (*W. W. Winter, Derby.*)

THE WARDWICK.

Turning the corner into the Wardwick, the line of progress was marked by Venetian masts, the conventional crimson of the poles being relieved at the base by a square box-like arrangement of blue, which had a pretty effect. The Free Library, in its way, was a *chef d'œuvre*, not indeed of the decorator's, but of the illuminator's art. It is not a building that lends itself to much upholstery. In fact, its beauties, like nature's, are "When unadorned,

adorned the most." The main thing was to show up to advantage the architectural outlines of the building, and this, too, was most picturesquely accomplished by Messrs. Defries and Sons, who picked out the windows and mouldings with lamps of many colours, the lower part of the building being lit up with festoons of the same, whilst the outlines of the roof and tower were effectively marked with naked gas jets. The lamps, as we have said, looked very pretty by day as well as by night, the effect, especially after they were lit up, being quite of a fairy-like character. Flags were displayed to advantage from the battlements of the tile-clad tower, and the front and back of the building were tastefully decorated with trophies, evergreens, etc. Mr. Eaton, grocer, and adjacent shop occupiers, displayed shields and banners; and the houses of Mr. Frank Iliffe, surgeon, and Mr. Vaudrey, surgeon, were tastefully adorned, the former with festoons of red, white, and blue, and the latter with red and white draperies, and the motto, "Long live our noble Queen," in white letters on a red ground. The quaint Jacobean house of Mr. Darwin Huish, solicitor, was appropriately decked with ancient shields of arms; and on the house of Mr. Francis, surgeon, was an effective tri-colour arrangement. Mr. Councillor Harrison and the Cash Tailoring Company had a brave display, and the premises of their neighbours, Messrs. Alton and Co., brewers, were pleasingly adorned. A novelty in the decoration of the Mechanics' Institution was the employment of a broad edging of white lace on scarlet cloth, which had a very tasteful appearance. The main entrance was surmounted by the letters "V.R.," and a St. George's cross, in a circle, surmounted by a royal crown in open gas jets. Mr. Linnell's drapery shop and the County Club above were nicely draped and flagged, and in addition to an illuminated St. George's star, the lower part of the building was lit up with a line of green and red lamps. The "Lord Nelson" was bright in blue and amber, and the whole street was gaily garlanded with bright flowers from side to side.

VICTORIA STREET.

The "Five Lamps" at the entrance to Victoria Street—opposite to the Post Office—was surmounted with a pretty pagoda-like structure of crimson cloth with fringings of amber, and shields of arms. It contained in panels attributes of "Justice," "Integrity," "Skill," "Honesty," "Worth," and "Energy," at the base being a blue flower stand, with border of rustic cork, whilst over its pretty floral canopy floated the Royal Standard. There was a spacious band stand, adorned with evergreens at its side, and a splendid floral arch was erected right across the road, with two suspended banners, inscribed, in amber letters on a crimson ground, "Health to Our Queen and Court," and "Let Derby Flourish." The Post Office Hotel was gay with banners and shields, and its doorway was surmounted with a crystal device. From Mrs. Ranby's shop depended long lines of bannerets and flags, and on the shop of Mr. Hirst, draper, was the device, in white letters on a red ground, "God bless our Queen." In similar colours, the shop front of Mr. Dearsley, fishmonger, contained the two inscriptions, "God Save our Gracious Queen," and "May she long live to reign." That part of the "Royal" which faces Victoria Street was effectively adorned, but, by a lack of co-operation on the part of the adjacent office occupiers, the decorations unfortunately stopped short at the Athenæum Room, the extensive newly-painted walls of which presented a very bare and naked appearance. In the upper show-room window of Messrs. Johnson and Son, jewellers, there was an æsthetic arrangement of beautifully shaded silks, and the premises were surmounted by a painted shield of the Royal Arms, surmounted by a trophy of banners, and flanked by the Royal Standard and Union Jack. The stand in front of the Congregational Church was tastefully adorned, and Mr. Stevenson, chemist, had a brave display. The Royal Standard floated from the Post Office, and the Venetian masts were connected by intertwining festoons of brightly coloured flowers, intersected with Chinese lanterns, floral baskets, and other devices of a highly tasteful and artistic nature. Mr. Hefford, hatter, and Messrs. Steele and Frazer, tailors, made suitable displays, whilst the premises of Mr. Smith (late Low's), restaurateur, and Mr. E. Clulow, stationer, were marked by draperies of an effective character.

THE DECORATIONS AT NORTH LEES.

North Lees, Duffield Road, the imposing residence of His Worship the Mayor, had been artistically decorated externally, in honour of the great and auspicious event which will long distinguish his year of office as one of the most memorable in local annals. Inside the grounds and running alongside the Duffield Road, eleven Venetian masts had been erected, and from these floated bannerets, whilst festoons of smaller flags connected the poles with one another. To each pole a shield bearing various arms had been attached, and these were surmounted by small flags. The illuminations took the form of a large crystal, by the side of which were the letters " V.R." Over the gateway an arch composed of evergreens had been erected, and above this was placed a large crown for illuminating.

At the Union Foundry, the Mayor's works, the decorations were of a similar character. A Royal Standard floated above the works, whilst between the windows shields and some flags were placed. Near the roof numerous flag poles had been fastened, and these were connected with festoons. Over the entrance to the works were the letters " V.R." for illuminating, and between these was a very fine centre piece.

STREETS NOT ON THE ROYAL ROUTE.

Outside the line along which the Royal procession passed many buildings had been decorated and illuminated, and in nearly every street in the town some show of loyalty was made, either by a floating flag or by a house decorated with bunting. Passing along the Irongate the first illumination to strike the eye was that on Messrs. Crompton and Evans' Union Bank. This consisted of a large crystal device, whilst on either side were shields and above it a number of flags. On Mr. Brigden's establishment there was a large star, and the letters " V.R." formed by gas jets, below which was a row of flowers, the pots in which they were planted being concealed by a nice arrangement of red and blue bunting artistically placed on a white ground. From Messrs. Cox and Bowring's and Messrs. Ward and Sons' business premises hung large flags, and in Queen Street the only illumination was a star of gas jets on Mr. Gilbert's premises, but along the street there were numerous flags, etc. Flags also floated from the towers of All Saints' and St. Michael's Churches, and the spire of St. Alkmund's. In King Street there were more decorations of a similar nature. Over the gateway leading to St. Helen's House hung two large banners, and the front of that spacious building was decorated with bunting of various colours, artistically arranged. There were also numerous shields on the House bearing the Royal and Borough Arms and other devices, and these were surrounded by small flags. At Mr. Styche's furniture warehouse a banner with festoons on either side set off the entrance. In Bridge Gate one could not fail to be struck with the decorations, which, although on a moderate scale, showed the loyalty of the people. In Friar Gate the Gas Company's offices were the chief attraction, and here the decorations and illuminations were of an extensive character. In the front of the buildings four rows of gas jets with coloured lamps ran up to the roof, and on the upper part similar rows of lamps surmounted the whole. In the centre of the building were the letters " V.R." and a large star, whilst on either side there was another star. The last mentioned lot of illuminations all had gas jets and formed a contrast with the coloured lamps on the other parts of the building. Right across the front of the building were two rows of blue cloth—one bright and the other of a darker hue, both being finished off with gold coloured fringe. On the windows were three large shields surrounded by flags, whilst large flags floated from the upper windows. Round the windows themselves a pretty effect was obtained by their being nicely decorated with the new art muslin in various shades. On the residence of Dr. Ernest Taylor red bunting had been used to advantage, whilst at Mr. Davis's the decorations took the form of festoons hung from the roof. The Friar Gate Coffee House had the words " Welcome to our Queen " in large gold letters on a dark red ground across the front of the building, in addition to some flags. The premises of Messrs. Crump and Co. were illuminated with a number of gas jets with coloured lamps on the upper part of the building, and at the Savings Bank several shields surrounded by flags formed the principal part of the decorations. Numerous flags floated from many private residences and business premises all along Friar Gate, and gave the thoroughfare a lively appearance. Curzon Street showed several banners. Beneath the windows of the Poor Law Offices in Becket Street,

Record of the Queen's State Visit to Derby.   103

The Derwent from St. Mary's Bridge.

red and white bunting formed the decorations, and numerous shields and flags were festooned. A large flag floated over the buildings, as also did one from the premises of Mr. Shenton, and from the Drill Hall. In St. Mary's Gate the County Hall was prominent by its illuminations, which were apparently those used in the Jubilee decorations in 1887. They consisted of the letters V.R.I. in front of the three windows, and two large stars of bare gas jets. There were no other decorations on the buildings. Flags were hoisted at the residence of Mr. Taylor, and at the offices of Messrs. Eddowes and Son, and Mr. Whiston, whilst at the latter place there was also the Royal Arms surmounted by flags. There was also another illumination in this thoroughfare, viz., at the office of Messrs. Robotham, Attwood, and Robotham. This illumination was of similar letters to those used at the County Hall, and

SPECIMEN OF ROYAL DERBY CHINA.

SPECIMEN OF ROYAL DERBY CHINA.

From a Photo. by)   THE ROYAL CROWN DERBY PORCELAIN WORKS.   (W. W. Winter, Derby.

also in bare gas jets. Along the Osmaston and Normanton Roads there were very few decorations beyond an occasional flag. The Arboretum Hotel, Osmaston Road, had the Royal Arms placed on it, together with the sentences, "God bless our Queen. Long may she reign." The arms were surrounded by flags, tastefully arranged. Several flags hung from the windows of the hotel, whilst in Regent Street the Prince Regent Inn had an exactly similar decoration to that on the above-mentioned hotel. Messrs. Cox and Sidley also had a device on which were similar words. In the same street, Mr. Smith, butcher, had a very effective arrangement. A line of cloth stretched across the front of his premises, and on it was an excellent representation of a Bible in gold clasps, and the inscription, "The Secret of England's greatness." Beyond Station Street, on the London Road, there were several decorations on a small scale and some flags, and in the streets branching off from the road nearer the St. Peter's Street end a flag or two could be seen. Coming to the Municipal Offices in Babington Lane, six banners were seen floating from the windows, whilst over the doorway were the Royal Arms, surrounded by Union Jacks and red, white, and blue bunting. In Albert Street the principal decoration was on the Co-operative Society's building. A flag floated over the top and from the pole festoons were carried down to the roof. The front of the buildings had two rows of red and white cloth, and presented a good appearance. On the Corn Exchange a number of shields and small flags were placed, whilst outside the Star Vaults was a full length portrait of the Queen, with the words, "Welcome, Victoria." Dr. Hough's residence in Full Street was nicely decorated with blue and yellow bunting round the lower windows, whilst at the upper ones were a number of flowers. The residence and works of Mr. Councillor Lowe, Stuart Street, were illuminated. At the end of the buildings were the letters " V.R.," and a large crown in gas jets, whilst in the front was a row of coloured lamps, with a star in plain gas. In Derwent Street, the Market Tavern and Mr. Smith's shop were decorated, whilst from Messrs. Mason's colour works and Mr. Johnson's shop there was a large piece of red bunting, bearing the words " God Bless our Queen." In Tenant Street and along the Morledge numerous flags floated, and in many other streets in the town there were signs of loyalty which gave a gay air and bright appearance to them all.

The following were the illuminations and decorations by Messrs. J. Defries and Son, London (Messrs. Crump and Co., agents, Derby) :—Midland Station and Hotel : A grand illumination in crystals and coloured garlands, large revolving star and " Welcome " in gas, and crystal " V.R.," together with a variety of medallion devices, stars, etc., the whole outlined with elfin lamps in various colours. The fronts of the Station and Hotel were elegantly draped with upholstered cloth and amber bullia fringe. These designs were settled, and the work carried out by Messrs. Defries, under the personal superintendence of Mr. G. H. Turner, the assistant general manager of the company. The Town Hall and Free Library : Splendid illuminations and decorations, etc., etc. Mrs. Warrington, George Hotel : Large medallion in crystal, with "V.R." monogram and a row of amber lamps. *Advertiser* Office, Market Place : Brunswick star and decorations, trophies, flags, etc. Mrs. Leech, London Road : Letters " V.R." in crystal, with double row of coloured lamps, also fairy lamps suspended to the trees. Derby and Derbyshire Bank, Corn Market : Large crystal medallion, with monogram " V.R.," surmounted by a crystal crown in purple colour, large letters " V.R.," and two crystal Brunswick stars, with row of coloured lamps on the top of the cornice. Messrs. Peters, Bartsch, and Co., Market Place : Crystal Brunswick star and suitable decorations. County Club, Wardwick : Crystal stars, with drapery and trophies ; shield over entrance, with County Arms. Henry Boden, Esq., The Friary : Crystal letters " V.R.," also a row of coloured lamps on the cornice. Messrs. G. and M. Linnell, Wardwick : Row of coloured lamps and suitable drapery. Messrs. Thos. Crump and Co., Friar Gate Works : The architecture of the building outlined with coloured lamps, and a crystal Brunswick star in centre. County Hall, St. Mary's Gate : The windows outlined with open gas jets ; large

Brunswick stars, one over each door, and windows filled in with " V.R.I.," the whole forming a most effective illumination.

Mr. Edwin Haslam, of St. Helen's Street, had supplied a large number of illuminations and decorations. Amongst the illuminations he fixed were the following :—A large crystal to the St. James's Hotel, and the decorations on the same building; the decorations on Dr. Hough's residence, Full Street, and a large crystal and the decorations on Messrs. Bemrose and Sons' establishment, Iron Gate. The illuminations, consisting of a large crown, the letters " V.R.," with a centre piece, on the residence of the Mayor, North Lees, Duffield Road, and also the letters " V.R." and three large crystals on the Union Foundry, City Road, the Mayor's Works. The large oval and star on the Conservative Club, and the gas jets which formed the Brunswick star and the letters "V.R." on Mr. Brigden's premises, Iron Gate, and also the large illumination and decorations at the Angel Inn, Corn Market.

Messrs. John Davis and Son, of All Saints' Works, had the opportunity, for the first time in Derby, of showing how pretty illuminations can be made to look with the aid of the electric light. They were responsible for the letters " V.R.," very prettily outlined in small lamps, over Messrs. Pountain, Girardot, and Forman's premises, and also for the 500 candle-power lamp which brilliantly illuminated Messrs. Bakewell and Wilson's premises in the Market Place.

THE VIEW FROM ALL SAINTS' TOWER

Gaius in comprehensiveness what it loses in effectiveness. It was by Messrs. John Smith and Sons' juvenile clockwinder—W. S. Gilbert would call him Lord High Clockwinder on the auspicious day—that the Man of Ink was piloted up the dark and devious stairway, and out upon the lower leads. The lad plays the *role* of the early bird who catches the silver

worm. The sun, in the warm heart of May, is also an early riser, and he had to borrow the well-known metaphor from Hudibras

——— long since in the lap
Of Thetis taken out his nap—

and ensconsed himself behind a cloudy pillar ere our representative essayed the Burnsian function of "takin' notes" with a view to "prent 'em."

The streets were alive with workmen, who were, after a busy night, occupied with putting the finishing touches on the labours of the past fortnight. Flags were being run up, and bunting was still an increasing quantity. The chronicler had too much work on hand to look far afield, but it took no more than twenty heart-beats to note that over Strutt's Park and beyond the rugged Chevin, where on clear days the purple prospect melts into nothingness, is Crich Stand, like a single tooth set on an inverted basin. To the right-about, in a favourable atmosphere, you can discern Breedon-on-the-Hill Church. In the centre of the South Derbyshire plain you may exercise the Johnsonian privilege to

> Let observation with extensive view
> Survey mankind from China to Peru

if Spondon be allowed for the Celestial Empire and Littleover for Guanaland. In the middle distance, crossed and recrossed by creamy pufflets of snail-crawling trains is the valley of the river Derwent, beside whose banks the Royal train could be traced from Derby to its vanishing point beneath the aforesaid Chevin. Derby town appears from here not unlike a child's puzzle of dull red toy houses. Some light grey stone built buildings stand out in sharp relief against the prevailing burnt umber of the bricks, while the blue slates of the new houses in the outskirts are in contrast to the ruddy tiles of the old town. Here and there church spires and the domes of some public buildings rise superior to the general level, and serve as landmarks to unravel the unfamiliar brick-and-mortar puzzle referred to. The size of everything below is as if the spectator were looking through the object glass of a small sixpenny telescope instead of through the eyepiece, and there is a corresponding diminution of sound. Ordinarily, especially on dull smoky mornings, Derby, from this coign of vantage, appears particularly quiescent. It has a chrysalis-like dulness. But from this chrysalis it had emerged as a gay multi-coloured butterfly—nay, numerous butterflies. You could not see much of the actual route of the procession, but it was fringed here and there, until distance destroyed its perceptibility, and the gauzy mist-veil obliterated minute objects, with bannerets and flaglings and devices, like butterflies strung on strings, or pinned on the walls. It would only have required the aid of an opera glass to have witnessed the presentation of the addresses in front of the Town Hall. There is no intervening obstacle, the crimson-covered stand, the raised daïs, and the canopy under which the Royal State Coach drew up being plainly discernable. The five-fold triumphal arch on The Spot, and the floral device at St. James's Street were also visible, while further on, the condemned Infirmary Buildings and the grand marquee were seen. The church towers and spires contributed to the joyous display, and from them all flew the festal flags of the period of Pentecost. One could not be quite sure, owing to the distance, whether a flag floated from H.M. Prison—that sombre collection of buildings is more intimately associated in the vulgar mind by a flag of another hue—the pennant of death. Viewed from aloft Venetian masts lose their effectiveness, and distance, which proverbially lends enchantment to the view, also insignificates the individual. By the assistance of magnifying lenses, however, the Royal progress could be well traced from and to the Spot, but without such visual aid Her Majesty's state coach was indistinguishable from what, in vulgar parlance, is known as the "common or garden growler." At this altitude vehicles are beetles and people flies. They are wandering along the streets and across the Derwent Bridge in streams. Further on, up Green Hill and against Christ Church, they are ants.

Derby, before this, has we all know welcomed many Royal personages. Rectification of the frontier was a favourite pastime with the pre-conquest barbarians; and as the line of demarcation between the struggling factions was shifted alternately now this side of Derby and now that, it is fair to assume that the semi-civilised sovereigns who personally led their forces, made sundry and manifold triumphal entries into the town. Derby was known in mediæval times as a Royal borough, and Litchurch, later on, as a Royal hamlet. The dulcet

From a Photo. by) THE OLD SILK MILL FROM DERWENT BRIDGE. (*W. W. Winter, Derby.*

chimes which played the sentiment of the day, "God save the Queen," were erected by that "great philosopher, mechanic, and worthy man," John Whitehurst, in 1745. Their tuneful strains first fell on Royal ears when bonnie Prince Charlie entered Derby, only to flee. For early on the following morning

> The bells they rang backward,
> The drums they were beat

for the retreat. During the last century or thereabouts this same tower of All Saints' has seen many occasions of general rejoicing, but none that can in any way be considered comparable to the recent one. Had not the noble house of Devonshire—the aged head of which is deeply interested in the scheme of the new Infirmary, and with whose family all

Derbyshire sympathises by reason of their recent loss—existed, the Glorious Revolution had never taken place, and the Prince of Orange never secured to Britain the lasting blessings of Protestantism. And then the centenary of that happy event, in which a barbecue of oxen and fatlings took place in front of the *Advertiser* Office, would not have occurred. But neither this event, nor the gift of the Arboretum to the town by Joseph Strutt, nor the previous visits of the Queen (semi-private as they were), nor those of the Prince of Wales when he came to fulfil an important function at Derby School, and attended the Royal Show in Osmaston Park—none of these events of first-rate importance were comparable with the recent State visit of Her Majesty Queen Victoria.

OLD MARKET STONE, DERBY ARBORETUM.

DISPLAY OF FIREWORKS AT THE ARBORETUM.

In commemoration of the auspicious occasion, a splendid display of fireworks was given in the grounds of the Arboretum, on the night of the Queen's visit, by Messrs. C. T. Brock & Co., the celebrated Crystal Palace pyrotechnists. There was a very large attendance, and to a "Venetian Fair," with accompanying promenade concert, succeeded a very brilliant and effective display of fireworks. No fewer than 20,000 coloured lamps and

THE FOUNTAIN, DERBY ARBORETUM.

lanterns were artistically arranged along the various walks, and presented a most picturesque appearance. The display, which was a most successful one, included an immense transparent fire portrait of Her Majesty, a monstre design in honour of Derby and its institutions, a Niagara of fire, the great Chromatropes, flights of shells and rockets, whistling fireworks, and a multitude of other devices. It was greatly appreciated by the large mass of sightseers which crowded the Arboretum on the interesting occasion.

THE EXCURSIONS.

The railway traffic was exceedingly heavy, and both the Midland and Great Northern Railway Companies ran a number of cheap excursion trains from various parts of the country crowded with people anxious to witness the auspicious event. The Great Northern Railway booked about four thousand passengers from Ilkeston, the Erewash and Leen Valley district, Grantham, Newark, Lincoln, Sleaford, Boston, Nottingham, Leeds, Bradford, Halifax, Doncaster, Burton, and from the smaller stations round Derby. Through the kindness of Mr. Wood, of the office of the Superintendent of the Line at the Midland Station, the following returns of their excursions have been furnished for publication:—From Sheffield, 1,250; Buxton, 340; Manchester, 308; Coalville and Ashby, 250; Birmingham, 320; Lincoln and Newark, 250; Leicester, 600; Mansfield and the Erewash Valley, 480. In addition to the above list the following bookings by ordinary trains took place:—From Ripley, 1,100; Wirksworth, 350; Melbourne, 600; Burton, 1,500; whilst 5,000 persons booked from the stations between Nottingham and Derby. The North Staffordshire Railway booked about a thousand from the Ashbourne district, whilst the London and North Western Railway ran several crowded trains from the Wolverhampton district. Some little difficulty was experienced in getting such a host off at night, but with good arrangement the whole had cleared out before twelve.

MILITARY AND POLICE.

The military arrangements have already been detailed, and it only remains to say that the military were most valuable adjuncts to the police in the maintenance of the line of route during the Royal procession, besides forming efficient guards of honour at various points, and adding greatly, by their presence, to the *éclat* of the occasion. The arrangements for the arrival and departure of the troops were under the experienced superintendence of Lieut.-Colonel MacLeod, D.A.A.G. of the North-eastern District. Colonel Hooke, commanding the 45th Regimental Depôt at Normanton, was in command of the troops, his staff for the day consisting of Colonel Gascoyne, Major Coney, and Captain and Adjutant F. C. Shaw. The police arrangements were admirable, ample provision having being made not only for the extraordinary exigencies of the line of route, but for the protection of the property of the ratepayers—a very necessary precaution on such an exceptional occasion, in the outskirts of the town. The six or seven hundred police from other places were admirably looked after, catered for, and despatched, with business-like method, to their several destinations when the special duties of the day and night were over. Their duties, as both the police and magistrates gladly testified, were most materially lightened by the general sobriety, orderly behaviour, and admirable good-humoured conduct of the immense crowds of people present in the streets on the occasion till a late hour. The whole of the police arrangements were in the very capable hands of Lieut.-Colonel Delacombe, Chief Constable of the borough, by whom they were most efficiently executed, with the assistance of Superintendent Jepson (who was indefatigable in his labours), Inspectors Adams, Claye, Dexter, Tinker, and Waldron, and the loyal co-operation of every man under their charge. The work of the detectives in Derby on these occasions is always of a most efficient character—so much so that the professional thieves, usually so largely in evidence at public demonstrations of this kind, were, on the occasion of the Queen's visit to Derby, chiefly conspicuous by their absence. Inspector Spibey and his men were assisted by some twenty detectives from several of the principal towns, notably Liverpool, Manchester, Salford, Leeds, Bradford, Sheffield, Nottingham, and Leicester, and the duties of these officers, though less ostentatious than those of the uniform men, were carried out in a manner that calls for the highest praise.

GRATIFYING ANNOUNCEMENTS FROM THE MAGISTRATES.

At the Derby Borough Police Court, on Friday, May 22nd, the day after the Queen's visit, the magistrates present were Mr. Alderman Hobson and Mr. Bottomley. Mr. Hobson, addressing the officials of the Court, said that in the absence of the Mayor, who had been

LIEUT.-COL. DELACOMBE, CHIEF CONSTABLE.
(*From a Photo. by W. W. Winter, Derby.*)

called away, he believed to the funeral of Lord Edward Cavendish, he should like to express, on behalf of the Bench, their felicitations on the admirable way in which the events of Thursday were carried out, and especially on the good order which prevailed throughout the streets, and the almost entire absence of drunkenness. He believed that he was stating a fact when he said that after five o'clock in the evening there was not a single case of drunkenness brought to the lock-up.—Colonel Delacombe (the Chief Constable): That is so. —Mr. Hobson, proceeding, said he was the more gratified by that fact as he happened to be the presiding magistrate on the Bench when the application was made by the publicans for an hour's extension on Thursday and Friday, and he had consequently been freely criticised by some of their temperance friends. Of course it was necessary to consider the public convenience in the way which they did, and he did not regret the course taken on that occasion. Mr. Bottomley said he could endorse the remarks made by Mr. Hobson. He had occasion to pass and repass the barriers several times during the afternoon, and he thought the order and goodwill of the crowds which were gathered round them was admirable, and that the best humour prevailed. He came down about eleven o'clock from the Midland Hotel, and he did not meet a single drunken man on the whole of the way. Mr. Hobson said he must also express their felicitations on the great and deserved honour which had been conferred by Her Majesty on their Chief Magistrate.

SIR ALFRED HASLAM IS PROUD OF DERBY.

Sir Alfred Haslam (the Mayor) presided at the Police Court on the following Monday, for the first time since the Queen's visit, and made some pertinent remarks relative to the important events of the past week. His Worship observed that it gave him the greatest possible satisfaction to make the announcement that during the visit of Her Majesty the Queen the order of the town had been of an exemplary character. He had been proud of Derby on many occasions, but he had never thought so much of the town and people before as he did at the present time. At least 200,000 people lined the route taken by the Royal procession, and, although intense excitement prevailed, excellent order was perceptible, and there were only three drunken cases for trial on Friday morning. He thought this was an answer to the uncharitable letters and remarks which had emanated from the Temperance party respecting his brother magistrates. He thought the people had justified the course the magistrates had taken. He would further say that the magistrates always endeavoured to do what was just, and that it would have been a mistake not to have given the extension of the licensing hours asked for. Indeed, if he had been on the Bench on the morning when the application was made, he should have given his cordial assent to the course the magistrates then pursued. He considered that when a body of gentlemen went out of their way to do what was right they ought to receive the support of the inhabitants of the town. The good order that was kept in the town on Thursday last reflected credit not only on the Bench, but on the town in general.

THE TOWN COUNCIL AND THE MAYOR.

A special meeting of the Town Council and Urban Sanitary Authority of the Borough was held at the Guild Hall, Derby, on Wednesday afternoon, June 3rd. His Worship the Mayor (Sir Alfred Haslam) presided, and the other members of the Council present were Aldermen Holme, Hobson, Higginbottom, Sowter, Newbold, Leech, and Councillors Hon. F. Strutt, Heathcote, Laurie, Bottomley, Fletcher, Percy Wallis, Chas. Wallis, S. Evans, Boam, Riley, Hart, Jackson, Cholerton, Wright, Bowring, Marsden, Williamson, Walley, Edwin Haslam, Sutherland, Butterworth, Foster, Ward, J. E. Russell, Unsworth, Cox, Doherty, Harrison, Hill, Duesbury, Dean, and F. E. Leech.

CONGRATULATION TO THE MAYOR.

Mr. Alderman Hobson craved the Mayor's permission to interpose for a few moments before the Council proceeded with the ordinary business of the day. He said he was sure he was acting in consonance with the feeling of every member of the Council when he rose to utter a word of congratulation to the Mayor personally, and to the town at large, upon the distinguished honour which Her Majesty the Queen had within the past few days conferred upon the Mayor as the civic head of the town. (Applause.) They all felt that the distinction and the honour were in this instance, as well as in some others, well deserved. (Applause.) Since the Mayor entered upon the important duties of his office, he had discharged the functions appertaining to every department of it with singular assiduity and attention. (Applause.) He also took upon himself, in connection with the Royal visit, duties of a most onerous and difficult character. The public were the best judges of the admirable manner with which he had fulfilled those duties, and had not been slow to award him their due meed of praise—(applause)—and he was confident he was echoing the sentiments of the whole Council when he wished the Mayor long life and health to enjoy the distinction which the Queen had been pleased to bestow upon him—(applause)—a distinction which he was proud to think did not stand alone in that Council, for it was within their knowledge that during the last seven years knighthood had been conferred upon three valued members of the Town Council of Derby. (Applause.) One of those members had, unhappily, passed away. He referred to the late Sir Abraham Woodiwiss; and another was not able to be present on that occasion owing to enfeebled health. The Mayor was happily present in the vigour of his manhood; the Council were proud that he had received such a distinction, and they hoped he would long live to occupy his high position. (Applause.) He moved—" That the cordial congratulations of this Council be offered to the Mayor on the distinguished honour which the Queen had conferred upon him in appointing him to a knighthood." (Applause.)

MR. ALDERMAN NEWBOLD, in seconding the motion, said after the very graceful observations of Mr. Alderman Hobson, its proposer, it would be an act of superfluity on his part to add anything to what had already been so well said. They one and all congratulated the Mayor on the honour he had obtained—an honour most worthily bestowed, and which redounded very greatly to the credit of this Corporation. (Hear, hear.) They might fairly claim to hold a position in this respect which few other Town Councils in the country could boast of, for not only had they had three knights, but a baronet created from amongst their ranks during the last few years. (Hear, hear.) He had exceedingly great pleasure in seconding the motion. (Applause.)

The resolution was then put by Mr. Alderman Hobson and carried unanimously, and with applause.

THE MAYOR, who was received with loud applause, said the resolution just passed had quite taken him by surprise, and he was sure he hardly knew what to say for himself after the very flattering statements which had been made with regard to himself—after the remarks so ably made by Mr. Alderman Hobson, so cordially seconded by Mr. Alderman Newbold, and which had received their unanimous approbation. They would remember that when he was elected to the Mayoral chair he said that he would discharge the duties which pertained to it as far as he could, and to the best of his ability. He had endeavoured, as far as his strength had allowed, to fulfil that undertaking. (Hear, hear.) He must confess he had not done what he should have liked—he should have liked to have done more. ("No, no.") He had done, however, what he could, and in the accomplishment of that purpose he believed he had only done what any other member of the Council who had occupied his place would have done under the same circumstances. (Hear, hear.) With regard to the visit of Her Majesty to Derby, he had no idea, when he accepted his present office, that he should be called upon to entertain the Queen of England—the first lady in the land. But circumstances developed, and he (the Mayor) took advantage of the opportunity, and made the most of it. (Hear, hear.) The Queen had been amongst them, and he ventured to say that in no town or city had Her Majesty been accorded a more hearty reception or a more loyal welcome. (Applause). He might say that he had received several letters, both from Buckingham Palace and from Balmoral, from the Queen's Private Secretary and from the Lord Chamberlain, stating that Her Majesty had referred with the greatest pleasure to her visit to Derby. (Applause). This showed that the visit had pleased Her Majesty—(hear, hear)—and he must say that it had made a very deep impression on his own mind, recognising as he did, with pleasurable pride, that no town could have risen to the occasion better than Derby did. (Hear, hear.) He tendered to this Council and to the town generally his very hearty and sincere thanks for the cordial manner in which they co-operated with him on this memorable occasion. The Decorations Committtee especially worked very hard to secure such admirable results, whilst private citizens performed wonders in the decoration of their premises, spending very large sums of money on their decorations, which were executed with exceeding taste. (Hear, hear.) He thanked, indeed, all who in any way contributed to the success of the day. It was pleasant to think that, in time to come, those who followed them would see with pleasure and pride that they had not only maintained the dignity of the town on this occasion, but had even excelled themselves, so to speak, and outstripped many other towns in the character of the reception which they had accorded to Her Majesty. (Hear, hear.) On this point the testimony of the Press might be accepted as conclusive, for certainly in connection with no Royal visit that he could remember had the London papers been so full in their descriptions and so loud in their praise of what had taken place. (Hear, hear.) He thanked them once more for the kind way in which they had received Mr. Alderman Hobson's remarks. He had endeavoured to do his duty, and if, in that endeavour, he had met with their approbation and the approval of the town—and the many letters of congratulation he had received (some of them, he was sorry to say, not yet answered) led him to hope and believe this was the case—he was amply rewarded. (Hear, hear.) The kind expressions made use of with regard to himself showed him that, at all events, the people of Derby appreciated what he had done. (Loud applause).

THE MAYOR afterwards announced that the Queen had replied to the address of the Corporation presented to Her Majesty on the 21st of May. He said that the reply was one which would give great satisfaction not only to the Corporation but to the town. The wording of it appealed most forcibly to everyone, and, if he might presume to say so, was couched in most beautiful language. All present had doubtless read the reply, and, therefore, they would doubtless agree for it to be taken as read.

This was agreed to.

THE MAYOR then said that before he sat down he should like to make a remark upon a subject which he had intended to mention when he was previously addressing them. On the 22nd or the 23rd of May he received a letter from the Chief Constable of Derby, and it was one of the most extraordinary letters it had ever been his lot to read. It referred to the fact that, although there were, roughly speaking, 200,000 persons in the town on the occasion of the Royal visit, and the streets were crowded till midnight, there were only three cases of drunkenness reported by the police. There was not a single accident, so that the resources of the Infirmary were not called into question, and there was no case of burglary. (Hear, hear). The Council would, therefore, be pleased to hear that order was observed, as well as the dignity of the town upheld, on that eventful occasion. (Applause.) He took the liberty of writing to Sir Henry Ponsonby to enquire if he thought the Queen would like to read the letter, and received a reply in the affirmative. The letter was therefore shown to Her Majesty, and he had since been informed that it gave her the greatest possible pleasure to read the statement it contained. He therefore thought that the character of the town had been thoroughly maintained. (Hear, hear.)

MR. MARSDEN hoped his Worship had also taken the trouble to point out to Her Majesty that two out of the three persons reported for drunkenness were visitors to the town. (Laughter.)

THE MAYOR said he did not do that, and if he had done so possibly it might have been thought that he was drawing it too strong. (Renewed laughter.)

THE QUEEN'S CARRIAGES AND HORSES.

The Queen's semi-state carriage, together with the other carriages and the horses to be used in the Royal procession, arrived in Derby at ten minutes past one on Wednesday, May 20th, from the Royal Mews, Pimlico. The horse boxes and trucks were attached to the ordinary train, which was met at the Midland Railway Station by four of Messrs. Holmes' men, who performed the task of unloading. Mr. Wm. Moreton, who was in charge of the equipages, arrived shortly afterwards. The Queen's carriage, which is the one she always uses on semi-state occasions, is an elegantly finished landau, drawn by four magnificent bays from the Queen's stud. Their harness is black, with the exception of a piece running across the front of the bridle, which is a bright red. It is gold mounted, and on each carriage door is emblazoned the Royal Arms. The carriages were at once taken to Messrs. Holmes' show rooms, where they remained until shortly before the time for Her Majesty's arrival. They were then taken in hand by the fourteen grooms from the Royal stables, and the Queen's coachman took the ribbons of the Royal team at the station, under the covered temporary passage way, at a quarter-past five. The total number of horses brought down was seventeen, one more than what was really required. The task of finding accommodation for the men and horses was left in the hands of Mr. Charles Holmes, and he very wisely secured the whole of the stabling at the St. James's Hotel. The stalls and loose boxes were scalded and bedded with sweet wheat straw, and the lair in each stall was fringed with a novel kind of edging, composed of wheat straw and red, white, and blue cloth interlaced, made by Mr. Walter Perkes, the head ostler. The stone portions of the yard were sanded, as well as part of the stable flooring. The window sills were also coloured red, white, and blue. The semi-state harness was conveyed from the station in a closed carriage, and one vehicle was entirely filled with horse rugs and clothing. We understand that the Queen's coachman was the guest of Mr. Holmes.

BANDS AND STATIONS.

By permission of their commanding officers (in the case of military bands), the following bands assembled in the Market Place at 2.0 p.m., and having unitedly played the National Anthem, in the presence of an immense throng of people, proceeded to their several stations, as undermentioned :—

Midland Railway Station—The Band of the 2nd Volunteer Battalion The Sherwood Foresters (Derbyshire Regiment).

At the Junction of Midland and London Roads—The Band of the Robin Hood Rifles.

Infirmary—The Band of the First Battalion The Sherwood Foresters (late 45th Regiment).

The Junction of Traffic Street and London Road—The South Notts. Temperance Band.

The Junction of London Road and St. Peter's Street—The Band of the 2nd Battalion The Cheshire Regiment (late 22nd Foot).

The Five Lamps, Albert Street—The Burton Volunteer Band.

The Market Place—The Band of the Grenadier Guards.

Near the Post Office, Victoria Street—The Band of the 4th Battalion the Lincolnshire Regiment.

Free Library—The Derby United Prize Band.

Sadler Gate Bridge—The Band of the 1st Volunteer Battalion The Sherwood Foresters (Derbyshire Regiment).

The bands played at intervals during the afternoon from two o'clock until dusk, and that of the Grenadier Guards, in the Market Place, naturally attracted an unusually large and appreciative audience. The school children were stationed at various stands along the line of route indicated below. They sang " God save the Queen " as Her Majesty passed, and patriotic and old-world songs in the intervals of waiting, and, as they had to be in their places a considerable time beforehand, were considerately refreshed with oranges and cakes by the Mayor, who also presented them with a handsome medal, manufactured in Birmingham, commemorative of the occasion. The arrangements throughout—though necessarily of an elaborate character—were admirably devised and carried out, and great praise is due to the Mayor and his committees, the Town Clerk and his assistants, the Borough Surveyor, Mr. William Crowther, Colonel Delacombe and the police, Colonel Hooke and the military—and, above all, to the hearty and loyal co-operation of the people themselves, for the smoothness with which everything ran, and for the admirable good order which prevailed throughout Her Majesty's visit to the ancient and loyal borough of Derby.

THE GENERAL ARRANGEMENTS.

The general arrangements have already been fully indicated, but it may be as well to recapitulate some of them, which are not given, in their chronological order, under other headings. The Mayor requested that all shops along the line of route should be closed at noon, but, as a matter of fact, many of them closed their premises long before that time, and thereby greatly facilitated the arrangements of those in authority. At two o'clock vehicular traffic along the line of route was stopped, and at the same time the Borough Police, augmented by about 700 additional police (including a strong contingent of the County Force), the whole under the command of Lieut.-Col. W. A. Delacombe, Chief Constable, were detached to their various stations along the route of the Royal procession.

CHILDREN AND TEACHERS.

Midland Road—Railway Servants' Orphanage, 250; St. Andrew's, 414; total, 664.

Infirmary, Front—Holy Trinity, 298; St. Chad's, 222; King Street, Wesleyan, 300; Canal Street Wesleyan, 500; total, 1,320.

Infirmary, Roe Timber Co.'s Stand—Traffic Street Board, 482.

Infirmary New Roadway—St. Joseph's, 65; St. Thomas's and St. Mark's, 162; Christ Church, 297; St. Dunstan's, 247; St. James's, 434; Firs Estate, Board, 564; St. James's Road Board, 842; total, 2,611.

St. Peter's Churchyard—Practising School, 64; Parliament Street Wesleyan, 86 Siddals Road, 274; total, 424.

Market Place—All Saints', 152; St. Alkmund's, 196; St. Anne's, 257; St. Mary's, 194; St. Michael's, 55; St. Paul's, 141; Gerard Street Board, 825; Ashbourne Road Board, 578; Orchard Street Board, 255; total, 2,653.

St. Werburgh's Churchyard—Curzon Street, 258; St. Luke's, 285; St. John's, 62; Nuns Street Board, 358; Wright Street Board, 121; Deaf and Dumb Institution, 67; Derby Union, 110; total, 1,261.

Total—4,574 boys, 4,844 girls, 497 teachers—9,415.

ITEMS OF INTEREST.

The refreshments provided by the Mayor for the children to partake of whilst waiting for the Royal procession, had been packed in bags under the supervision of the teachers. Two-thirds of a pound of plum and plain cake were given to each child, together with an orange.

RAILWAY SERVANTS' ORPHANAGE.

The cake, which was supplied by Mr. John Wells and Mr. W. Fletcher, weighed nearly three tons. The oranges were purchased from Mr. Rowley, fruiterer, of Green Lane.

The medals presented by the Mayor to the school children who took part in the proceedings were specially struck by Mr. Joseph Moore, of Birmingham, and obtained through Messrs. Bemrose and Sons, Derby. To the last-named firm was reserved the sole right of publishing the "Official Programme," which commanded a large sale on Wednesday and Thursday. On the medals a beautiful head of Her Majesty is surrounded by the words "Derbyshire Infirmary. Foundation stone laid by H. M. Queen Victoria. May 21, 1891." On the other side are the Borough and County Arms and some handsome ornamental work, and the words "A. Seale Haslam, Esq., Mayor." One in gold was specially struck for Her Majesty.

In commemoration of the Royal visit, Messrs. Brock and Co., the celebrated Crystal Palace Pyrotechnists, gave a grand display of fireworks in the grounds of the Arboretum in the evening. There was a Venetian fete from 6 to 9 o'clock, at which hour the display of fireworks—which were of an unusually magnificent character—commenced.

Her Majesty has notified, through Sir Henry Ponsonby, her acceptance of a copy of Mr. W. Foster's (Derby) book, "The Subject-Testament" (London : Simpkin, Marshall and Co., Limited), a special copy of which was bound by Mr. Howard Wilkins, of St. Peter's Street, Derby, in best morocco, gilt edges extra.

Mr. James Harwood issued on the eve of the Queen's visit an artistic bijou souvenir of the great event. It contained a number of interesting illustrations, together with a variety of reading matter, and was very nicely got up.

The streets throughout the entire route of the Royal procession were barricaded, the distance covered being about three miles. For this work the timber was supplied by Messrs. Graham and Bennett, of Stuart Street.

On Thursday afternoon a telegraph clerk found himself in rather an awkward predicament. A telegram, simply addressed "The Queen, Derby," had just arrived, and been placed in his hands for delivery. How to convey the missive to the Queen was naturally beyond his knowledge. A way out of the difficulty presented itself. Meeting in the streets a well-known member of the Reception Committee, he handed it over to him to be conveyed to the proper officials, and it reached its destination safely.

The influx of visitors to the town on Wednesday and Thursday was so great that all the accommodation furnished by the various hotels and lodging-houses was speedily taken advantage of, with the result that on Thursday a bed could hardly be obtained in the town "for love or money."

COMPLIMENT TO A DERBY MUSICIAN.—The Queen has been pleased to accept a copy of Dr. Corbett's latest composition, Duets for the Pianoforte ; also of his songs, "The Organist" and "The Reaper and the Flowers," and the book compiled by him for the Jubilee Service held in All Saints', Derby, June 21st, 1887.

Messrs. Elkington, of Birmingham, sent £3,000 worth of plate to the banquet, as a compliment to the Mayor.

AN HEREDITARY LITTLE LOYALIST.—Among the juveniles on the chief platform, for whom the Mayor kindly found a place, was a little one named "Loyalty" Cater, a granddaughter of Mr. R. Ramsey Dinnis, a representative of one of the Derby newspapers. The Christian name was that borne by Mrs. Dinnis's mother, who was so christened, at the instance of her parent—a staunch "King and Constitution man"—in the fateful days when the effects of the French Revolution of 1789 were felt in this country, and gave such a violent shock to old institutions.

During their stay in Derby in connection with the Queen's visit, the Band of the 45th Regiment, who stayed at Normanton Barracks, were a source of great attraction in Derby, where they made many friends. On Saturday afternoon and evening, May 28rd, they were engaged by the Mayor (Sir Alfred Haslam) to give a concert in the

Market Place, which was attended by a large and appreciative audience. The Mayoress (Lady Haslam) was present in her carriage. The Mayor presented Mr. Bradley, the talented bandmaster, with a bronze medal in velvet case, and each member of the band with a medal, as an interesting souvenir of the occasion.

CALKE AND TICKNALL.—The labourers employed by Sir Vauncey Crewe at Calke Abbey, and on the estate at Ticknall, were much gratified on Thursday, May 21st, by having a holiday granted to them in honour of the occasion of Her Majesty's visit to Derby, the wages of each being ordered by Sir Vauncey to be paid as usual.

The day was a general holiday at Ripley, Belper, Matlock, and other places in the county, a great number of people coming into the town by road and rail.

Mr. William Sharratt has received a graceful acknowledgment from Her Majesty of his poem, " Welcome to Her Majesty."

In addition to the special gold copy of the children's medal presented by the Mayor to the Queen, bronze copies of the same, in handsome cases, were given by His Worship to members of the Reception Committee.

Two handsome new banners were carried in the procession of the Reception Committee. They were artistically painted by Mr. T. Sharratt, St. Peter's Street—one being a Corporation banner, with the borough arms, and the Mayor's banner with His Worship's arms, crest, and motto emblazoned on it.

The gracious permission of Her Majesty having (through the Mayor) been previously obtained from Sir Henry Ponsonby, an album consisting of a series of interiors of Hardwick Hall, was presented to the Queen by the Mayoress on behalf of Mr. Keene, and Her Majesty was so much pleased with the book that she took it with her into the Royal carriage.

A special copy of a new song, " Welcome, Victoria," written by Mr. Charles Walker, and arranged by Mr. Frederick Hainsworth, for presentation to Her Majesty, has been beautifully printed on white satin by Messrs. Chadfield and Son, Friar Gate, and ornamented with old gold fringe by Miss Brealey, of Iron Gate.

In connection with the splendid illuminations executed by Messrs. J. Defries and Co., of London—whose local agents were Messrs. W. T. Crump and Co.—mention should be made of the excellent services of Mr. Lionel Mosedale, gas fitter, of 10, High Street, Deritend, Birmingham, who acted as their efficient foreman in these matters. A substantial supper was given to the numerous staff and employés of the firm, at the George Hotel, Midland Road, in appreciation of their arduous labours, and in commemoration of the occasion.

The chairs used by Her Majesty in the Infirmary Pavilion were lent for the occasion— that on the platform by Mr. Alderman Bemrose, J.P., and that in the retiring room by Mr. G. Sutherland. They were handsome chairs of the Henri IV. or Renaissance period, of dull unpolished walnut, the carving of heads, figures, rams' heads, and all details beautifully executed ; the backs and seats were upholstered in tapestry *applique*. The arrangements for the laying of the memorial stone had been admirably carried out by Messrs. Walker and Slater, builders, of Derby.

The trowel, spirit level, and mallet, presented to the Queen at the Infirmary, were on exhibition for a short time in the window of Messrs. Johnson and Son, Victoria Street, and attracted considerable attention and much appreciation from the admiring crowds which inspected them, alike from the beauty of the materials employed in their manufacture, and from their exquisite finish and admirable workmanship.

The officers of the various regiments down for duty in Derby on the occasion of the Queen's visit, May 21st, were—by a thoughtful decision of the committee, which was of a purely social and non-political character—made honorary members of the Derby and Derbyshire Conservative Club for the occasion, which means that they had the same advantages as ordinary members enjoyed in obtaining refreshment, etc., at the commodious club premises in the Corn Market.

Popular penny medals were numerously sold in commemoration of the occasion. They contained on the obverse side a profile portrait of Her Majesty, similar to that stamped on the Jubilee coinage, with the superscription, on a raised rim, "Victoria, Queen of England and Empress of India." The reverse side bore, in relief, the inscription, "To commemorate laying the foundation-stone of the new Infirmary, Derby, by Her Majesty, Queen Victoria, May 21st, 1891." The whole was suspended from a shield, or fastener, stamped with the arms of the borough of Derby.

Mr. Freeman, of Curzon Street, Derby, supplied all the carriages used in the Corporate procession with the exception of the Royal carriages and the High Sheriff's carriages, and a splendid turn-out they were. The smart appearance of the equipages and their drivers created a most favourable impression, being the subject of general praise amongst the thousands of sightseers.

The stone to be employed in the new Infirmary is known as Bentley Brook, so named from the quarry where it is obtained, belonging to Mr. Drabble, stone merchant, Matlock Bridge, and which is situated at the north end of Darley Dale, and about a mile-and-a-half north-east of Matlock Bridge Station, on the edge of Matlock Moor. The stone is a beautiful pale-brownish or yellowish compact grit, very uniform in tint, and capable of being worked into either the most delicate tracery or the plainest arris. It belongs to that particular subdivision of the great millstone grit series of North Derbyshire, known to geologists as the third grit. Although worked at the Bentley Brook Quarry as far back as a century ago, it was not brought into extensive use till about fifty years ago, since which time it has rapidly grown in favour, until, at the present moment, it is used all over the country, both for ornamental work and for the more common purpose of viaducts, railway bridges, landings, stairs, window sills, etc. This stone has been adopted by Her Majesty's Board of Works for the erection of Post Offices, Savings' Banks, and other public buildings in London, Birmingham, Sheffield, Manchester, and other large centres of industry. It is also being employed by the London County Council in the erection of the new Metropolitan Asylum at Claybury, in Kent, the contract for which amounts to £300,000. The foundation-stone of the new Derbyshire Infirmary is composed of a block of this Bentley Brook stone, four feet by two feet by one foot six inches, and the memorial stone laid by the Queen, which consists of Aberdeen granite, rests upon this.

A CRIPPLE'S OFFERING.—TOUCHING INCIDENT.

As many accounts have been given of the rug used by Her Majesty to stand upon, at the laying of the foundation-stone of the Infirmary, and of the touching circumstances under which it was given by an afflicted Derbyshire woman, we give the following statement, *verbatim et liberatim*, of a gentleman well acquainted with all the facts of the case, feeling sure that it will be of interest to our readers :—" Bessie Taylor, a native of Melbourne, now living with her widowed mother at King's Newton (who is about 70 years of age), was over 40 years ago struck in the back with a stone thrown by a boy at play, which so injured the spine that she has never walked since, and has had to be helped and lifted about from that time. A fortnight ago I was at her home at King's Newton on a visit, when she said, ' You will have a busy week at Derby at the Queen's visit.' I said, ' Yes. I am pleased Her Majesty will honour the cause of the Infirmary by her presence; it will do a great deal of good. She (Bessie) said—' I have for nine or ten months been making a rug; it is just finished, and I should like to make a present of it to the Infirmary.' I said I should like to see it. She then said, ' Mother, bring it and let Mr. ——— see it.' The mother fetched it. I was very pleased with it. Bessie Taylor then said, ' There is one thing I should like.' I said, ' What is that ? ' She said, ' If ever a poor creature needed the benefits of an Infirmary and good medical treatment it was me, and I am anxious to help on this noble cause; but before that I should like the Queen to stand on my rug. I should feel I had not lived for nothing then. Do you think it can be done ? ' I was very much struck with the idea, but made the remark, ' I think that is rather a large order.' I stopped about an hour with them, and just before leaving said to Bessie, ' You had better leave that matter for a short time, and do not mention it to anyone, and if it can be done it shall.' On Sunday night, the 10th May (the above conversation was on Saturday, the 9th May), I wrote a letter descriptive of the case to His Worship the Mayor, who at the time was in Buxton. On reflection, I thought that, as I was unknown to the Mayor, I must get someone of wealth and influence to back me up. I wrote Mr. J. Crompton (under whom I serve), described the case to him, and asked him to kindly use his influence to accomplish the desired result. The next day I received a letter from Mrs. Arkwright, saying that her father (Mr. Crompton) had been very much interested in the case of Bessie Taylor, and would do his best to gratify her wishes. He at once wrote to the Mayor, also to Dr. Ogle. The Mayor wrote to the Queen, making known the poor invalid's request, and describing her case. Her Majesty at once ordered a telegram to be sent to the Mayor, saying how pleased she would be to gratify the poor invalid, Bessie Taylor's wish, and that she would use the rug when she laid the foundation-stone. I think the kind action of these gentlemen in this matter is beyond all praise, as also the womanly feeling of the first lady in the land for one of the afflicted of her own sex: I do not know whether I am at liberty to use the name of the gentlemen above-mentioned, but I can do nothing wrong in mentioning the action of the Queen, which ought to commend her to the hearts of all Derbyshire men and women."

Dr. Ogle, who was asked to interest himself, as above mentioned, wrote to the Editor of the *Advertiser* as follows:—"Bessie Taylor, living at King's Newton, is nearly 50 years of age. Over 40 years ago she was struck on the spine by a stone thrown by a boy while at play. She has never walked since. She can use her hands, is very intelligent, and has borne her terrible affliction in the most exemplary and even cheerful way possible. She forgets her own trouble by sympathising with, and devising means to help, others who are in trouble. Her mother, who is about 70 years old, is of a similar spirit, and the rug presentation is but one of many such examples of it, which came about in this way. Bessie Taylor said to a working man (Mr. Briggs) last Saturday week (the 9th inst.) 'I have one ambition.' He said 'What is that?' She said 'Nine or ten months ago, I started on a drawing-room rug. I have just finished it, and I want to make a' present of it to the Infirmary. But I want the Queen to stand on it first, and, if possible, while she is laying the foundation-stone, and then whatever is thought best to be done with it is to be done.' She said, moreover, that her own case was one of the most striking proofs of the necessity for a good Infirmary and good medical attendance, and although it was too late to do her any good, if she could help anyone else she should be proud to do so. Mr. Briggs wrote to the Mayor, who, with his usual promptitude, communicated with the Queen's Private Secretary, Sir Henry Ponsonby, and received in reply a telegram to say that Her Majesty would stand upon the rug." Dr. Ogle visited Bessie Taylor so as to be able, if necessary, to vouch for the truth of these particulars.

AMBULANCE STATIONS.

The practical suggestion made at a meeting of the Town Council by Dr. Gentles, relative to the location of Ambulance stations along the route of the Royal procession, was adopted. The congested state of the streets arising from the numerous influx of visitors from adjacent towns and villages, naturally led those conversant with the matter to expect casualties ; while the value of first aid in these contingencies has been abundantly proved since ambulance work came to be so generally taught, as it happily now is, in our midst. Dr. Gentles, with the aid of other ladies and gentlemen, and with the hearty co-operation of owners and occupiers of premises, was enabled to secure twenty-two ambulance stations, which were manned by the members of the Brigade Bearer Co., members of the Regimental Ambulance Corps, the Midland Railway Ambulance Corps, and the P.S.A. Ambulance Corps. All the men were under the efficient management and supervision of Surgeon-major Gentles. Each station was distinguished by a flag bearing a red cross, and there were ambulance appliances at each for giving first aid to any person who might meet with an accident. There were about forty cases dealt with at these ambulance stations, most of them "faints," and none of them, happily, of a serious character. The sense of security, however, derived from the presence of these systematic aids to cases of accident, which are so very possible, and, indeed, probable on such occasions, when large crowds of people are massed together, was so appreciably felt by the authorities and by the public, that the new departure is felt to have been fully justified, and, doubtless, it will become an established and recognised institution on all such occasions in future. The following is a list of the stations:—Mr. Sturgess' Hotel, Midland Road; the Cocoa Rooms, Midland Road; Dr. T. L. Gentles' residence, London Road; Wesleyan School Room, London Road; Nurses' Institute, London Road; Dr. Cassidi's Residence, London Road; Congregational School Room, London Road; "Temple," School Room, London Road; Messrs. Earp's Mart, London Road; Babington Music Warehouse, St. Peter's Street; Mr. C. F. Hoare's premises, St. Peter's Street; Mr. Wells's Café, St. Peter's Street; Mr. Wells's Shop, Corn Market; the Cocoa Rooms, Corn Market; the Town Hall; Slack's Restaurant, Market Place; St. James' Hotel; Messrs. George and Dean's, The Strand; Mr. Sinclair's premises, Cheapside; Dr. Vaudrey's residence, The Wardwick; Congregational School Room, Victoria Street; Mr. Wells's premises, Victoria Street.

THE DECORATIONS COMMITTEE.

With reference to the Official Decorations, a detailed account of which appears elsewhere, great credit was due to the Decorations Committee, which was composed of the following gentlemen:—Mr. Councillor James Wright (Chairman); Mr. W. Bemrose, J.P.; Mr. Councillor Edwin Haslam; and Mr. George Holme, jun. These gentlemen, with the invaluable assistance of the Borough Surveyor (Mr. R. J. Harrison), superintended the whole of the public decorations in the town, and, as might be expected, their labours were of an arduous character, but throughout they worked most harmoniously and successfully together.

DESCRIPTION OF THE CASKET PRESENTED TO HER MAJESTY THE QUEEN FROM THE BOROUGH OF DERBY.

The Casket was of unusually large size, and was made in ivory with massive gold parts and figures. It bears the following inscription :—

THIS CASKET

Containing the Loyal and Dutiful

Address of the Corporation of Derby,

was presented to and graciously

accepted by

THE QUEEN,

On the occasion of Her Majesty's

First State Visit to the Borough,

in order to lay the Foundation Stone

of the new

DERBYSHIRE GENERAL INFIRMARY.

Dated this 21st day of May, 1891.

ALFRED SEALE HASLAM, Mayor.

The Casket was made unusually large in order to take the bound book (12 in. by 9 in.) which contained the illuminated address of the Corporation to Her Majesty the Queen. The task of the designer had been, therefore, to relieve the apparent flatness which a plain box of that shape and character has, and also to give lightness and elegance. The first had been done by the arrangement of the lid, which after several richly decorated ivory and gold mouldings commenced a series of ovals which gradually rose, becoming bolder as they neared the top, upon which was placed a stag in pale, the armorial bearings of the borough of Derby. The stag is carved and enamelled boldly upon a rising green mound, surrounded by a gold palisade and a gate in the centre. Then descends from the simple element of the palisade a richly fluted dome. Below this comes a circle of English Tudor roses which are interesting as being not only Royal emblems, but being also the county symbol, the white rose centre representing York and the other Lancaster. Below this is another moulding interspersed with small gold roses followed by a rich acanthus oval which completes a series of oval mouldings on the flat of the lid. The four corner spaces have massive gold plates, each an embossed representation of the borough chain, indicating the office and the occasion. Further mouldings complete the lid and bring us to the box itself. The elegance of the box has been secured by raising it up on four cross arches of ivory, and these four arches also support gold emblematic figures—1st, Britannia, holding a trident and Union Shield, as on the bronze coins of the realm. On the other side appears a figure of Derby herself, holding a shield bearing the Borough Arms and presenting an address. On the other side of the box the two corner figures represent respectively—Charity, holding in one hand the symbol of the heart, and in the other a long subscription list, and Hope, with the emblem anchor in her hand. There are various gold emblems relating to each of the figures, viz.:—Sporting dolphins Britannia, stag in pale Derby, heart and cross Charity, and the heart and anchor device that of Hope. The body of the box is mainly decorated with eight enamelled panels, containing views of the town of Derby and the vicinity, but the centre of each of the three faces has an enamelled device, the centre of the reverse being devoted to the inscription. The Royal arms occupy the obverse centre, and the crest and monogram of Sir Alfred Seale Haslam, the present Mayor of Derby, the other two. The front views are the Town Hall on one side, and on the other the Infirmary, while those on the reverse are Exeter House and Derby School. The enamelled panels at the sides contain views of St. Mary's Bridge, the Old Silk Mill—one of the first founded in England, the Market Place, and Derby from Exeter Bridge. Between each of these enamelled panels is a series of charming miniature panels in *repoussé*, each of them having relation to the various subjects illustrated; thus we have the Rose, Shamrock, and Thistle, a miniature copy of the civic mace, and also the Mayor's chain, the unwreathed sceptre of Victoria, the heart with palms and celestial crown, the cross of Faith amid rays of the celestial crown, and the anchor of Hope, all being suitably treated. The effect of the ivory and gold in combination was very fine. The enamels were treated as works of art, and gave additional richness to the effect. The whole was finished in best style and taste and manufactured by Messrs. Elkington & Co., Limited, Birmingham.

The attendance at the Art Gallery while the Royal addresses and casket were on view was something altogether unexampled. On Friday, May 15th, before the matter was generally known, 422 paid for admission; on Saturday, 1,034; on Whit-Monday, 8,145; on Wednesday, 8,914; while on Whit-Tuesday, when admission was free, the enormous number of 10,696 persons passed the turnstiles. The total number of visitors was thus 19,211. The addresses exhibited were much admired, and included, beside that of the Corporation, those from the Borough Magistrates, the County Magistrates, the Derby Guardians, the School Board, the Clergy, the Medical Profession, the Nursing Association, Repton School, Derby School, Chamber of Commerce, Friendly Societies, Teachers of Elementary Schools, and the Temperance Society.

DESCRIPTION OF THE GOLD TROWEL.

The handle, of ivory, is surmounted by the Imperial Crown, and a figure of Charity is embossed on the handle. On the reverse are the County and Borough Arms. On the trowel, engraved, are the Royal Arms, with "V.R.I." under. On either side Æsculapius and St. Luke. Again the County Arms, and "May 21, 1891." In a scroll round the trowel is the following inscription :—

"This Trowel was presented to Her Majesty the Queen by the President and Governors of the Derbyshire General Infirmary, on the occasion of the Laying of the Foundation Stone of the New Buildings by Her Majesty."

The design was by Messrs. Young and Hall, the architects for the new Infirmary, whilst its execution was entrusted to the skilful hands of Messrs Edward Johnson & Son, Victoria Street, Derby.

THE PULPIT AND THE QUEEN'S VISIT.

When Her Majesty's visit was first announced, it was thought that it would be a fitting introduction to the important ceremonies and festivities of May 21st, if a general service of a hearty congregational character was held in All Saints' Church on the morning of the eventful day. The Reception Committee, however, found it impossible to include this desirable and praiseworthy suggestion of the Rev. Canon Knight, the deservedly esteemed and respected vicar of All Saints', in the programme of the day's proceedings. The Town Council, nevertheless, accepted an invitation from the vicar to attend the morning service at All Saints' on Whit Sunday; he accordingly placed himself in communication with the Bishop of Southwell, who had promised to preach on that memorable occasion, but, as will be seen below, his Lordship was unable to fulfil his engagement, owing to his regretted indisposition. A bitterly cold wind, with occasional showers of snow and sleet, ushered in a day more resembling Christmastide than Whit Sunday, and this, together with the prevailing epidemic, militated considerably against a large attendance of either members of the Corporation or the general congregation. There was, however, a fair muster of the Corporation and of gentlemen interested in the Infirmary, including Sir James Allport, Knt., J.P.; Mr. Cox. J.P. (Brailsford); and Mr. H. J. Wood, J.P. (Breadsall); all of whom had travelled from their country seats to support the Mayor. As usual the civic body assembled in the Grand Jury Room at the Town Hall, where they formed in procession attended by the mace bearers, halberdiers, and other officials, as well as a large body of policemen. The Mayor, who wore the gold chain of office, was accompanied by Sir James Allport, Knt., J.P.; Mr. Cox, J.P.; Mr. H. J. Wood, J.P.; Mr. Alderman Roe, M.P.; Mr. Alderman Hobson, J.P.; Mr. Alderman Sowter, J.P.; Mr. J. Wright Baker, J.P.; Councillors Bottomley, J.P.; Butterworth, S. Bennett, Jackson, E. Haslam, Roome, C. Ward, F. Stone, G. Foster, Unsworth, Lowe, Wallis, J. Walley, Duesbury, and Ann, Mr. T. W. Coxon (deputy Town Clerk), Mr. W. Crowther (curator of Free Library and Art Gallery), and Col. Delacombe (Chief Constable). The Mayor, Magistrates, and Town Council occupied the Corporation pew, in front of which were placed the mace and other insignia of civic authority. As the procession entered the Church, from the tower of which floated the Royal Standard, they were met by the clergy, the Rev. Canon Knight (vicar), the Rev. F. Orton, and the Rev. J. Seymour Hill (curates), and the National Anthem was sung as the visitors passed down the centre aisle and took the places allotted to them by the churchwardens (Messrs. Blunt and Smith), who had made admirable arrangements for the service. As it was Whit-Sunday, the service for that important festival of the Church of England was used. Hymns bearing upon it, and breathing a spirit of thankfulness for past and present mercies and blessings, were creditably sung by the choir, Dr. Corbett presiding with his usual power and ability at the organ. Prayers were said by the Rev. F. Orton, the lessons being read by the Rev. J. Seymour Hill, and both these clergymen officiated at that portion of the communion service usually read during the morning service. The Rev. Canon Knight preached an interesting and appropriate sermon. Before commencing his discourse, he said he apologised

9

to the congregation for the absence of the Bishop of Southwell owing to indisposition. Canon Knight then selected as his text a part of the fourth verse of the second chapter of the Book of the Acts of the Apostles—"They were all filled with the Holy Ghost."

He said :—This day is the birthday of the Christian Church. All that the Son of God came down on earth to do had been accomplished. That wonderful life had been lived, the influence of which is growing amongst men daily; that death of shame, by which atonement was made for our transgressions, had been suffered ; that victory over the grave, which stands alone in the annals of the world, had been won. Sin and death had been conquered for men, and Paradise regained. All this had been done, and yet without the coming of the Holy Spirit, all was done in vain.

On this day a new order, a spiritual order began. A new Person, the Third Person in the ever blessed Trinity, was made known. True, He had lived in God's Saints of old, and wrought in them whatever of holiness and goodness they possessed ; true also, He had spoken for many ages in the Prophets. But now He was revealed as never before, and a new order of things began.

All that Jesus Christ had taught and effected for men's salvation must be proclaimed throughout the whole world. How shall it be done ; so done that men everywhere shall not only hear, but be convinced ? You see that little company in their upper room at Jerusalem, "the number of names, together, were about one hundred and twenty," what can they do ? They have no influence, no great stock of wisdom, no money, no power. What can they do ? How shall men in other lands hear in their own tongues the tidings they have to tell ? Nay! How could they succeed, even in their own land ? Prophets of old for many generations had spoken and witnessed for God, but they had failed to convince and save their own countrymen. What force shall accompany the new message, so that they shall gain access to the hearts and life of all men over the whole globe ? The Holy Spirit shall come upon them, and they shall be endued with a new power, which the world knew not. We sometimes, I am disposed to think, are in the habit of speaking of the advance of Christendom, and we forget the power by which alone it can make true progress. We expect that Christ's Kingdom should grow, and the Lord be served, and we do not ask, how is this to be done ? We expect it, I say ; rather, should I not ask, do we expect it ? This day for example, this birthday of the Christian Church, are you looking for the gift of the Holy Spirit ? Do you, does the Christian Church itself, believe that this mighty power of the Holy Ghost is really at hand for all who will receive it ?

Let us, then, go back in thought to-day to the first Pentecost. There was to be no manner of doubt in men's minds concerning the gift of that day. And so a stupendous miracle was wrought. Suddenly there is heard throughout the City of Jerusalem the sound as of a rushing, mighty wind ; the whole house, where Christ's people are assembled, is filled with it. They are all baptized into the Holy Ghost. Tongues of fire are seen distributed on every brow, and they begin to speak with other tongues as the Spirit gives them utterance. Now are they equipped for service ; now that for which their Lord and Master bade them wait, has come. A new power is given to them. They are able, while the spiritual influence rests upon them, to speak with languages otherwise unknown to them, so that men of many nations may hear in their own speech the wondrous story, the meaning, and power, and efficacy of Christ's life, and death, and resurrection for the salvation of men.

It was, indeed, a mighty sign, repeated in some form, as you will remember, at the house of Cornelius, to indicate that Gentile as well as Jew shall share the gifts of the Father's love, and be made members of the new Kingdom of Christ.

But more than this. Granted that the Lord's disciples speak with new tongues, how shall they touch the hearts and consciences of men ? It is not enough that the speaker be filled with power and zeal ; it is not enough that it shall be plain that a new force is at work. How shall hearts be touched, and consciences roused, and wills moulded, and affections stirred ? That same Holy Spirit, speaking through the lips of the Apostles, shall deal in a convincing manner with the hearers' hearts. When the speaker and his companions spoke to the crowd around them of Christ, of His life, and death, and resurrection, of pardon freely given and sealed in His blood, they were "pricked in their hearts." The word made use of by St. Luke signifies *deep conviction* of soul. The sins of the past life are seen as they have never been seen before; the deep need of pardon and of renewal of heart and life are now perceived. They have helped to crucify the Son of God, and the cry they utter is, "Men and brethren, what must we do to be saved?"

It is so still. Whenever in faith and love Christ is set forth to men, Christ crucified for their sins, and rising again for their justification, the Holy Spirit takes these precious truths and brings them home to the hearers' hearts. And it is such people, my brethren, people made to know by the Holy Spirit's power, Jesus Christ as Lord and Saviour; it is people constrained by the Holy Spirit, for Christ's sake to hate sin and to love holiness; it is they who truly belong to Christ's Church, and can really take up and carry out Christ's work and service.

"The fruit of the Spirit is love." His highest, best, chiefest gift—gift that includes all others—is love. Of this holy affection St. Paul speaks at length in 1 Cor. xiii. When this love exists and lives in the heart, it will show itself in many ways, and prominent amongst them is loving care for the weary bodies and sin stricken souls of our fellow-men. I know that the Apostle in that same chapter plainly teaches us that it is possible for a man to "give all his goods to feed the poor" and yet have no true love; that it is possible that other motives than the great high motive of love may move his heart. Some, for example, may be forward to build a hospital, because they know the terrible burden of bodily pain and sickness. Either they have felt these themselves, or they have seen them at work in others; or they know that the hour is coming when they must bear their share of the sufferings of humanity: they can sympathise with bodily suffering; they will give to alleviate bodily pain. But while this is quite true, I venture to claim for the Gospel of Christ, for the work of the Spirit of Christ, the very existence of hospitals, and especially when they care—as rightly conducted they do care—not for the body only, but for the soul also.

We know that before Christ came there were no hospitals. You might have gone through great Babylon, or learned Athens, or mighty Rome, or wealthy Antioch, and you would have found none. We know that hospitals are the outcome of Christianity, the fruit—one of the fruits—of the Gospel of Jesus Christ; and more especially when they rest, as they ought to rest, on a religious basis, and to care for the body and care for the soul.

In founding or renewing a hospital, are we not following the example of the Lord Jesus Christ Himself? "He went about doing good, and healing all that were oppressed of the devil." He came to save the whole man, body, soul, and spirit; and at this day in our work in the mission-field we find a Christian hospital perhaps the most effectual means of preaching Christ. When men see that you care for the body, and try to heal the body, they are led also to believe that you care for the soul, and desire to heal and save the soul.

And thus, my brethren, I take it as a happy omen that the foundation-stone of the new Infirmary is to be laid in this Whitsun-week, and that our inauguration service—as I venture to call this service—has fallen on Whit Sunday. Let us regard the work in this light. Let one and all look upon it as spiritual work—work to which our Lord and Master summons us, and which, because he summons us, must be done in the very best way. Let us to-day resolve, each and all, that we will not cease to commit the whole work to God, that it may indeed be begun and continued and ended in Him.

It is a happy thing, Christian brethren, for a people to be of one heart and one mind in any work; and this also, remember, is a spiritual gift. Nothing in my experience have I known so to knit together a people as this great, resolute, united effort which we are now making. May the hospital and the building of it thus in God's goodness exercise a healing power on our people, and bind us together heart to heart. It is a happy thing also, that the Royal lady, so long and so deservedly esteemed, and loved, and honoured, has consented to visit us, and by so doing to set her seal to this great work, and to encourage us to complete it.

While we pray that the work, so auspiciously begun, may be happily, speedily, royally completed, we shall also pray (I pledge you one and all to this) that the Divine protection, with every blessing, earthly and heavenly, may rest on Her Royal head; and that though in years well advancing, she may still long be spared to us, and enabled still to hold sway over us.

Many like works there are yet to be done in the land which she will foster, and so mark yet more to generations to come the happy season of prosperity and peace, of the growth of knowledge and science—knowledge and science slowly "broadening down," and rightly used for God's honour and man's welfare; of care, moreover, and love one for another, which have to so great an extent already stamped her reign.

Though you have already given, and have promised to give again, use the opportunity now before you, which will not recur, and give with no niggard hand to-day. Let there be to-day some fresh sign of gratitude for all the mercies God has given you. Labour all for that gift of the Holy Spirit which is the crown and top stone of all heavenly gifts, out of which comes all love and charity, without which you do not really live, and dare not die.

Above all may God grant unto us in this church—in this town rather—the gift of the Holy Spirit, that the words of the text may be fulfilled, "they were all filled with the Holy Ghost"; and, therefore, full of love, full of sympathy, full of good works, full of humility, full of praise to the honour and glory of that great and gracious God, "in whom we live and move and have our being."

At the close of the service the Corporation and their officers returned in procession to the Town Hall.

On Sunday, May 24th, the subject of the Queen's visit was very naturally and properly referred to in various places of worship in Derby, the Vicar of St. Alkmund's (Rev. J. Stanley Owen) devoting the whole of his evening's sermon to the religious and social lessons to be derived from the interesting and memorable occasion. The Mayor (Sir Alfred Seale Haslam) was present at All Saints' Church in the morning, when the Rev. Canon Knight chose as his text Haggai ii. 18, 19.

He said:—There is one subject which is paramount in all minds and hearts to-day. The visit of our gracious Queen and the noble work which she has thus encouraged, the spirit in which all the arrangements have been undertaken, the success by which they have been attended, and the honour done to the town in the person of its chief magistrate, these things are paramount in our thoughts to-day.

The laying of a foundation-stone is spoken of both actually and figuratively in the Bible. You will find not a few references to it. When, for example, I was looking through the Psalms for this day, my eye rested on the 22nd verse of Psalm cxviii.—"The stone which the builders refused is become the head stone of the corner," and my heart at once said to me, "That is the topic about which you must speak on Sunday."

Moreover, this is Trinity Sunday, and it speaks to us of the subject of the Christian Creeds—the Unity of the Godhead and the co-existence of the Three Persons in that Godhead—the Father, the Son, and the Holy Ghost. That great truth is the foundation truth of the Christian Church, and it may be summed up in the fulness which is in Christ, our Mediator and Redeemer.

In Isaiah xxviii. 16 we read: "Behold, I lay in Zion for a foundation, a stone, a tried stone, a precious corner stone, a sure foundation: he that believeth shall not make haste."

"This is the stone," said St. Peter, on the Day of Pentecost, quoting Psalm cxviii., with reference to the resurrection of the Saviour, ("which was set at nought by you builders, that is become the head of the corner."

"Other foundation," writes St. Paul to the Corinthians, " can no man lay than that is laid, which is Christ Jesus"; and in a later Epistle, that to the Ephesians, he adds that the Church " is built upon the foundation of the Apostles and Prophets, Jesus Christ Himself being the Head corner stone."

And it was, thank God, in a religious spirit that we, as a people, gave ourselves to the work accomplished last week. I claim our united service of last Sunday, which had the special sanction and presence of the authorities of the town, as a token of this. How should we begin such a work but in the spirit of prayer? The work itself, again, the laying of the foundation-stone, was done in prayer, and the tone and spirit of those prayers commended them to all who heard them. This, depend upon it, brethren, is the spirit which the Lord will bless.

Has it not always been so? The house which Solomon built, that great example of a grand work, perhaps the greatest and most splendid building ever erected, was built for God, in dependence on God's favour, and dedicated to His service. And when, through the sins and follies of kings and people, their beautiful city had been overthrown and their temple destroyed, and it was permitted them after years of suffering to return home once more, and again to raise up their holy House for divine worship, the laying of the foundation-stone was specially marked by Divine blessing. It is to this our text refers: Haggai ii. 18, 19. " Consider now from this day and upward, from the four and twentieth day of the ninth month, even from the day that the Lord's temple was laid, consider it. Is the seed yet in the barn? yea, as yet the vine and the figtree, and the pomegranate and the olive tree have not brought forth, from this day will I bless you."

My brethren, it is so still, for us here in England, as for Israel in days past—for Israel's God is our God; and there have been manifest to all who have eyes to see many tokens that God is working in the midst of us. If the union of the hearts of a people for a good and noble purpose, if a spirit of large liberality for a great and Christian work, if a resolute heart to accomplish a benevolent design in the best way, if the utmost is to be done that can be done for the relief of the sufferings of humanity, if these things are in accordance with the mind of God, then God has been working—does anyone doubt it?—amongst us.

For my part, I do not hesitate to say that the spirit which has been called forth will yield abundant blessing. On the one hand, the Queen's visit has evoked a spirit of loyalty in itself good; and most happy it is for us that the occasion of this visit has been such that if disloyalty had dared to lift its head, it could only have done so by seeming to be opposed to a work of charity which naturally appeals to the hearts of all men; and on the other hand, the spirit of loyalty evoked cannot fail to give an impulse to the cause, and will, we may be quite sure, redound in blessings to this town and people. Let us, men and brethren, go forward in this spirit, and God will never fail us. Bring into His treasury all the stores He gives you for the purpose, and He will repay you again for yielding to the impulse of His blessed Spirit of Love. Let us be quite sure that He will never fail. " From this day," we may say with boldness and confidence, "from this day He will bless us."

We are, perhaps, too apt to confine our pulpit addresses to the individual aspects of Divine truth, the needs of individual souls and God's supply for them. There are aspects of Gospel truth which belong to the community and the nation, which are, perhaps, too often set aside. We have turned our thoughts to some of these to-day. But you will, I am sure, agree with me that it is not right in this place and on this day to refer only to the general aspect, as I may call it, of the truth before us. We must not put aside the individual application of the Scriptures we are considering. You and I, brethren, are builders, soul builders, builders for eternity. The eternal welfare of body and soul depend on building rightly. There is a foundation on which you can build surely. What it is has been already indicated. "Other foundation can no man lay than that is laid which is Christ Jesus." If foolish builders neglect this, we will not. We will not build on self, however pure and true we may strive to be. We will not build on ordinances, however solemnly and elaborately they may be arranged. We will not build on the Lord's own sacraments instead of the Lord Himself.

The foundation is Christ—Christ as the Revelation of the Triune God. The Father has sent the Son; the Father and the Son send forth the Holy Spirit. The Holy Spirit reveals to us the Son; and the Son brings us back reconciled to our Father. This is the doctrine of the Trinity. Any view of truth which fails to grasp this is imperfect, deficient, and will tend to ruin. To build without this foundation is to be like the man, of whom the Lord Himself has spoken, who erected his house on the sand, "and the rain descended and the floods came, and the winds blew and beat upon that house, and it fell, and great was the fall of it." Brethren, it is only when the whole circle of truth is taken hold of and appropriated that peace will come and holiness will come. This, then, is the foundation. See the importance of it. It has been laid for you. You have but to depend on it. You may with all confidence rest on it the whole weight of your salvation and the whole erection of your character. Depend upon it. It will stand, for God has provided it, and it meets all His requirements. Build on Christ, brother, build on Christ. He will never fail you. Neglect Him in His salvation and He becomes to you "a stone of stumbling and a rock of offence." Ah! Yes! It was said of the infant Christ, "This child is set for the fall and rising again of many in Israel." To some He is the savour of life unto life, and to others the savour of death unto death. See that you, one and all, rest and abide in Him.

This being also the Queen's birthday (the 24th May), "God Save the Queen" was sung at both morning and evening services at St. Werburgh's, St. Andrew's, St. Luke's, etc., whilst the National Anthem was played at other churches.

THE PRESIDENT OF THE INFIRMARY.

(SIR WILLIAM EVANS, BART.)

IR (THOMAS) WILLIAM EVANS, Bart., President of the Derbyshire Royal Infirmary — a striking and characteristic portrait of whom will be found on another page—is the only child and heir of the late William Evans, Esq., of Allestree Hall, county Derby, J.P. and D.L., High Sheriff 1829, and M.P. for 16 years for that shire, and also for the borough of Leicester; by Mary, daughter of the Rev. Thomas Gisborne, of Yoxall Lodge, county Stafford, Prebendary of Durham. He was born on the 15th of April, 1821, and was educated at Trinity College, Cambridge, where he graduated B.A. in 1842 and M.A. in 1846. On the 21st of May, 1846, he married Mary (his first cousin), who died in 1889, eldest daughter of Thomas John Gisborne, Esq., of Holme Hall, county Derby. In his thirty-second year he essayed, on the retirement of his father from the representation of North Derbyshire in 1853, to represent that division of the county in Parliament in the Liberal interest, but was defeated by Mr. Pole Thornhill. In 1857, however, he was returned at the top of the poll for South Derbyshire, as the colleague of the late Mr. C. R. Colvile; and again, in a similar pre-eminent position, for the same constituency in 1859, on the memorable occasion when Mr. Mundy, who was second on the poll, defeated the Hon. Augustus (afterwards the late Lord) Vernon by one vote, and that his own. In 1865, Mr. Evans was again successful as the colleague of Mr. Colvile; but in 1868, on the Irish Church question, Mr. Evans and Mr. Colvile were defeated by Mr. Rowland Smith and Sir Thomas Gresley. At the close of the year, however, Sir Thomas Gresley died; and, after another sharp contest, Mr. Evans was defeated in January of the following year by Col. (now Sir Henry) Wilmot. A little later on, Mr. Evans suffered defeat as Liberal candidate for the borough of Stafford, near which a portion of his property is situate. During his temporary absence from Parliament Mr. Evans devoted himself with great assiduity to local affairs, becoming, besides Chairman of Quarter Sessions, Deputy Lieutenant of the county and an active county magistrate—a position he had long occupied—Mayor of the borough (1869-70), High Sheriff of the county (1872), and chairman of the Derby School Board, on which he was the chief representative of the Church interest at the time when the celebrated "25th Clause" of the Education Act was a great bone of religious contention. In 1874, Mr. Evans was again returned to Parliament as member for South

Derbyshire, being next on the poll to Sir Henry Wilmot, and defeating Mr. Rowland Smith. In 1880 he was once more returned for South Derbyshire, this time without opposition, as the colleague of Sir Henry Wilmot. In 1885, upon the redistribution of seats, Mr. Evans retired from the representation of South Derbyshire, and, though he issued his address, in anticipation, for Mid-Derbyshire, he was not sufficiently advanced for the wire-pullers of that division, and did not go to the poll. In 1886, at considerable inconvenience, and with little chance of success, he patriotically yielded to the solicitations that were made to him, and contested, unsuccessfully, the borough of Derby as a Unionist, against Sir William Harcourt and Mr. Roe. On June 21st, 1887, as part of the somewhat limited honours that were conferred on the occasion of the Queen's Jubilee, Mr. Evans was created a baronet, as Sir (Thomas) William Evans, of Allestree Hall, Derbyshire, and the event was made the occasion of much local rejoicing. Sir William is an alderman (the senior alderman) and J.P. (the senior magistrate) for the borough of Derby, and is well known as an earnest advocate and liberal supporter of all local, benevolent, philanthropic, religious, and educational movements. With regard to no institution has this been more marked than the Derbyshire Royal Infirmary, of which—like his father (the late Mr. William Evans, M.P.) and maternal grandfather (Prebendary Gisborne) before him—he has been, all his life so to speak, a staunch friend and supporter. He was first elected President of the Infirmary in November, 1857, in succession to the late Mr. M. T. Bass, M.P., and as the immediate predecessor of the present Duke of Devonshire, who was appointed in the following year. A long interval elapsed before he again accepted the office—indeed there is only one instance on record (since 1851) of the same gentleman being twice elected President of the institution, viz., its great friend and most generous benefactor, the late Francis Wright, Esq., of Osmaston Manor. In November, 1889, Sir William was again persuaded to accept the high and honourable position of President of the Infirmary, and at that time anticipated a very quiet and conventional year of office. He accepted the position, to borrow his own words, "with a very light heart," thinking that his year of office would be a conventional one, and that the main responsibilities it would entail on himself would consist of presiding over the quarterly meetings of the governors, giving the customary donation of £100 to the Infirmary, and attending the meetings of the Weekly Board as often as he conveniently could. He was soon, however, undeceived. Illness of a serious character broke out amongst the staff of the Infirmary, and a searching inquiry was instituted into the sanitary condition of the institution by several eminent experts, with the result that it was discovered to be in a most unsatisfactory state, and the rebuilding of the hospital was found to be a work of absolute necessity. This was the alarming state of things—a veritable crisis, it will be admitted, in the history of the institution—which existed at the time when Sir William Evans arrived at the end of his year of office, and all eyes turned to the worthy baronet as the one of all others who could successfully take the helm in such a great town and county undertaking as the rebuilding of the Infirmary, at a cost of from £60,000 to £70,000, would necessarily involve. Many a man would have shrunk from a task so arduous, but Sir William Evans was not made of the stuff which leaves men or institutions in moments of their greatest peril to take care of themselves, and, at the unanimous and pressing wish of the governors, he again, last November, agreed to accept the office of President for another term, being the second year in succession, and the third in the last thirty years—an unexampled honour in the history of the institution. What followed is matter of recent history. Sir William's stirring appeal to the men of Derby and Derbyshire on behalf of the rebuilding of the Infirmary, which he practically backed up with a princely donation of £3,000; the business-like method which he has displayed in organising the movement in every town and village and hamlet of the county; and his well-known influence with Lord Hartington, which has done so much to ensure the success of the movement, and the crowning honour and stimulus of the Queen's visit to lay the foundation-stone of the new Infirmary—all these points are yet fresh in the memory of our readers, and add yet still more deeply to the lasting obligations which the local community are under to Sir William Evans for his praiseworthy efforts on behalf of this and every other benevolent and philanthropic work in our midst. It only remains to wish him—as, in our representative capacity, we most heartily do—long life, health, happiness, and an increase of those honours which a grateful Queen and country have bestowed upon one of their most deserving patriots and zealous public servants.

SIR ALFRED S. HASLAM, KT., J.P.

(MAYOR OF DERBY.)

A SKETCH OF HIS CAREER.

IR ALFRED SEALE HASLAM, Kt., J.P., the Mayor of Derby, whose portrait, in his chain of office, accompanied by that of Lady Haslam, will be found at the commencement of this Record, is one of our most enterprising and successful citizens. By dint of natural talent and unceasing industry, combined with praiseworthy perseverance and good fortune, he has at a comparatively early age won for himself a high position, not only amongst his fellow townsmen but also in the wider field of commerce. On Thursday, May 21st, he experienced a brilliant and memorable honour—one which but few heads of our great municipalities have ever been privileged to enjoy—viz., that of receiving and welcoming in our midst, in the name of her devoted subjects, our illustrious and well-beloved Sovereign Lady, Queen Victoria. That Sir Alfred Seale Haslam proved the proverbial "right man in the right place" is admitted by all classes of local society. To him is due the credit of conceiving the brilliant idea of a State Visit from the Reigning Monarch in furtherance of the noble scheme for building the new Infirmary. The sum required to erect a new institution on the most modern and scientific principles, an institution which we have it on the authority of Sir Douglas Galton will be second to none in the kingdom, either in sanitary excellence or general efficiency, is necessarily very considerable. Now, the Mayor rightly judged that nothing could possibly exceed the impetus which would be imparted to the movement if only Her Majesty could be induced to come to Derby and lay the foundation-stone of the new pile of buildings. Sir Alfred is essentially a man of action; it is not his custom to allow grass to grow under his feet.

He proceeded, therefore, without delay to take the initial steps in the matter. Fortunately, the town and county of Derby possess an influential friend at Court in the person of Lord Hartington; and it is an open secret that the Mayor placed himself in communication with his Lordship, to whose kindly offices there is no doubt whatever the town owes the great honour and distinction just bestowed upon it. It must not, however, be supposed that there were no difficulties to be surmounted in obtaining the gracious consent of Her Majesty to pay a State visit to Derby. Such visits are, like those of angels, "few and far between;" and, with advancing years, Her Majesty exhibits a growing, albeit a natural, reluctance, to take a prominent part in public demonstrations. *Apropos* of this fact, we may observe that only recently the Queen felt compelled to withhold from the very important and populous neighbouring town of Birmingham a similar mark of Royal favour to that just conferred upon our own town. Moreover, although not generally known, it is a fact that when the invitation from the Mayor of Derby was first laid before Her Majesty she failed to see her way to make an exception in behalf of our borough. But the Mayor was not to be daunted. Her Majesty was approached a second time, with the happy result that the *Derbyshire Advertiser* was able to announce in its issue of Thursday, March 26th, to the great surprise and delight of its readers, that Derby was to receive the rare and signal honour of a State visit from our Queen and Empress. Elsewhere will be found a full and graphic account of the brilliant pageant. In this article we are merely concerned with it in so far as it affects the Mayor and Chief Magistrate. It is universally acknowledged that Sir Alfred Seale Haslam has performed the important functions which fell to his lot, as the head of the Municipality, with unqualified success. At an important epoch in the history of our borough he has upheld its honour and dignity in a manner which entitles him to the warm thanks of the community. By the way, this is not the first occasion upon which Sir Alfred Seale Haslam has had the honour of entertaining Royalty. Some time ago he had the honour of being present with the late chairman of the New Zealand Shipping Co. to receive His Royal Highness the Prince of Wales on board the *Ionic* in the Royal Albert Dock, when the Prince made a close inspection of the vessel, and the Patent Refrigerating Apparatus.

Sir Alfred, as will be gathered from our opening remarks, is a self-made man, and one of those great captains of industry who form so splendid an example of inventive genius and untiring devotion to duty. The fourth son of the late Mr. William Haslam, who for more than half a century had been connected with the iron trade of Derby, and who for many years was a member of the Corporation, the subject of this sketch was born on October 27th, 1844. He was educated in Derby, and displaying at an early age a marked taste for engineering pursuits—a taste which he doubtless inherited from his father—he served his apprenticeship at the works of the Midland Railway in Derby. Needless to say he availed himself to the fullest extent of the opportunities there afforded of acquiring a thorough acquaintance with the most practical forms of engineering. Conscious that his success in life would depend upon his own exertions, and determined to carve out for himself a prosperous and honourable career, he threw himself heart and soul into his daily work, with the object of learning everything there was to be learnt, and thus equipping himself with the most powerful weapons for the battle of life—viz., knowledge, ability, and experience. His first engagement was with the well-known firm of Sir William G. Armstrong and Co., London and Newcastle-on-Tyne. Hydraulic machinery principally occupied his attention whilst in the employment of this firm. Amongst a number of important undertakings entrusted to him was the erection of the extensive hydraulic apparatus at Broad Street Station. In 1868 Sir Alfred returned to his native town, and commenced business for himself at the Union Foundry. With the aid of a staff of workmen, which for some time did not exceed twenty—at the present time we may parenthetically remark he employs above five hundred—he carried on for some time a general engineering business on a comparatively small scale. Shortly afterwards his attention was directed by discussions both in and out of Parliament to the great desirability, since grown into an absolute necessity, for machinery by which perishable food supplies could be transported to this country. With our vast and ever-increasing population it is of supreme importance not only that the most abundant supplies, but also that the cheapest and most nutritive food stuffs should be placed within easy reach of all classes. Sir Alfred decided that he would never rest until he had solved the problem, or, in other words, until he had invented the necessary apparatus for opening up, as it were, the rich pasture lands of Australia and New Zealand, with their beef and mutton at 2d. or 3d. per lb., to the teeming populations of our great cities.

"The principle," as the *British Trade Journal* lucidly explains, "which Sir Alfred sought to apply, and ultimately succeeded in applying with brilliant success, was one discovered in its theoretical form some 150 years ago. It is based on the fact that air which has been compressed, dried, and cooled, will, when suddenly allowed to expand, fall in temperature to a degree below freezing point corresponding to the density of the point to which it has been compressed. The difficulty experienced by Sir Alfred as an engineer, was practically to apply this philosophical truth. The mechanical difficulties proved almost insurmountable. But the field was open, and the rewards of success stimulated this inventor, as others have been similarly encouraged, where important mechanical achievements and discoveries have been at stake."

"In the autumn of 1881 Sir Alfred had the pleasure of boarding the Orient Steam Navigation Co.'s Steamship *Orient* on its arrival in the Thames from Sydney, with a cargo of mutton and beef, which had been preserved in a cold air chamber maintained at the requisite low temperature by one of his freezing machines, one of the first which had ever been put on board ship practically to solve the question of our meat supply. It must have been a source of infinite satisfaction to find how successfully his cargo turned out, and how well the machinery had worked, without even a momentary stoppage, during the six weeks' voyage, the greater part under a tropical sun. From that day to this the frozen meat trade has been steadily developing—not, however, for meat alone, but for the conveyance of ice, fish, milk, fruit, and vegetables; and we now receive supplies of fresh perishable provisions regularly from Australia, New Zealand, the River Plate, Canada, the United States, and other parts, all of which, with the exception of hardly a fraction, has been brought to us by Sir Alfred's dry-air refrigerating machinery. Auxiliary to the Frozen Meat Companies for conveying meat, there have been established at all the ports of export and import vast stores or cold-air chambers and cellars, in which the meat and other articles are kept before being placed on board ship or sent to the market for sale to the butcher. The dead meat market at Smithfield is also thus supplied, and such stores are fitted with the Haslam Company's machinery, which works day and night for months at a time, reducing the temperature to the necessary degree. The Haslam machines are also used for cooling hospitals and public buildings in hot countries, for cooling rooms in breweries, dairies, chocolate factories, and other establishments where a cold, dry air is required. All kinds of perishable food, meat, butter, eggs, milk, and fruit, may be preserved indefinitely whether on land or at sea, in temperate climates or in tropical. In the bacon curing industry also refrigerating machinery is of the highest importance, and special machines are made by the Haslam Company for the establishments of wine growers and for the manufacture of ice. For the last-named purpose the British Government employed them during the Egyptian campaign, and the Italians have used them for a similar purpose with reference to the troops at Massowah. Among the numerous shipping companies and ship-owning firms who have vessels fitted with refrigerating machinery by the Haslam Engineering Company, are the Peninsular and Oriental; the Cunard; the White Star Line; Messrs. Henderson and Co.; the Orient; the Pacific Steam Navigation; the Shaw, Savill, and Albion Company; Messrs. Donald Currie and Co.; the New Zealand Shipping Company; the British India Steam Navigation Company; the Guion Line, and other important lines. Of the meat stores fitted with such refrigerators we may mention those at Smithfield, capable of holding about 2,000 tons of meat, and others at the Victoria, the East and West India, and the London and St. Katherine's Docks, at the establishments of Messrs. Nelson Bros., and at all the leading meat-storage companies' premises. In New Zealand, Australia, and the River Plate, numbers of the machines are at work, as many as twenty being used by a single company."

In 1884, Sir Alfred achieved one of his most striking successes, which has been fraught with immense benefit to our colonies. A full description of the "new departure" inaugurated by Sir Alfred was given in the following terms in *The Times* of Jan. 30th of that year.

"The New Zealand Shipping Company's steamer *Ionic*, had then just left Gravesend with a consignment of 60,000 salmon eggs, packed on an entirely new principle, in order to keep down the temperature and retard the development of the germ in fish eggs. The method hitherto adopted in sending out consignments of ova to the Colonies had been to surround the cases in which the eggs are deposited with blocks of ice, which it was too often found, besides taking up a large space and adding much to the cost, melted *en route*, causing the destruction of the eggs it was intended to preserve. Even if the supply of ice did not become exhausted, the excessive saturation of the moss in which the eggs were packed, by the percolation of the ice water, and the impossibility of effecting a change of the atmosphere in the packages, led to chemical action, or to the development of fungoid growths, which equally often proved fatal to a large proportion, if not the whole, of the eggs. The new system adopted was a modification of Haslam's Refrigerating Machinery. By an ingenious contrivance invented by Sir Alfred, the air, though kept at a steady temperature of from 30 to 40 degrees—low enough to retard the development of the eggs without actually freezing them—was also so thoroughly saturated with moisture, that a piece of dry flannel, being hung up in the chamber in which the eggs were deposited, became quite damp in the course of a few hours." The experiment proved an immense success, and Sir Alfred's invention in this direction has proved an incalculable boon to our colonies, whose rivers, as the result of being stocked with ova conveyed by his process, now teem with salmon.

An important function in connection with Sir Alfred's invention took place at Deptford so recently as Friday, May 29th last, when the Lord Mayor, accompanied by Mr. Sheriff Farmer and Mr. Sheriff Harris, attended at the opening of a new "chill room" which has been erected in the Deptford Cattle Market, over which the Grand Markets Committee of the Corporation of the City of London has control. The carcases of animals slaughtered as they arrive at the waterside market place are taken by means of a simple running apparatus to a "chill room," where as many as 800 sides may be left to hang in a freezing temperature. This, it is stated by the experts in such matters, not only improves the meat, but causes it to keep better when passed on from the wholesale man to the retailer. The new machinery by which the cold air is pumped into the freezing rooms and the used air drawn out, has been supplied by Sir Alfred Haslam, its inventor, patentee, and manufacturer. Mr. Alderman Phillips, Sir John Monckton, Mr. Sly, Mr. Knott, Mr. Wallace, Dr. W. H. Wray, of the United States Department of Agriculture, and the representatives of New Zealand were among those who minutely examined the details of the working of the machinery. Mr. C. J. Cuthbertson, the chairman of the Cattle Markets Committee, gave some interesting information concerning the rise and progress of the Deptford Cattle Market, and the necessity for the present addition to its resources. Last year, of a total of 306,878 animals entered, 159,058 were cattle, showing a large increase, but there was a decline in the sheep, owing to the compulsory stoppage of the German supplies. Yet the lairage and market dues amounted to £46,646, as compared with £39,886 in 1889. Mr. Cuthbertson further pointed out that the market was of great advantage to the poor, as one bullock supplied edible offal sufficient for 44 people's dinners, and a sheep for eight. The chill rooms, he added, would hold 800 sides of beef, and when the meat was thus cooled much waste was prevented, and it reached the consumers in the primest condition. This striking statement as to the immense volume of business transacted at the market was supplemented by the Lord Mayor, who expressed himself proud of the work performed by the Corporation in furnishing the metropolis at large not only with supplies of meat, but with fish, vegetables, poultry, and hay. After a few words from Mr. Lindsey and Mr. Greenwood, the guests were entertained at a luncheon. In the course of other speeches, Sir Alfred Haslam, the inventor of the cold-air machine, described the difficulties which had attended its introduction, but there were now six steamers fitted with the apparatus, having a capacity of 64,000 carcases, and others were in hand to carry 100,000 each. Cheese and butter were coming to hand in hundreds of tons from New Zealand, and a few days ago the steamship *Ballarat* brought 24,000 cases of apples, worth £17,600. One such case he had the honour of presenting to the Queen at Derby, who expressed her great gratification at receiving a present of this character from her colonies. In further illustration of the possibilities of the refrigerating system, Sir Alfred mentioned that Norwegian fish was about to be supplied to Egypt, and Mr. Low stated that, in a few days, a large consignment of frozen rabbits from New Zealand would arrive. In this colony, it was added, meat could be got at 1d. per pound. Cold-air storage, it was shewn, places these boundless food supplies at our command.

In 1876 Sir Alfred's business was converted into a limited liability company, under the title of the Haslam Foundry and Engineering Co., Sir Alfred being its managing director and principal shareholder. The works now cover some four acres of ground, and, as already

THE HASLAM FOUNDRY AND ENGINEERING WORKS.

indicated, furnish employment for some 500 hands. Both the situation of the works and their construction are all that could be desired. Within easy communication of both the Midland and Great Northern Railways, they have also the advantage, thanks to the river Derwent, which lies adjacent, of canal and river navigation. The new buildings were constructed on the most modernised principles, being designed for the purpose of turning out the best possible work on the largest conceivable scale. By the way, not the least interesting portion of the works is the original "Haslam Foundry," the *fons et origo*, so to speak, of the present gigantic concern. The old foundry, where the Mayor carried on his experiments and completed his inventions, remains still in use, and will, it may be taken for granted, ever be preserved, on account of the old and cherished associations bound up with it. The *façade* facing the road is of regular design, the main entrance being immediately in the centre; and the wings right and left of this, occupied as fitting and machine shops, filled with the most modern tools and appliances. Directly over the entrance are the general offices, manager's room, drawing offices, and stores. Close by are the pattern makers' and joiners' shops, and behind these the smiths' shop. The fitting-shop to the right of the main entrance has a gallery, in which the small work is carried on. From the gallery, as well as from the drawing offices, the whole of the fitters in the department can be seen busily employed at their work. The sight is both an interesting and impressive one. As the stoppage or breakdown of the refrigerating machinery might be attended with the most serious losses, the aim and object of the company is to attain the highest possible point of perfection in manufacture. Since 1878 Sir Alfred has almost exclusively devoted his attention to the invention, perfection, and manufacture of the cold-air refrigerating machinery, which has brought him such fame as well as prosperity. The part played by Sir Alfred in the matter has by no means been restricted to the production of the machines. It required great faith and enthusiasm, as well as great persistence and ability, in order to induce the steamship companies to embark in the frozen meat trade. To Sir Alfred is due the credit of convincing them of the great opening for such an enterprise, and of pioneering it to such astonishingly successful results. *Apropos* of this point, the following remarks, made by the Mayor on the occasion of the banquet at which he entertained his workpeople, will be read with interest:—" Some people said that these wholesale importations of provisions would do a serious amount of harm to the agricultural industry of this country; but nothing of the kind occurred. Indeed, if it had not been for these importations he did not know what would have happened. It was evident that many poor people must have gone short of such necessaries of life as beef and mutton. It was well known that this little island could only produce an insufficient amount of food for the ever-growing population, and unless supplies could be obtained from the colonies, the home food supply in the shape of meat would have to come from America and the Continent of Europe. Now, however, that refrigerators had become an assured success, British ships could not only bring meat from the colonies, but take from this country to them manufactured goods. Each country was therefore receiving surplus articles from the other, and each was therefore receiving and conferring mutual advantage. The ships never went away empty, but conveyed cutlery,

Irish goods, linens, calicoes, etc., so that that industry had not only been important to himself and workmen, but also of great national importance, helping to unite England and her colonies in a manner not known before."

Another important advantage derived by this country, it may be pointed out, is the important business connected with the bringing over by the refrigerating apparatus of cheese and apples. It was only last year that the steamship *Ballarat* arrived from the antipodes with the first cargo of apples. It contained no fewer than 24,000 cases, and every case was in splendid condition. A large number of ships are now loaded with cases of apples from the colonies. In 1889, Sir Alfred was presented with the freedom of the City of London—a rare and honourable distinction—in recognition of his position and reputation in the world of commerce. He is also a liveryman of the City of London, and connected with the company of Coachmakers and Coach-harness makers.

In spite of his numerous business engagements, Sir Alfred Haslam has devoted much time and energy to local public affairs, ever being prominent in advancing the interests of his native town. He entered the Town Council as a representative of Derwent Ward, in which his works are situate, in 1879, and has continued to represent the same ward up to the present time. In 1886 he was appointed a Justice of the Peace for the Borough, and so recently as July 1st last he qualified as a County Magistrate, having been placed on the Commission of the Peace by the Lord Lieutenant of the County, His Grace the Duke of Devonshire. Amongst other local offices which Sir Alfred fills are those of Director of the Derby and Derbyshire Bank, President of the Children's Hospital, and Governor of the Derby and Derbyshire Royal Infirmary. For several years he has occupied the position of Vice-President of the Chamber of Commerce, and on Wednesday, June 10th, of the present year, succeeded to the Presidency of that important body. Mr. Geo. Holme, in proposing the election of Sir Alfred Haslam, expressed the desire, on behalf of the Chamber, to congratulate Sir Alfred upon the well-merited honour conferred upon him by Her Majesty. The motion was seconded by the Hon. F Strutt, and carried unanimously. Sir Alfred, in reply, stated that he had been a member of the Chamber for 21 years, and had therefore attained his majority. His time was fully occupied, but he should always be ready to devote what was necessary to the duties devolving upon him in connection with the Chamber.—Having for a long period taken a deep interest in all movements affecting the welfare of the town, Sir Alfred's election as Mayor and chief Magistrate in November last was generally felt to be in accord with the eternal fitness of things. Alderman Sir William Evans in proposing his election, observed that " for eleven years Mr. Haslam had been an active member of the Council, and had also taken a full share of the work of the committees, where, they all knew, most of the business of the Corporation was transacted. He was a gentleman of the highest possible private character, he had lived all his life in the town, he was an excellent business man who had built up a large and most important commercial undertaking, and was consequently a large employer of labour. He (Sir William) had always been struck with Mr. Haslam's courtesy and forbearance towards his colleagues, and his remarks in the Council had always been characterised by clearness and ability."

The Hon. F. Strutt, in seconding the motion, also bore eloquent testimony to Sir Alfred's eminent fitness for the post. "Not only," he said, "was Mr. Haslam a native of this town, not only had he served in the Council for many years, and served as well and usefully as any gentleman who could be named, but his father before him was known and respected by the fathers of many gentlemen present. Although the industry which the late Mr. Haslam conducted was not so extensive as the business now carried on by his son, it was an honourable one. The present Mr. Haslam, however, had been instrumental in introducing to Derby an industry which had made itself known, not only in this town and country, but throughout the entire civilised world."

In returning thanks for the honour bestowed upon him, Sir Alfred delivered a very interesting address, in which he indicated various town improvements which he hoped to carry forward during his term of office. The Mayor, *suo more*, threw himself heart and soul into his new work, displaying an activity and ubiquity in the performance of his duties which have rarely, if ever, been surpassed. Mindful that generosity, like another excellent quality, begins at home, he commenced his civic hospitalities by inviting his workpeople and their wives, to the number of some seven hundred, to a great banquet in the Drill Hall on Saturday December 20th, 1890. The affair was a brilliant success, and will long be remembered with pleasure and satisfaction by this army of horny-handed sons of toil and their worthy helpmeets. The workpeople took the opportunity of presenting their employer with a highly artistic congratulatory address, towards which every individual workman had contributed. In returning thanks, the Mayor aptly remarked that on becoming Mayor, " it occurred to him that one of his first public duties ought to be to recognise the faithful services of nearly five hundred men. He thought that if anybody deserved that post of honour it was his workpeople, and he desired in a public manner to recognise the valuable assistance he had received from them all from day to day for many years past." The kindly words of the Mayor were cheered to the echo, and the utmost enthusiasm prevailed throughout the memorable proceedings. Another magnificent entertainment, given by the Mayor and Mayoress, long talked of and eagerly looked forward to, was the Children's Fancy Dress Ball, which was held in the Drill Hall, on Tuesday evening, February 3rd, 1891. The novelty of the event, the picturesque dresses of the children, the splendid hospitality dispensed, and last, but by no means least, the bright countenances of the children radiant with happiness, contributed to form a brilliant *tout ensemble*.

At a quarter to eight o'clock, the Mayor and Mayoress, leaving the reception-room, proceeded with their family to the other end of the hall, all rising to their feet as the band struck up the well-known notes of the National Anthem—the signal for the commencement of the children's dances. The sight of the little ones, in their many-coloured, grotesque, and nymph-like costumes, dancing together, with all the joyous exhilaration of childhood and youth, was a sight never to be forgotten by the adults who so pleasurably witnessed it. Excellent order and a clear space for the youngsters within the barriers were admirably preserved, owing to the efficient and zealous efforts of Mr. T. Roe, M.P., who was the experienced M.C., ably assisted by the following stewards :—Mrs. Stormont, Mrs. Shaw, Mrs. B. W. Pike, Miss Shaw, Miss May Taylor, Miss M. Cox, Major C. C. Bowring, Mr. G Brigden, Lieut.-Col. Gascoyne, Mr. R. J. Harrison, Mr. W. G. Haslam, Mr. H. M. Haywood

Mr. E. Horne, Major Monkhouse, Dr. Macphail, and Major Newbold. A small committee, consisting for the most part of the stewards, efficiently superintended all the arrangements, the details of which were most admirably carried out, without a hitch, by Mr. W. Crowther, curator of the Free Library and Art Gallery, as a most efficient, painstaking, and courteous hon. secretary. Special praise is also due to Mrs. Shaw and Mrs. Stormont—on whom much of the preliminary preparation of the children in dancing and deportment had fallen—who marshalled and directed the little ones for the various dances in a manner which was beyond all praise, and whose general services to the undertaking were invaluable in their character. The procession was, probably, the prettiest sight of the evening, enabling the onlookers to see, as at a review, all the children in their picturesque costumes. The youngsters, headed by the Mayor's son, in a naval officer's uniform, paraded in step to the strains of a suitable march, which was played by the band, the Mayor—accompanied by the Mayoress, who carried a magnificent bouquet of lilies of the valley—efficiently beating time for them, and acting withal as reviewing officer. The performance was highly appreciated, and, at its close, the little ones were loudly applauded. The assembly of adults, including the leading citizens of the town, with their wives and families, and many of the leading residents of the county, was a particularly brilliant one, and, amongst several civic dignitaries from a distance, the Right Worshipful the Mayor of Lincoln (Mr. Edwin Pratt), wearing the magnificent diamond pendant, which, with its ruby cross of St. George, centred with a gold fleur-de-lis, is the armorial ensign of his office—was the recipient, together with Mrs. Pratt, of many warm greetings from a host of old Derby friends and acquaintances. From half-past eight o'clock, and during the remainder of the evening, supper was served in the annexe, or glass-covered yard at the Becket Street entrance to the hall. The apartment itself was adorned in keeping with the decoration of the interior of the hall, both walls and roof being draped with red, white, and blue cloth, festooned with pink and white, whilst the beautiful plate and glass and artistically-garnished dishes of the tables were lit up with the subdued rays of oil lamps, moderated with red shades. Mr. Rayner, of the Bell Hotel, with the aid of his noted *chef*, provided, in really splendid style, a banquet which was replete with every delicacy.

The latest brilliant functions in which the Mayor has taken so leading a part are fully described elsewhere. Reference to one pleasing feature of the proceedings on the memorable 21st of May must not, however, be omitted in this sketch. It is almost unnecessary to say that we refer to the knighthood bestowed upon His Worship, under such extremely complimentary circumstances, at the conclusion of the Queen's visit. It formed a most fitting *finale* to the great event of the day, adding to it a finishing touch which afforded the greatest gratification to the entire community. No honour was ever more fully deserved, and in conferring a knighthood upon the Mayor, Her Majesty paid a highly-appreciated compliment to the municipality of which he is the head. The official announcement of the distinction appeared in the *London Gazette* in the following terms :—" Derby, May 21st, 1891. The Queen was this day pleased to confer the honour of knighthood on Alfred Seale Haslam, Esq., of North Lees and West Bank, in the county of Derby, Mayor of Derby, Liveryman and citizen of London." Sir Alfred was presented by the Earl of Lathom at the levée held on Friday, June 5th, at St. James's Palace, to the Prince of Wales, on behalf of Her Majesty.

Amongst the numerous flattering and well-deserved recognitions of his pre-eminent services in reference to the Queen's visit which Sir Alfred has received, the following resolution, unanimously adopted by the Weekly Board of the Derbyshire Royal Infirmary, at their first meeting after the eventful day, is of special value, coming as it does from the managing body of the institution in whose behalf the great event was planned and consummated with such brilliant success :—" That the hearty thanks of the Weekly Board be given to his Worship the Mayor of Derby for his successful labours on the occasion of the visit of Her Majesty the Queen to lay the foundation-stone of the Infirmary." His recent appointment as a County Magistrate was also a graceful recognition on the part of the official head of the county of the admirable manner in which, as the head of the municipality, Sir Alfred received the Queen on the occasion of Her Majesty's State Visit.

In the discharge of his arduous duties, Sir Alfred has ever found a true co-operator and warm sympathiser in his highly esteemed wife, Lady Haslam (neé Miss Tatam, of the Elms, Little Eaton), who gracefully unites with him in dispensing hospitality to their numerous friends at their residence, North Lees, Derby. Sir Alfred has gathered around him an immense number of works of art and beauty, selected with the taste of a *connoisseur*, and the "household gods" at North Lees form a collection of whose possession any nobleman might be proud. Sir Alfred and Lady Haslam have four children—namely, Master Alfred Victor Haslam, aged 15, who is being educated at Repton School ; Master Eric Seale, and the Misses Hilda and Edith.

THE KNIGHTHOOD OF SIR ALFRED HASLAM.

"It is just upon ten years ago that the first cargo of frozen meat arrived in the Thames from Sydney. Such a cargo was rendered possible by the energy and skill of one man, whose indefatigable will had overcome all obstacles, and who had at last succeeded in proving the practicability of keeping the English market supplied with fresh meat from the Antipodes. Probably the majority of people in the country have not realised how great and far-reaching is the revolution he effected. To the working and middle classes it means that the price of meat has been kept within reasonable limits : and the colonist has had opened to him a vast market for his surplus cattle. This has enabled him to increase his purchases of British manufactures, from which, again, our working population derive support. The originator of such magnificent results—the achievement of twenty years incessant effort—has, as all the world is aware, just been knighted by the Queen. Perhaps it is a gratifying sign of the times that such honours are conferred more and more upon those who have done the State some service, not as leaders of armies, but as captains of industry. Among these Sir Alfred Seale Haslam takes foremost rank, for seldom has the honour of knighthood been more worthily bestowed."—*British Trade Journal*.

THE MAYOR'S ARMORIAL BEARINGS.

A correspondent well versed in heraldic matters writes as follows :—It may be interesting to your readers, in view of the prominent part taken by the Mayor of Derby in the reception of Her Majesty the Queen, to give you some account of the armorial bearings of His Worship, particularly as they happen to be of a singularly unique and appropriate character. Without being too technical and using terms which would not be generally understood, the following will give a very good popular idea of the insignia in question. To begin with—as we might expect with a man who is the honourable architect of his own fortunes—the grant of arms to Sir Alfred Seale Haslam from Her Majesty's College of Arms in London is a comparatively recent one. At the same time the prevailing idea—the *motif de piece*, if I may so call it—of the arms is not a new one, being taken from a much older grant to the Irish family of Haslam, with which, of course, it is quite possible that, in some collateral and remote degree, the Derby family of the same name is connected. The arms are what is designated in heraldry as "canting" arms—*i.e.*, they contain a punning and symbolical reference to the name of the family to which they pertain. The reference is rather far fetched, it is true, but it is so patent on the face of it that "he who runs may read." This will be at once understood when I say that the characteristic charges on the shield—or rather on the "chief" of it—are two hazel leaves and a lamb. Blend the words and you get at it directly—*Hazel-lamb*, which only wants abbreviating and softening and you get "Haslam" without further difficulty, which it must be admitted is rather a good way of expressing a proper name in type and symbol. Then, lower down in the shield—

and this is a peculiarity of the new as distinguished from the older arms of Haslam—we get what are called in heraldry "two bars wavy, *azure*"—typical, one would suppose, of the blue waves of the sea across which our worthy Mayor, in his refrigerated ships, brings in such large quantities sheep and lambs from the pastures of the antipodes. The crest, as is usual in such cases, embodies the leading charges of the coat of arms which it surmounts—that is to say we again get the lamb and the hazel-leaf, though with a somewhat different and more effective arrangement, and the introduction of what I take to be yet another piece of symbolism, new and peculiar to the present Mayor, and not present in the older grant to which I have referred. The crest, then, consists of an eagle, with a "slipped" hazel leaf in its beak and with a shield suspended by a ribbon to its neck, bearing a lamb similar to that which figures in the shield beneath. Thus we have, in symbolic language, the name of "Hazel-lamb" *(Haslam)* repeated, with the further emblem of the eagle, which is a great carrier of lambs, as indeed, the Mayor, in his vast business operations from New Zealand to this country, may be very fitly said to be. The motto of the Mayor—following that of the more ancient family of the name—is, like the arms and crest already described, a "canting" one—*i.e.*, it plays on the principal charge on the shield and on the second syllable of the name, "lam(*b*)." In the Latin it runs thus, "*Agnus Dei, Salvator Meus*," which, at the same time that it refers to the armorial *lamb* above mentioned, gives expression to a very pious and proper declaration of belief and trust in "the Lamb of God" as "the Saviour of the World." All of which taken together—arms, crest, and motto—goes, I think, to make up as pretty and expressive a bit of symbolic wit and punning fancy as, if we search them from end to end, we shall find in the pages of heraldry.—The Mayor's knighthood makes no difference to his coat of arms, except that between his shield and crest he will be entitled to a knight's instead of an esquire's helmet.

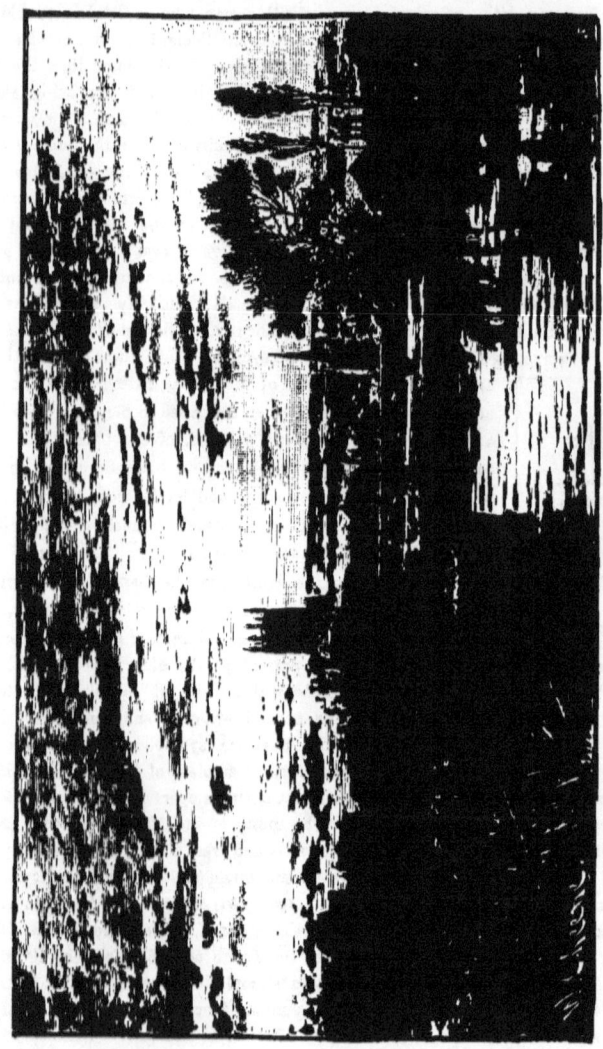

Derby from the "Long Bridge."

DERBYSHIRE GENERAL INFIRMARY.

DESCRIPTION OF THE NEW BUILDINGS.

The New Hospital will consist of thirteen blocks of buildings, which, for the purpose of description, may conveniently be numbered as follows :—1, Front Administration. 2, Back Administration. 3, Laundry and Engine House. 4, 5, 6, 7, and 8, Ward Pavilions. 9, Out-patients' Department. 10, Chapel. 11, Operation Room. 12, Home for Nurses. 13, Mortuary.

THE PRESIDENT OF THE INFIRMARY. THE MAYOR OF DERBY.
(Sir T W. Evans, Bart.)   (Sir Alfred Seale Haslam, Kt.)
(From Photos. by W. W. Winter, Derby.)

The central block round which the wards and other buildings are grouped is No. 1, the Front Administration. This is a three-storey building, and contains on the ground floor the main entrance to the Hospital, with the Secretary's office, waiting-room, porter's office, and room for Medical Staff closely adjacent. The eastern part of the ground floor is devoted to the Casualty Department, with its separate entrance, waiting-room, consulting-rooms, and a small ward for cases of urgency. On the first floor is the Board-room, with the residential quarters for the Medical Staff and the Matron. The second floor is devoted to bed-rooms for the servants.

This building is connected to the Back Administration (block No. 2) by a corridor, and again to the main Hospital corridor, which, running at right angles, divides the block in question into two unequal parts. The lower or larger part of the block contains on the ground floor the stores, linen rooms, etc., and on the upper floor the kitchen offices and larders. The upper or smaller part contains on the ground floor the nurses' dining-room, servants' hall, and pantry, and on the upper floor bed-rooms and sitting-rooms for the porters.

Block No. 3 contains the Laundry, with a separate wash-house for infected linen, the Boiler House, Engine Room, Disinfecting House, and Cremator for refuse.

Blocks Nos. 4 and 5 are similar in all respects, so that a description of one will suffice for the other. Each block is approached from the main corridor by a covered bridge, with free ventilation at each side, and of sufficient height only to afford proper head room. The object of this arrangement is to isolate each ward from aerial contact with the other wards, and thus to prevent the connecting corridors being channels for the conveyance of air from one ward to the other.

At the entrance to the Pavilion will be found spaces for coal bunkers, cupboards for ward linen, patients' clothes, and food ; a w.c. for the use of nurses ; and a cupboard for brooms, pails, etc. Close to the entrance to the ward on one side of the corridor is a separation Ward, capable of holding two beds, and on the other side a nurse's·duty room or ward kitchen.

The wards are 127 ft. long, 29 ft. wide, and are arranged to hold 24 beds each. Each bed is separated from its neighbour's by a window, and each patient will have 145 ft. floor space and 1,890 ft. cubic space. The floors will be laid with teak, or some similar hard wood, bedded directly on concrete, and the framework of the floors and ceilings will be of iron, bedded in concrete. In the finishing of the walls, floors, ceilings, windows, and doors, all internal angles will be rounded, in order to provide no avoidable lodging-places for dust. The wards will be warmed partly by open fire-places placed in ,the centre with descending flues, and partly by steam coils placed in window recesses, and provided with fresh air from outside.

At the further end of the wards are two towers, connected with the wards by covered bridges, containing the sanitary offices and the bath rooms. Between these towers are balconies for the use of convalescent patients.

Block 6 is on the ground floor, exactly similar to Nos. 4 and 5. On the upper floor it contains six small wards for one bed each, and a general ward for 10 beds, all of which will be allotted to the Gynæcological department. Block 7 is similar in all respects to Nos. 4 and 5.

Block 8 is a two-story building, and will be devoted on the ground floor to Diseases of the Eye. It contains two wards for six beds each, and has in addition to the usual ward offices, a separate operation room, with a recovering room attached. The upper floor of this block contains two wards for children, with the necessary offices.

The Out-Patients' Department, No. 9, is at the extreme south-east end of the main corridor, and is a one-storey building.

The entrance for patients is in the centre of the front, facing the London Road. Immediately inside the entrance are two small waiting lobbies for new patients, separated from each other by the porter's office. From these access is obtained to the General waiting hall. Off this hall are placed the four consulting rooms, each of which is provided with a small examining room. From these consulting rooms the patients will go to a second waiting room, where they will wait their turn to receive their medicines from the Dispensary. Behind the Dispensary is the Pathological Department and Museum.

The Chapel (No. 10) is placed midway between the Back Administration and the Eastern Ward Pavilion (blocks 4 and 5).

In the corresponding position to the last, on the western side of the Administration block, is the Operation Room. Beside the operation room itself, there is a room for the administration of anæsthetics, and a room for the staff. The operation room will be lined with marble slabs up to a height of between seven and eight feet, above which the walls and ceilings will be painted and varnished. The floor will be laid with "mischiati," which consists of marble chips bedded in cement, and forms a very hard impervious surface. In all its details every effort will be made to secure as entirely "antiseptic" conditions as possible.

The Home for Nurses (Block 12) is a detached building, and will afford accommodation for 48 nurses. Each nurse will have a separate bed-room and separate sitting-room, and reading-rooms will be provided for the staff nurses and probationers respectively.

The Mortuary Block (No. 13) is also a detached building, and will contain, in addition to the Mortuary and Post Mortem Room, a separate chamber where bodies will be placed for friends to view, and an ambulance house and stable.

Externally the buildings will be faced with red bricks, with Bentley Brook stone mullions, cornices, and mouldings. The style adopted is late Elizabethan.

THE ARCHITECTS.

The gentlemen whom the governors of the Infirmary have been fortunate enough to secure as architects of the new building—we say fortunate, because of their great abilities and special experience in such matters—are Messrs. Young and Hall, the eminent hospital architects, of 17, Southampton Street, Bloomsbury, London, W.C. Of their private lives, owing to their own very proper modesty and reticence in such matters, we know little, and, indeed, perhaps it would be hardly germane to the subject of their architectural abilities to enter into such genealogical items and personal *minutiæ*. But this much we may say, and with propriety, that they are old school-fellows, that they have been associated for many years, and have carried out many hospital and sanitary works, a list of some of the most important of which is here appended:—Miller Memorial Hospital, Greenwich; Hastings, St. Leonard's, and East Sussex Hospital, Hastings; Great Northern Central Hospital, London; Cheshunt Cottage Hospital, Cheshunt; Branch Hospital, Royal Albert Docks, for the Seamen's Hospital Society, London; Sanatorium at King Edward VI.'s School, Sherborne; Warwick Joint Infectious Hospital, Leamington; Isolation Building, London Fever Hospital; Alterations to Eastern Hospital, Homerton; Institute for Trained Nurses, Middlesex Hospital, New Buildings for Medical School, Residential College, New Mortuary and Post Mortem Room, London. Works in progress :—Royal South London Ophthalmic Hospital, London ; Fever Hospital, Harrow School, Harrow ; Sanatorium, Blundell's School, Tiverton : Warneford Hospital (additional), Leamington ; Derbyshire General Infirmary (re-building), Derby ; Isolation Hospital for the Right Hon. W. H. Smith, M.P., Henley-on-Thames, Sanitary Work ; Re-drainage of Eastern Hospital, Homerton, London ; Re-drainage of South Eastern Hospital, Deptford ; Re-drainage of West London School, Ashford ; Re-drainage of St. Mary's Orphanage, North Hyde. Mr. Keith D. Young also holds the appointments of Hon. Architect to the London Hospital and Architect to the London Fever Hospital.

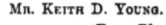

Mr. Keith D. Young.   Mr. Henry Hall.
From Photos. by W. W. Winter, Derby.

THE NEW HOSPITAL AT DERBY.

[From the *British Medical Journal*, May 16th.]

" The old-fashioned county town of Derby, true to its reputation of being ' slow and sure,' is at last astir. In regard to its infirmary, as it was practically condemned in the Government Blue Book of 1864 by Messrs. Bristowe and Holmes, it may have been said to have been very slow ; but, if so, it is now doing its best to be very sure. There is, in a word, to be a new hospital, built on the most approved principles by Messrs. Young and Hall. The most recent hospitals in London have been visited, so as to adopt their merits and avoid their blunders. The Queen will lay the foundation-stone on May 21st. The Mayor of the town has thrown himself most heartily into the undertaking, and has taken the most energetic steps to give Her Majesty a right royal reception. His donation to the building fund is but a fraction of what he is spending, and in addition he is giving time and energy to the work without stint. There is, in fact, fair promise of the money—between £70,000 and £80,000— being raised with comparative ease. Circumstances have combined in a very remarkable manner to bring this about. It is less than twelve months ago, on the outbreak of typhoid fever amongst the nurses—and alas! the death of one of them—that the alarm was raised. The Weekly Board, presided over by Sir W. Evans, Bart., acted with promptness and energy, and determined that no half measures should be trusted. It is only bare justice to add that the honorary medical staff has proved itself equal to the occasion. Besides spending time and money on the elaboration of the details—which have subsequently been submitted to the careful consideration of the most distinguished hospital experts, Miss Nightingale, Sir Douglas Galton, Mr. Burdett, and others—they have collectively promised more than two hundred guineas, and they are well aware that their labours are only just begun. Everything, in fact, at the present moment gives abundant promise of a result in the highest degree satisfactory to all parties, and fully worthy of the county, that, as the home of Miss Nightingale, is entitled to stand first in all that concerns hospital improvement."

HISTORY OF THE INSTITUTION.

It was on the 19th November, in the year 1802, that the Rev. Thomas Gisborne, of Yoxall Lodge, in a letter to Francis Noel Clarke Mundy, Esq., of Markeaton, then an active magistrate for the county, suggested the erection of an Infirmary at Derby, offering to contribute largely to the object out of a fund left in the hands of himself and of Mr. Hawkins Browne for benevolent purposes. Mr. Mundy communicated the proposal to his brother magistrates, and to the Mayor and Corporation of Derby, by whom it was favourably entertained. He then submitted the project to the Lord-Lieutenant of the county, His Grace the Duke of Devonshire, who also viewed it with favour, and wrote to Mr. Mundy, proposing to contribute £2,000, and expressing the satisfaction it would afford him to aid in the accomplishment of so desirable an object. A meeting of the leading inhabitants of the town and county was convened by the High Sheriff at the County Hall, on the 5th of April, 1803, liberal contributions were promised, and the result was the erection of the present Infirmary, designed by Mr. William Strutt, and surmounted by a statue of Æsculapius, modelled by Mr. Coffee. On Monday, the 4th June, 1810, the anniversary of His Majesty's birthday, the Infirmary, then considered to be one of the best of its kind in the kingdom, was opened for the reception of patients. An appropriate sermon was preached on the occasion in All Saints' Church by the Rev. Charles Stead Hope, after which the Governors met at the Infirmary and admitted the first patient, Ellen Brailsford. "Since that time," says the fiftieth annual (or jubilee) report of the institution in 1859, "nearly eighty-four thousand persons have participated in its benefits, either as in or out-patients, the larger proportion of whom have been either wholly cured or greatly relieved. The amount of suffering alleviated and comfort afforded in time of severe affliction to so large a number of persons it is impossible fully to estimate. . . . . Its founders have long since entered into their rest, but their descendants are now amongst the warmest and best of its friends, and there are still found on the list of annual subscribers several individuals whose names appeared in the list first published in the year 1810, and who have so continued uninterruptedly from that time to the present." The hereditary interest thus manifested in the welfare of the Infirmary is still characteristic amongst the governors of the institution. The first anniversary meeting of the Infirmary was held under the presidency of His Grace the (then) Duke of Devonshire, and it is a gratifying circumstance that the present venerable head of that noble house presided over its fiftieth anniversary, and is now, forty-one years later, not only the most munificent contributor towards its annual support, but recently convened the great county meeting to further the re-building of the Infirmary, to which he has also generously contributed the very handsome sum of £3,000. Another instance, scarcely less notable, of hereditary interest in the Infirmary is furnished in the case of the practical founder of the institution, the Rev. Prebendary Thomas Gisborne, of Yoxall, whose maternal grandson, Sir William Evans, Bart., is the present president (for the third time) of the Infirmary, and is heading the movement for the re-building of the institution, to which he also has contributed £3,000. To recur, however, to the opening of the Infirmary in 1810, we find that the total amount raised—a most creditable sum for those days—was £31,239, including the sum of £5,361 4s. 4d. in the hands of the Rev. Thomas Gisborne and Mr. Hawkins Browne abovementioned, and the still more munificent donation of £6,837 2s. 10d. from "An Unknown Friend." This sufficed to purchase the fifteen acres of land on which the institution stands— land purchased at £200 an acre, which must now have increased in value to an enormous extent—to erect the main building at a cost of £18,081, and the fever wards at an additional outlay of £4,789, leaving the very satisfactory and substantial balance in hand of £13,368 15s. 8d., with which to commence its beneficent operations. It began by providing accommodation for 80 patients, not including those afflicted with infectious diseases, but it was many years, in those anti-railway days, before even that available space was occupied. As to the means by which it was supported, we have already indicated that it started with a good balance in hand. But the interest on that amount was not, of course, sufficient to defray the ever-increasing expenses of this noble institution. Besides the annual subscribers, who from the first liberally contributed to the funds of the Infirmary, Triennial Musical Festivals—such as even now survive in the west of England—were held on its behalf, with very gratifying financial results. That held on the occasion of its first anniversary in 1811 realised £1,200, and that in 1819, under the helpful patronage and presence of H.R.H. Prince Leopold, £1,890. These festivals, producing an average income of about £1,000 a year to the funds of the charity, were continued till 1831, when a loss for the first time was sustained, and the festivals—the trial of which might well be resumed, under happier auspices—were discontinued. The anniversary (comprising Divine Service, with a sermon at All Saints' Church ; a musical performance, a dinner, and a sale of work) also added to the resources of the institution, but, one by one they fell off, till only the anniversary service remained. In response, however, to an eloquent appeal by the Rev. Canon Abney in 1853, the town of Derby—which had hitherto been somewhat backward in its support of the Infirmary, proportionately to the benefits it received—came forward nobly in the matter, and all classes, from the highest to the lowest, vied with each other in the heartiness of their support to an institution from which the community at large derived such incalculable benefit. The clergy, prior to this— in 1838—had warmly taken the matter up, and doubtless the interest they thus early displayed in the welfare of the Infirmary led, later on, to the Infirmary Sunday Fund, which is now so valuable an assistance to the funds of the institution. Out of this grew that still more extensive contribution to the funds of the Infirmary—now amounting to about £1,200 a year—which is made by the working classes, through the Infirmary Saturday Fund. The ladies also held an annual sale of work on behalf of the charity, and that reminds us that, before the rebuilding of the Infirmary is completed and paid for, we shall almost certainly have to face the inevitable bazaar to help us out of our difficulties, and it is safe to predict that, if it comes off, it will be at once by far the largest and most successful event of the kind which has ever taken place in the town and county of Derby. Various interesting developments of sanitary science are chronicled in contemporary records. Baths (similar to those at Buxton and Bath) were established in 1811, and discontinued in 1835 as no longer profitable. Gas was introduced in 1825, and an anatomical museum was established in 1830. The management seems, on the whole, to have been very good, and though an inquiry into alleged abuses was held in 1852, very few tangible grievances were discovered. The demands on the accommodation of the institution grew with the population of the town and county, and year by year the space available was utilised till, in 1826, the annual report states that the accommodation was insufficient. Nothing much, however, in the way of enlargement seems to have been done till 1848—just about the time of the advent of railways—when the main building seems to have been added to considerably, new fever wards for the accommodation of forty patients, and lock wards for twenty-two patients being erected at a cost of £7,000. In 1857, £600 was spent in improving the ventilation, but this was found in 1864 to be still very imperfect, and in 1865 a new wing was suggested, a committee being appointed to procure plans for that purpose. The practical result was attained in 1869, when the "Nightingale Wing" (so called after Florence Nightingale, the celebrated Derbyshire nurse of the Crimea), with chapel, kitchens, and other buildings, were erected, and formally opened by the late Lord Vernon, on November 12th of that year, being the sixtieth anniversary of the foundation of the institution. The total cost of these extensive additions amounted to upwards of £25,000, but there was a deficiency of about £5,000, which the Governors, as a matter of principle, declined to pay out of their invested capital. The difficulty was met, however, by the generosity of the late Mr. Francis Wright of Osmaston Manor (twice President of the Infirmary), and, later on, of three of his sons, who, on the occasion of his lamented death in February, 1873, gave a donation of £1,000 each (thus wiping off the remainder of the debt), "in memory of the deep interest their late father always took in the charity." When the Prince and Princess of Wales visited Derby, on December 17th, 1872, they visited the Infirmary on their return from the Drill Hall—where they had been presenting the prizes to the boys of Derby School —and two of the wards of the Nightingale wing were named the "Albert Edward" and "Alexandra" wards, in commemoration of the occasion. With recent events, which are yet fresh in the minds of our readers, it is not necessary to deal. Suffice it to say that, from its foundation in 1810 till the present time, the Infirmary has been a source of untold blessing to countless thousands of the sick and suffering poor, who, as in or out patients, have obtained health and healing within its walls. The march of sanitary science has, indeed, rendered a new hospital necessary, but in the accomplishment of this purpose, all-important though it be, we must never forget the charitable beneficence of our forefathers in the early part of the present century, which designed and founded this noble institution, nor the buildings—thought to be perfect in their day—in which, for eighty-one years, its truly Christ-like and benevolently useful work has been carried on, with the evident blessing of God, and the ever-increasing support of a grateful people, to the incalculable benefit of the community at large.

THE MEDICAL STAFF OF THE DERBYSHIRE INFIRMARY.

The re-building of the Infirmary being the *raison d'être* of the Queen's Visit to Derby, it will doubtless be interesting to many of our readers to receive some information relative to the staff of that important institution. We therefore append the names of the medical officers, the date of their qualification, and other items.

PHYSICIANS.

William Ogle, Esq. (M.A., Oxon.); 1858; M.D. (Cantab.); F.R.C.P., London; the Senior Physician of the Institution, who was presented to the Queen at the ceremony of laying the foundation-stone, on Thursday, May 21st, 1891. Dr. Ogle was appointed physician to the Institution on the 27th of August, 1860. Since that time he has continuously devoted his great medical skill to the alleviation of pain and suffering, and striven earnestly to promote the welfare of the Infirmary.

Charles Augustus Greaves, Esq., LL.B.; 1858; M.B., London; M.R.C.S., Eng.; L.S.A., Lond. Dr. Greaves, who is Medical Officer to H.M. Prison at Derby, became one of the physicians of the Infirmary on the 28th of July, 1884.

Winfred Benthall, Esq., 1879; M.B. (Cantab.); M.R.C.S., Eng.; L.S.A., Lond. Dr. Benthall was appointed House Surgeon of the Infirmary in 1880, but resigned in December, 1888. A few months later, viz., on the 28th of July, 1884, he was elected one of the physicians to the Institution.

CONSULTING SURGEON.

John Wright Baker, Esq., 1850; M.R.C.S., Eng.; L.S.A. In May, 1868, Mr. Baker was appointed one of the surgeons of the Infirmary, and held that responsible position for many years. On his retirement the governors conferred upon him the distinction of Consulting Surgeon. Mr. Baker was placed on the Commission of the Peace for the Borough of Derby in 1890.

SURGEONS.

William Grafton Curgenven, Esq., 1882; M.D., St. And.; M.R.C.S., Eng. Mr. Curgenven was appointed House Surgeon in 1878. He resigned in 1880, when he was succeeded by Dr. Benthall. He was elected as one of the surgical staff on the 28th of July, 1884.

John Adolphus Sharp, Esq., 1868; L.R.C.P., Lond. He was House Surgeon from November 21st, 1870, until February, 1874, when he resigned, and about thirteen years later, viz., on the 25th July, 1887, succeeded, as one of the Surgeons, the late Mr. A. H. Dolman, who had vacated the office through ill-health.

OPHTHALMIC SURGEON.

Edward Collier Green, Esq., L.R.C.P., Lond.; M.R.C.S., Eng.; L.S.A., 1881. Became House Surgeon on the 11th of February, 1884, and after retaining the position for some years, retired and devoted himself to the treatment of ophthalmic diseases. In 1888 he became the first Ophthalmic Surgeon appointed to the Institution.

HOUSE SURGEON.

Charles Henry Taylor, Esq., M.B., Lond., appointed 17th July, 1889.

DISPENSER.

Mr. Francis W. Bassano, who was appointed on May 12th, 1890, in succession to Mr. Wilson, who retired after many years of valued service.

MATRON.

Miss Mary Pratt, formerly matron of the Cardiff Infirmary. Appointed May 14th, 1888, in succession to the late Miss Probyn.

SECRETARY.

Frederick Luke Sowter, Esq., Accountant, Corn Market, Derby. Mr. Sowter is the principal member of the firm of Messrs. Watson, Sowter, and Co., the well-known Auditors and Accountants, and was appointed Secretary to the Governors on the 4th of August, 1890, in succession to Mr. Samuel Whitaker, who resigned the appointment after holding office for upwards of half-a-century.

CAPTAIN PARRY, CHIEF CONSTABLE OF DERBYSHIRE.
From a Photo. by W. W. Winter, Derby.

A BRIEF SKETCH OF QUEEN VICTORIA'S REIGN.

ER MAJESTY QUEEN VICTORIA ascended the throne on the 21st of June, 1837, having succeeded thereto on the death of her uncle, King William IV., very shortly after Princess Victoria attained her regal majority.

William IV. died at earliest dawn, and the birds were in full song in Kensington Gardens when the Archbishop of Canterbury and the Lord Chamberlain and four other gentlemen came from Windsor with the news. Miss Wynn, in her diary, says: "They knocked, they rang, they thumped for a considerable time, before they could rouse the porter at the gate. They were again kept waiting in the courtyard, then turned into one of the lower rooms, where they seemed forgotten by everybody. They rung the bell and desired that the attendant of the Princess Victoria might be sent to inform her Royal Highness that they requested an audience on business of importance. After another delay, and another ringing to enquire the cause, the attendant was summoned, who stated that the Princess was in such sweet sleep that she could not venture to disturb her. Then they said: 'We are come on business of State to the Queen, and even her sleep must give way to that.' It did, and to prove that she did not keep them waiting, in a few minutes she came into the room in a loose white nightgown and shawl, her nightcap thrown off, and her hair falling upon her shoulders, her feet in slippers, tears in her eyes, but perfectly collected and dignified."

The announcement was briefly made to her, and the first words spoken by the young Queen were to the Archbishop of Canterbury :—" I beg your Grace to pray for me !" They knelt down together, and thus the reign of Victoria was inaugurated.

At length the Queen went away to finish her toilet, and talk to the Duchess of Kent, and then followed the Council described by Disraeli in the following words:—

"A hum of half-supressed conversation which would attempt to conceal the excitement which some of the greatest of them have since acknowledged, fills that brilliant assemblage ; that sea of plumes, and glittering stars, and gorgeous dresses. Hush ! the portal opens ; she comes ; the silence is as deep as that of a noontide forest. Attended for a moment by her Royal mother, and the ladies of her court who bow and then retire, Victoria ascends her throne ; a girl, alone, and for the first time amid an assemblage of men.

"In a sweet and thrilling voice, and with a composed mien, which indicates rather the absorbing sense of august duty than an absence of emotion, the Queen announces her accession to the throne of her ancestors, and her humble hope that divine Providence will guard over the fulfilment of her lofty trust.

"The prelates and captains and chief men of her realm then advance to the throne, and, kneeling before her, pledge their troth, and take the sacred oaths of allegiance and supremacy.

"Allegiance to one who rules over the land that the great Macedonian could not conquer ; and over a continent of which even Columbus never dreamed ; to the Queen of every sea, and of nations in every zone."

On the following day the ceremony of Proclamation took place from St. James's Palace.

Having taken up her residence at Buckingham Palace, the Queen, in the month of July (on the 17th), went to prorogue Parliament. Her Majesty's part in the ceremony is thus described by Fanny Kemble, the actress, who was present : " The Queen was not handsome, but very pretty, and the singularity of her great position lent a sentimental and poetic charm to her youthful face and figure. The serene, serious sweetness of her candid brow and clear soft eyes gave dignity to the girlish countenance, while the want of height only added to the effect of extreme youth of the round but slender person and gracefully moulded hands and arms. The Queen's voice was exquisite, nor have I ever heard any spoken words more musical in their gentle distinctness than ' My Lords and Gentlemen,' which broke the breathless silence of the illustrious assembly, whose gaze was riveted on that fair flower of Royalty. The enunciation was as perfect as the intonation was melodious, and I think it is impossible to hear a more excellent utterance than that of the Queen's English by the English Queen."

Coronation day arrived, and at seventeen minutes past three on the morning of the 28th of June, 1838, a Royal salute of 21 guns announced that the sun was opening the day of rejoicing. The whole populace was awakened and soon astir. At four o'clock the carriages blocked the streets, which were even so early almost impassable. At six o'clock the struggle for places to view the procession had begun. At a quarter-past ten the Queen entered her carriage on her way to the Abbey. She was attired in a Royal robe of crimson velvet, furred with ermine, and wearing the collars of her Orders. A band of gold encircled her head, and her train was upheld by eight daughters of peers, all of them about Her Majesty's own age. Besides the personal attendants on the Queen, and the Royal Princes and Princesses, a long array of gentlemen and pages followed, having their respective vocations in the ceremony. The Queen, ascending to the daïs, passed on to the Chair of State, and, kneeling on the faldstool, offered her private devotions, and then, rising, took her seat ; the bishops standing on each side bearing the Bible, the chalice, and the patina ; the noblemen bearing the four swords, viz. : the pointed Sword of Temporal Justice, the pointed Sword of Spiritual Justice, the curtana, or Sword of Mercy, and the Sword of State, borne by Viscount Melbourne, who stood nearest Her Majesty.

After her devotions, and upon the Queen taking her seat, the organ pealed forth an anthem, the singing being rendered by the vicars choral and the choristers. At the conclusion of this the Archbishop demanded the "Recognition." This was done by his Grace repeating in a loud voice four times—to the east, north, south, and west—the following words :—" Sirs, I here present you unto Queen Victoria, the undoubted Queen of this Realm; wherefore all of you are come this day to do your homage ; are you willing to do the same ? " This completed, Her Majesty, who had been standing, resumed her seat. The Bible, the chalice for the wine, and the golden patina for the bread, were placed by the Bishops on the altar, and they then retired to their seats. Two officers of the Wardrobe then spread a rich cloth of gold on the steps of the altar for Her Majesty to kneel upon. The Archbishop of Canterbury proceeded to the altar, put on his cope, and stood on the north side. The two bishops who were to read the liturgy, with the Dean of Westminster and the noblemen carrying the swords, and others bearing the regalia, consisting of St. Edward's Staff, the Golden Spurs, the Sceptre, with the Cross, the Orb, and St. Edward's Crown, going before the Queen to the altar. Her Majesty then kneeling, made her " first offering " of an altar cloth of gold, and an ingot of gold weighing one pound, while a prayer was said by the Archbishop. The regalia was delivered to be laid on the altar, the swords were retained by their bearers, and the Queen returned to the Chair of State.

The Service of the Church was then gone through, and was followed by Her Majesty being conducted to the altar, where the Coronation Oath was taken.

The crowning followed. The Dean of Westminster carrying the Crown, the Archbishop of Canterbury placed it on Her Majesty's head, the Abbey resounding with shouts of " God Save the Queen."

The old Crown used by George IV. and William IV. weighed seven pounds, and was too large for the Queen's head ; so another had been made of less than half the weight—a cap of blue velvet with hoops of silver, brilliant with diamonds, pearls, rubies, sapphires, and emeralds. Above it rose a ball covered with small diamonds, surmounted by a Maltese cross of brilliants, with a splendid sapphire in the centre. In front of the crown was another Maltese cross bearing the enormous heart-shaped ruby once worn by Edward the Black Prince. The precious stones in the diadem of all sizes numbered 2,166, and were worth nearly £118,000. The famous Koh-i-Noor had not yet been obtained.

"The Enthronization " next took place, the Queen being lifted into the Throne, all the great officers of the State and noblemen bearing their swords, surrounding her. The exhortation, " Stand firm and hold fast," was pronounced by the Archbishop.

The tenderest scene of all this gorgeous ceremony was " The Homage," inasmuch as the Dukes of Sussex and Cambridge, the Queen's uncles, to whom she had ever looked with reverence for their age, ascended the steps of the throne, knelt before her, and placed their coronets at her feet.

There was merrymaking all over Great Britain, and amongst English residents all over the world.

The Queen's first Drawing Room has been described as a scene like fairyland. All the youthful beauty of the United Kingdom, entitled to the honour of a reception, assembled there, and the Duchess of Kent stood by the side of her young daughter during the whole function.

"Poor little Queen," said Carlyle with rugged kindliness, "she is at an age at which a girl can hardly be trusted to choose a new bonnet for herself, yet a task is laid upon her from which an archangel might shrink."

The rapid passage of time brings us nearer that important epoch in the life of the Queen—her marriage with Prince Albert.

The marriage of Her Majesty with His Royal Highness Prince Albert was performed with adequate and befitting ceremony on Monday, the 10th of February, 1840, in the Chapel Royal, St. James's Palace.

The Archbishop of Canterbury officiated, and the Bishop of London made the responses. At the moment the Prince placed the ring on his wife's finger the cannon fired the royal salute, which was answered by the Tower artillery, and all the bells in the good cities of London and Westminster simultaneously rang out a joyous peal of gratulation. The service over, the Duke of Sussex kissed her Majesty on the cheek, and the Queen stepping across to the other side of the altar, similarly saluted the Queen Dowager. The attestation of the marriage was signed first by the Duke of Sussex, and afterwards thirty other signatures were appended. On returning to Buckingham Palace the Royal pair were enthusiastically cheered, as they were likewise *en route* to Windsor, where they drove after the wedding breakfast.

Lady readers will be especially interested to know that her Majesty's wedding dress was of white satin, with a very deep trimming of Honiton lace. The body and sleeves were richly trimmed with the same material. The train, also, was of white satin, lined with the same material, and was trimmed with orange blossoms. On her head she wore a wreath of orange blossoms, and a veil of Honiton lace, with a necklace and earrings of diamonds. The cost of the lace alone on the Queen's dress was £1,000, and the satin, which was pure white, was manufactured in Spitalfields. Her Majesty wore an armlet, having the motto of the Garter *Honi soit qui mal y pense* inscribed upon it. She also wore the Star of the Order. The lace of the bridal dress, though popularly called Honiton lace, was really worked at the village of Beer, which is situated near the sea coast, about ten miles from Honiton.

The year 1840 was remarkable for a trio of events of considerable importance in the Royal life, viz., the first attempt to shoot the Queen, the attainment by Prince Albert of his majority, and the birth of the Princess Royal.

About six o'clock in the evening of Wednesday, the 10th of June, the Queen and Prince Albert left Buckingham Palace by the garden gate, opening from Constitution Hill, for a drive. After the carriage had proceeded a short distance up Constitution Hill, so as to be quite clear of the crowd, a young man, on the park side of the road, presented a pistol and fired it directly at the Queen. He then set himself back again, drew a second pistol with his left hand from his right breast, presented it across the one he had already fired, which he had in his right hand, and fired again, taking very deliberate aim. The would-be assassin was seized. He was quite calm and collected, and at the police station gave the name of Edward

Oxford. He was a pot-boy, aged 17, and at his lodgings were found the rules of a secret society, styled " Young England," prescribing among other things that every member should, when ordered to meet, be armed with pistols and a sword, and a black crape cap to cover his face. Her Majesty was much alarmed, but rising to show that she was unhurt, ordered the postillions to drive to her mother's house, the Duchess of Kent, who had taken up her abode at Ingestre House. For several days popular enthusiasm knew no bounds; their Royal Highnesses were accompanied in their drives by a voluntary bodyguard of hundreds of ladies and gentlemen on horseback, whilst sympathising crowds cheered enthusiastically. Oxford was confined as a lunatic during Her Majesty's pleasure; but we have heard of him so recently as 1882, when the following paragraph appeared in *Vanity Fair:* "The young man Oxford, who shot at the Queen in 1840, and who was found insane and lodged in Bedlam, and then in Dartmoor, is now earning his living as a house-painter in Australia. Oxford, who was never insane at all, always declared that there was no bullet in the pistol he fired—and certainly none was ever found—and explained his act as having been prompted by sheer vanity and desire for notoriety. He was released a few years ago on condition that he would go to the Antipodes."

On Tuesday, the 9th of November, 1841, the Queen gave birth to the Prince of Wales. So unbounded was the joy at the Palace at the birth of a prince, that the ceremonious officials got into a state of extraordinary confusion.

The christening of the Prince, which took place on the 25th of January, 1842, and at which the King of Prussia stood sponsor, and the subsequent celebrations, festivities, etc., are stated to have cost £200,000.

We may appropriately here give the further issue of Her Majesty and Prince Albert:—H.R.H. Alice Maud Mary, born 25th of April, 1843; H.R.H. Alfred Ernest Albert, Duke of Edinburgh, born 6th August, 1844; H.R.H. Helena Augusta Victoria, born 25th May, 1846; H.R.H. Louise Caroline Alberta, born 18th March, 1848; H.R.H. Arthur Patrick William Albert, Duke of Connaught, born 1st of May, 1850; H.R.H. Leopold George Duncan Albert, Duke of Albany, born 7th of April, 1853; and H.R.H. Beatrice Mary Victoria Feodore, born 14th April, 1857.

A second attempt to shoot Her Majesty was made on Monday, the 30th of May, 1842, by a man named John Francis, who was tried on the 17th of June, and sentenced to death. On hearing the sentence, he fell insensible into the arms of one of the turnkeys, and in that state was carried out of court. Scarcely had Her Majesty exercised her clemency towards Francis, and commuted the sentence, on the 2nd of July, to transportation for life to Tasmania, when another attempt was made upon her person. The very day after, on the 3rd of July, a deformed youth, named John William Bean, levelled a pistol at the Queen as she going from Buckingham Palace to the Chapel Royal, St. James'. Fortunately, although the weapon was loaded, it did not go off. Bean was sentenced to eighteen months' imprisonment in Newgate. In this connection, we may mention that on the 12th of July a bill was introduced by Sir Robert Peel, and became law the following Saturday, making attempts on the Queen's life punishable as high misdemeanours, by transportation for seven years, or imprisonment with or without hard labour for a period not exceeding three years, the culprit "to be publicly or privately whipped, as often and in such manner and form as the court shall direct, not exceeding thrice."

In the year 1851, the Exhibition was the event in England, and Prince Albert had the infinite satisfaction of seeing his most sanguine anticipations far exceeded. The Queen speaks of it as a complete and "beautiful triumph," and one "which I shall ever be proud of for my beloved Albert and my country."

In 1860 the Queen experienced the most acute sorrow of her life up to that time by the death of her mother, the Duchess of Kent, which occurred at Frogmore, in the presence of Her Majesty, Prince Albert, and the Princess Alice. Her Majesty, however, was destined to suffer the most terrible trial of all ere the following year expired. The Prince, never very strong, began to experience a frequency of gastric attacks and fits of sleeplessness. He nevertheless worked with his customary energy, and endeavoured to master his bodily feelings, as had been his wont, by sheer force of will. The last time he appeared in public, however, was on the 28th November, and on the Sunday following he went to church, though looking very ill. After that evening he did not join the family. The Queen and Princess Alice day after day read to him in his room. By the 12th of December the physicians felt actual alarm, and though on the night before the 13th there was a slight rally, it was thought expedient to send for the Prince of Wales from College. Death rapidly advanced upon the sinking frame, and the Prince died peacefully just before eleven o'clock, his last words to his now broken-hearted widow having been, "*Gutes fraulein!*" "Good little wife."

The Prince was buried as quietly as possible at Windsor, and on the 17th of March, 1862, the Queen laid the first stone of a mausoleum, where by the end of the year the remains were transferred. Her Majesty and family always observe the anniversary of Prince Albert's death.

Her motherly heart was full of joy when she discovered that the Prince of Wales had formed an attachment with the loved and lovely Princess Alexandra of Denmark. The excitement aroused in the country was intense, and the general gratification extreme. March 10th, 1863, was the date fixed for the nuptials, and the Princess arrived at Gravesend three days previously, being welcomed with unparalleled enthusiasm.

On March 10th, 1863, Her Majesty was present at the marriage of the Prince of Wales to the beautiful Princess, which took place in St. George's Chapel, Windsor. Amid the strains of inspiriting music the pageant with waving plumes and flaming jewels presented a magnificent spectacle.

The Queen has taken an equally loving interest in all the other marriages connected with her family; and the last child of the Queen, Princess Beatrice, was united about six years ago to Prince Henry of Battenberg.

Her Majesty's years of widowhood, so far as the inner and private life of the Royal circles is concerned, have been quiet and peaceful. The domestic tranquillity of the household has been occasionally intruded upon by those troubles which come to every family, and which have been met by the Queen with patience and fortitude. The illness of the Prince of Wales was perhaps the most vital period of suffering endured by the whole Royal Family, as well as by the nation at large, although the deaths of the Princess Alice and the Duke of Albany spread a deep gloom over the whole country.

It is pleasing, however, to turn aside from these darker pictures to that feature of Her Majesty's life which has given her a nobler office upon earth

> "Than arms, or power of brain, or birth,
> Could give the warrior kings of old."

We refer to the earnest interest she has always taken in the welfare of her subjects.

During the last few years Her Majesty has emerged somewhat from the voluntary retirement which was most in harmony with her life's sorrow; and occasionally, very occasionally, takes part in public demonstrations. No wonder, then, that Derby feels proud to have been the recipient of so rare an honour as a State visit from Her Majesty.

FORMER ROYAL VISITS TO DERBYSHIRE.

LTHOUGH possessing a somewhat ambitious heading, this article does not profess to record the numerous visits made to Derbyshire by past monarchs. It simply glances at the times when this county and its ancient metropolis have been honoured with the presence of our own beloved Queen, and the members of her illustrious family. Otherwise this sketch would occupy a greater space than is desirable at the present moment, when our minds are filled with intense enthusiasm and devoted loyalty to Queen Victoria, who has just condescended to pay us a state visit, and given us another proof of her sincere sympathy with the numerous charitable and philanthropic institutions which happily abound in this highly-favoured country. We may, however, pause for a moment to briefly recapitulate the names of some of the royal visitors who have entered the county town. Alfred the Great doubtless came here, inasmuch as his daughter Ethelfreda drove the Danes from it, and re-established the Saxon authority. King John, whose character and memory are held up to scorn by historians, visited it, and gave the burgesses a charter conferring upon them various privileges. A warlike visit was made by Henry III. (accompanied by Prince Edward); and Edward II., with his army, stayed at Derby before the battle of Boroughbridge. James I. was the next English monarch who visited Derby, although his unfortunate mother, Mary Queen of Scots, had previously remained one night at Babington House, when being removed from Wingfield Manor to the now ruined and dismantled castle at Tutbury. Charles I. was at Derby repeatedly. First as Prince of Wales, when he accompanied his father. Again in 1635, when, in returning to Yorkshire, he was entertained by the corporation, and slept in the town; and a third time in 1642, when he marched at the head of his army to Nottingham. A visit of equal national importance was made to Derby in December, 1745. This was the arrival of Charles Edward Stuart, the "Young Pretender," who, although not a member of the reigning dynasty, still had royal blood flowing in his veins, and whose object was to regain the throne of his unfortunate ancestors. The "Young Pretender," at the head of his Scottish adherents, entered Derby by way of Friar Gate, having travelled from the north through Ashbourne. The Prince, as his followers called him, took up his quarters for the night at Lord Exeter's house. This historic mansion formerly stood in Full Street, but was pulled down upwards of 25 years ago, to the great disappointment of antiquarians, and its site now forms an unsightly street. Next morning the army proceeded on their journey

southward. They only went a few miles, however, and on reaching Swarkestone Bridge, a council of war was held, at which it was determined to retire northward. Thus commenced a retreat which ended most disastrously for all engaged in the expedition. The Young Pretender, after many marvellous adventures and hairbreadth escapes, found himself an exile, and the hopes and aspirations of the unfortunate and ill-fated Stuart dynasty, so far as

His Grace The Duke of Devonshire, K.G.

the English throne was concerned, became for ever blighted and destroyed. Many a long year passed away before Derby again entertained royalty, and it was reserved for Queen Victoria to be the first reigning sovereign who had entered it in State for upwards of two hundred years. She had, however, visited it on previous occasions, and it is to these visits, as well as those of her illustrious eldest son, that we will now direct attention.

THE QUEEN'S FIRST VISIT TO DERBYSHIRE.

It is nearly sixty years since the Queen first honoured our picturesque and beautiful county with her presence. She was then the Princess Victoria. A writer of the time describing her personal appearance says — "The young Princess is an interesting and intelligent looking child; the upper features especially are particularly good, and bear a strong resemblance to the late Princess Charlotte and some other members of her illustrious dynasty." The Princess, accompanied by her mother, the late Duchess of Kent, had been making a tour of North Wales. On their return they visited the ancient and interesting city of Chester, with its remarkable "rows" and wall and numerous antiquities. From Chester their Royal Highnesses travelled by road to Macclesfield and Buxton, which was full of fashionable visitors. They did not stay at Buxton, but drove direct to Chatsworth, where they were magnificently entertained by the then ducal owner. The new and magnificent dining room of this mansion was opened for the occasion, and in the evening a large and distinguished party had the honour of dining with the Duke of Devonshire's Royal Guests. Various points of interest were visited during their stay. These included Haddon Hall, Hardwick Hall, and the various scenes of romantic and picturesque beauty abounding in the Peak. A memorable and gratifying incident connected with their Royal Highnesses stay in Derbyshire was their inspection of the extensive cotton manufactory of the Messrs. Strutt, at Belper. The route taken was by Matlock, where extensive preparations were made to ensure a hearty reception for the Royal party. A number of large trees were removed from the Heights of Abraham, and placed on each side of the road. From these trees were suspended wreaths and garlands of evergreens and flowers of the most tasteful variety. Flags and banners floated from the precipitous High Tor, the church and the houses; while bands of music paraded the streets. Accompanying the Royal party were the Duke of Devonshire, Lord and Lady Cavendish, Miss Cavendish, Lord Waterpark, and other distinguished persons. The duke's state carriage was drawn by six horses with outriders in rich liveries, and there were four other carriages, each drawn by four horses. The Duchess of Kent, the Princess Victoria, Lady Blanche Cavendish, and the Duke of Devonshire occupied the state carriage. As the distinguished visitors entered Matlock, a general cheer burst from the assembled throng, mingled with the pleasing cry of "Welcome" from numberless voices. The Royal party did not stop at Matlock, but passed slowly through it, preceded by a band of music. Their progress through the villages lying between Matlock and their immediate destination produced many loyal demonstrations, and not a little surprise, amongst the rural population. At Belper, the party and the retinue received a real Derbyshire welcome. An esteemed correspondent of the *Derbyshire Advertiser* recently gave a graphic description of what occurred when the Duchess and Princess visited Messrs. Strutt's Mills. He said: "The girls of the mills were all arrayed in white aprons, and placed in tiers on raised platforms, between which the Princess passed. The effect was very striking, and the youthful future Queen was highly amused and delighted as she passed between the girls. The illustrious visitors were deeply interested in all the various processes of cotton spinning as developed by Messrs. Strutt, and it was officially placed on record that 'with the sight of these mills the Duchess and Princess were highly gratified.' The date of Her Majesty's visit is observed as a red letter day by the firm

CHATSWORTH. (*From a Photo. by*) (*W. W. Winter, Derby.*)

at the present time. After going over the mills, the party honoured Mr. and Mrs. George Benson Strutt by partaking of luncheon at Bridge Hill." The same correspondent mentioned other interesting incidents relating to Her Majesty. He said that her visit to Derbyshire in 1832 "was no doubt recently brought to the Royal recollection by a Belper lady, much honoured and loved amongst Belper people for her kindness of heart and generosity, who begged Her Majesty's acceptance of several unique specimens of picture frames, made by Mr. John Hibbert, of Belper, from the macramé cord, so largely produced by Messrs. W. G. and J. Strutt. Her Majesty, in graciously accepting these now fashionable frames, asked to be favoured with other specimens, and it is more than probable that in viewing Messrs. Strutt's manufactures her memory recalled the girlish visit to 'Good old Belper,' and these celebrated mills." He further says:—" Her Majesty is a close observer, and she may have noticed another little incident on her second visit to Derbyshire. Mr. Jedediah Strutt was then High Sheriff of the County, and in that capacity he received Her Majesty. In his haste and loyalty, however, he ran with the carriage across from the station to the hotel, much to the amusement and satisfaction of the huge crowds assembled." On returning to Chatsworth in the evening, the Duchess and Princess stayed at several of the spar shops at Matlock, where they purchased specimens of the remarkable geological formation of the district. They also inspected Mr. Pearson's petrifying well, after which they drove forward to Chatsworth. Before leaving, however, the Duchess and Princess expressed themselves highly delighted with the welcome accorded to them, and also with the scenic beauty of Matlock. A few days later their exceedingly enjoyable visit to Chatsworth terminated. They then started for Shugborough, the seat of the Earl of Lichfield, being escorted as far as Ashbourne by the Wirksworth troop of Yeomanry Cavalry, under the command of Captain Goodwin. The inhabitants of the little Peak town provided for the Duchess and their future Queen a right loyal reception. The civil authorities were in attendance, the streets were profusely decorated, and the visitors were received amid the ringing of the fine old church bells and the enthusiastic acclamations of the people. It was, indeed, a "red letter" day in the old town. From Ashbourne the Duchess and Princess drove to Alton Towers, the charming and beautiful seat of the Earl of Shrewsbury, where they were magnificently entertained. From Alton the royal party proceeded through Uttoxeter, being escorted thither by a troop of the Staffordshire Yeomanry Cavalry, under the command of the Hon. George John Vernon. Lichfield and Shugborough were subsequently visited, and the royal party, at the termination of a most pleasant and memorable tour, proceeded to the seat of the Earl of Liverpool, in Shropshire.

THE QUEEN AND PRINCE ALBERT AT CHATSWORTH.

Her Majesty's second visit to Derbyshire was paid towards the close of the year 1843. It was a most auspicious and memorable event in the county annals, deeply interesting to the Queen and her beloved Consort, who accompanied her, and was the cause of much loyal enthusiasm amongst her devoted subjects. The Queen and Prince Albert, her husband, were making a tour through the midlands. Towards the end of November they were the guests of Sir Robert Peel at Drayton Manor, the illustrious statesman's beautiful seat near Tamworth.

From thence the royal pair journeyed into Derbyshire, Her Majesty and her husband having graciously accepted the invitation of the late Duke of Devonshire to become his guests at Chatsworth, the palace of the Peak. The royal train left Tamworth on the morning of December 1st, 1843, amidst the plaudits of the inhabitants of that district of Staffordshire. The distinguished party travelled by what is now known as the Midland Railway, the train being in charge of Mr. Matthew Kirtley, an official of the company long since passed away, but whose memory is still honoured and respected by the older citizens of Derby and the neighbourhood. The distance between Tamworth and Burton-on-Trent, thirteen miles, was accomplished in the same number of minutes. Burton station was decorated in honour of the distinguished travellers, and both at that town and Willington the Queen received many loyal demonstrations of affection. The inhabitants of Derby were not to be honoured with a prolonged stay from the Queen, but they nevertheless accorded to Her Majesty a sincerely warm and fervent welcome. About two thousand persons assembled inside the station, to which they had been admitted by ticket, and the Queen was received with the greatest enthusiasm on her arrival. No stoppage was made further than to allow time for a change of carriages. When Her Majesty was received on the platform, the staff of the militia, the recruiting parties, and pensioners, who were under the command of Captains Dixon and Jones, presented arms. Twenty rounds of ammunition were fired from the cannon located at the county gaol, under the direction of Mr. Sims (the governor). The church bells rang out merrily, and there was great rejoicing at even this brief visit to the town of the reigning Sovereign. The engine which drew Her Majesty's train from Derby was decorated, and upon it was fixed a beautiful flag, lent for the occasion by John Stevenson, Esq., railway contractor, of Derby. The Queen only remained at the station about ten minutes. Both she and Prince Albert are described as looking remarkably well. It may interest our lady readers to know that Her Majesty wore a black satin dress, and a bonnet of the same colour, but we regret to be unable to furnish a description of the fashion in which those important articles of attire were made. The royal train departed northward, amidst the enthusiastic cheers of the assembled multitude at the station, there being similar demonstrations from the spectators on the bridge over the river Derwent, and on each side of the railway outside the town. Directly after the termination of this brief Royal visit to our ancient borough, the Duke of Wellington—the hero of the Peninsular War—arrived by the ordinary train from London. He was on his way to attend the Royal party at Chatsworth, and it became necessary, owing to the traffic arrangements in operation, for him to alight and wait at the station. During the interval which intervened before he resumed his journey, the Duke inspected the station and the numerous objects of interest it contained, besides entering into conversation with Mr. Douglas Fox, a former prominent citizen of Derby, and other gentlemen. The Queen travelled from Derby to Chesterfield by railway, and thence to Chatsworth by road. In the town of the crooked steeple the preparations for Her Majesty's visit were upon a most extensive scale. The streets presented a perfect blaze of decoration and embellishment. Triumphal arches were erected along the line of the Royal procession at the public expense, and four other arches were erected by gentlemen at their own private cost. Flags, garlands, and emblematic devices were exhibited, and it is stated that the town was made to assume an appearance of gaiety and jubilee such as had not been witnessed within the memory of the oldest inhabitants. All business was suspended. From the early morning bands of music paraded the streets, and conveyances of every conceivable kind, full of passengers, poured into the town. Three troops of the Derbyshire Yeomanry Cavalry were present. The Derby and Chaddesden troop were under the command of Captain Story; the Radbourne troop was commanded by Lieutenant Hurt; and the Repton and Gresley men were under the orders of Captain Colvile, M.P. These troops were drawn up in double lines along the road which the Royal carriage had to take, and assisted in preserving order during the day. Chesterfield Railway Station presented a charming and graceful scene. The platform was covered with elegant carpet, and ornamented with plants, trees, and shrubs from the conservatory of Lord Scarsdale, of Kedleston Hall. On the walls were suspended stags' heads, in allusion to the Devonshire coat of arms, as well as banners, on which were represented the arms of Lord Vernon, Lord Scarsdale, Sir George Sitwell, and other county magnates. When the Royal train drew up to the platform, the Queen was received by the Duke of Devonshire and other notabilities. Leaning on the arm of his Grace she was conducted to a reception room, followed by Prince Albert and the members of her suite. During the brief retirement of the Queen and her consort, an Address from the Chesterfield Corporation, and three others from different public bodies, were presented by the mayor (Mr. Thomas Clarke) to the Earl of Jersey (Master of the Horse) for Her Majesty's acceptance. After the presentation of the Addresses, the Queen re-appeared, again leaning on the arm of the Duke, and entered the splendid State carriage provided for her accommodation by her honoured host, after which they drove through the town streets, which were lined with spectators. At night there were brilliant illuminations at Chesterfield, and a public dinner, in celebration of the visit. The Royal party were escorted through the town and along the road to Chatsworth by detachments of the Derbyshire Yeomanry Cavalry. The arrival at Chatsworth was distinguished by the firing of a royal salute from guns posted at the foot of the Flag Tower. Her Majesty was received by the Duke and Lady Louisa Cavendish, and escorted to his Grace's private apartments in the west front of Chatsworth House, which were appropriated exclusively to Her Majesty's use during her stay at this magnificent Derbyshire seat. During the day Her Majesty went to the south of the Italian gardens, where a scene of deep interest, of which she was a principal enactor, was witnessed in her more youthful days. Eleven years before, she and the Duchess of Kent each planted a tree, which was in a flourishing condition then, although shorn of the foliage by the winds of the preceding autumn. Prince Albert accompanied Her Majesty to this memorable spot, and having selected a sycamore from a number of other trees, planted it, as a writer of the time tells us " with the tact of a practised aboriculturist." The arrangements for the Queen's entertainment had been made upon a scale of great splendour and magnificence. On the evening after her arrival she and the Prince dined with a large and distinguished company, many of the guests being members of prominent county families. Next day, the Queen and her Consort visited Haddon, the finest old baronial hall in this or many adjacent counties. The royal party passed through the whole range of rooms, and were deeply interested in this venerable mansion. The return journey was made through Bakewell, where there were triumphal arches and decorations. The fine old peal of bells rang out merrily, and the royal party seemed much delighted with their reception. The progress was through Pilsley and Edensor. Soon after their return a deputation, consisting of the High Sheriff (William Mundy, Esq., of Markeaton), the Hon. and Rev. Alfred Curzon, and the county members of Parliament, Lord George Cavendish, Mr. William Evans, Mr. E. M. Mundy, and Mr. C. R. Colvile, had the honour of an audience with Her Majesty and the Prince, and presented them with an address from the county meeting held at Derby in the previous week. In the evening the Queen and her husband, accompanied by the Dukes of Wellington and Devonshire, and other distinguished guests, visited the grand conservatory, which was brilliantly lighted with lamps, the scene being indescribably beautiful. The dinner which followed was a brilliant gathering, and the dining room presented a gorgeous spectacle. The display of gold and silver plate was truly magnificent, and a flood of light from upwards of a hundred candles was poured on the dazzling scene. The evening concluded with a display of fireworks. The next day (Sunday) was one of quiet and repose. The Queen and the Prince attended the services in the noble duke's private chapel, where the Rev. R. C. Wilmot, his grace's chaplain, had the honour of preaching before the Royal party. The Queen and her suite terminated their enjoyable visit to Chatsworth on Monday, December 4th. They drove to Chesterfield, where there was another enthusiastic reception, and then travelled by train to Derby, where between 30,000 and 40,000 persons assembled adjacent to the railway. The Midland station at Derby was partially decorated with evergreens; flags floated from the Town Hall and other public buildings; there were tasteful displays of flowers and bunting on private houses, and the church bells rang merrily. Unfortunately the police arrangements failed. There was consequently great confusion on the platform, and the presentation of Addresses from the Corporation, signed by the Mayor (the late Mr. Ald. Barber), and from the clergy, did not proceed according to the usual form. The train only waited a few minutes, and then departed in the direction of Nottingham.

HER MAJESTY REVIEWED THE YEOMANRY CAVALRY.

Derby was honoured with the presence of the Queen and Royal Family in October, 1849. On their return from Balmoral they broke their journey here, and stayed for the night at the Midland Hotel. The Royal party consisted of the Queen, Prince Albert, the Prince of Wales, Prince Alfred, the Princess Royal, and Princess Alice, with the members of their suite. The station was splendidly decorated, and a triumphal arch was erected immediately over the spot where the Royal party alighted. The Queen was received by the High Sheriff of the county (the late Mr. Jedediah Strutt), and the Mayor of Derby (the late Mr. Robt. Forman). The High Sheriff and the Mayor escorted the Queen and her husband to the Sheriff's carriage, which was in waiting at the entrance, and on their appearance in front of the station the Royal party were received by the multitude with deafening cheers, which were renewed again and again as the royal party proceeded to the Hotel. Before the departure from the station, the Mayor and Corporation were received by Her Majesty, to whom a loyal Address, with a beautifully illuminated border with the rose, thistle, and shamrock entwining the borough and Royal arms, was presented by the Mayor. An address from the clergy (a large number of whom attended in their gowns) was also presented by the Rev. E. H. Abney, rural dean of Derby. Her Majesty graciously acknowledged these manifestations of loyalty. The whole suite of apartments on the principal floor of the hotel were appropriated to the use of the Queen, all being elegantly decorated, and superbly furnished. Various buildings in the town were illuminated, and at night the public were admitted to a grand display of fireworks at Abbot's Hill, the residence of the Mayor. The Royal party did not enter the borough on this occasion. The rain poured down in torrents on the following morning, but it did not cool the ardent loyalty of the inhabitants of Derby, who as early as seven o'clock might be seen— some in carriages, and others walking—proceeding in the direction of the station. After breakfast, the Hon. G. H. Cavendish, M.P. (Deputy-Lieutenant of the county), and the Mayor were presented to Her Majesty and the Prince by Sir Geo. Grey, Bart. Her Majesty informed both the High Sheriff and the Mayor that she was highly gratified with the reception given to her by the loyal people of Derby, and also with the arrangements for her reception and accommodation. She afterwards appeared at the drawing-room window and reviewed the Derby and Chaddesden troop of Yeomanry, who had taken a part of the military duty, and she expressed, through the Earl of Cathcart, her approbation of the corps and the loyal devotion they had manifested by rendering a voluntary attendance on that occasion.

PRINCE ALBERT AT MESSRS. HOLMES' COACH WORKS.

The Queen visited Derby again in September, 1852. She was then on her way to Scotland. When it became known that she had graciously decided to spend the night here, the directors of the Midland Railway Company made arrangements for her suitable reception at the station. Galleries, capable of accommodating several hundred persons, were erected on the platform, admission to which was by tickets judiciously distributed by the directors. Rich carpets were placed on the platform for the Royal party to walk upon, and elaborate arrangements for the decorations and illuminations were carried out under the direction of Josiah Lewis, Esq., resident director. Very complete arrangements were also made by the town authorities. Two companies of the 77th Regiment of Foot acted as a guard of honour. In addition to these a troop of the 8th Hussars, the Derby and Chaddesden troop of Yeomanry, under Captain Wilmot; the Radbourne troop under Captain Chandos Pole ; the enrolled pensioners, under the command of Captain Jones, and the militia staff, under the direction of Captain Dixon, were in attendance. The band of the 77th Regiment was also present, and played a choice selection of music. The Royal party travelled from Birmingham, reaching Derby shortly after six in the evening, the arrival being announced by the church bells. The Duke of Devonshire was in attendance. The High Sheriff of the County (Sir Henry S. Wilmot, Bart.) was represented by W. Mundy, Esq., M.P. ; and the Mayor of Derby (the late Mr. Alderman Dunnicliffe), the Recorder (the late J. Balguy, Esq.), and the Corporation of Derby, with their officers, were grouped in a central position. When the Royal train had stopped, the Mayor was presented to the Queen by the Earl of Malmesbury, and he then requested her gracious acceptance of an Address from the inhabitants. The

Address, which was beautifully written on vellum, and surrounded by an illuminated border, was a model of brevity. It nevertheless eloquently conveyed to the Queen the continued loyal devotion of Derby to Her Majesty's person and throne, as well as a prayer for the blessing of God on the Queen, for the health and happiness of the Prince Consort and the Royal children, and for the long continuance in peace and prosperity of Her Majesty's reign. Her Majesty received the Address very graciously, bowing repeatedly to the Mayor. On alighting from their carriage the Royal party were met by the Duke of Devonshire, the Earl of Burlington, the Hon. John Cavendish, General Arbuthnot, and other gentlemen. As the Royal pair proceeded from the train to the High Sheriff's carriage at the entrance hall, they and their illustrious children were enthusiastically cheered. On emerging into the streets the band played the National Anthem, and the populace, who had assembled in thousands, rent the air with their plaudits. The Royal party again condescended to honour the Midland Hotel with their presence and patronage. They were accordingly escorted there, and on alighting were loudly cheered by the populace. The hotel, which was, as on the former occasion, tenanted by Mr. Cuff, had been specially decorated for the reception of the Royal family. The corridors and lobbies were tastefully decorated with choice exotic flowers. The dining room was laid out with great elegance, and the table and sideboard exhibited a gorgeous display of beautiful silver plate. The chief ornament on the sideboard consisted of a magnificent flower stand and candelabrum. There was an elegant candelabrum at each end of the dinner table, the centre of which was occupied by a superb epergne, raised on a pedestal of burnished silver; and between each of the candelabra stood an elegant flower stand, all of these being surmounted by bouquets of rare beauty. The drawing-room presented a well-arranged profusion of splendid furniture, in rosewood, papier maché, and silver. The chairs, couches, and music stool were done up in amber-coloured damask satin, the carpet and hearth rug displayed a rich and beautiful arrangement of colours, and the table, with its massive yet chaste cover of crimson, edged by a floral design in gold, harmonised admirably with the rest of the display. On the centre table in this apartment were placed a magnificent silver candelabrum, surrounded by an elegant array of fancy books, prints, etc. Her Majesty had placed at her disposal a piano of new mechanism and design. The other Royal apartments were furnished in a similar elegant and sumptuous manner. Shortly after the Royal party had entered the hotel, Prince Albert, accompanied by the Earl of Malmesbury, appeared at one of the drawing-room windows, and was much applauded, a courtesy which he acknowledged by bowing repeatedly.

Later on, Prince Albert commanded a vehicle to be prepared to convey him, the Prince of Wales, and Colonel Phipps to Messrs. Holmes' Carriage Manufactory, on the London Road, where, to the surprise and gratification of the proprietors, they arrived about half-past six. The Royal visitors were conducted through the dried timber store, and then through the various departments of the manufactory, and after examining the processes with care, entered the show rooms. Several of the finished carriages attracted the notice of the Prince Consort, who, with the Prince of Wales, entered such of them as by the novelty of their arrangement gave promise of unusual comfort and convenience. The Prince remained in this manufactory more than an hour, and repeatedly expressed his satisfaction in observing the order and neatness which pervaded it, remarking that it gratified him the more because his visit was an unexpected one. It was most interesting, we are told by the *Derbyshire Advertiser*, to witness the untiring attention paid by the Prince of Wales to everything that came under his notice, to hear his intelligent enquiries, and to observe that he took with him some specimens of wood and iron worked in his presence by the machines. On their Royal Highnesses leaving the premises they were enthusiastically cheered by the workpeople, who had formed in line on each side of the carriage way. In the evening the town was right loyally joyous. From tower and steeple the church bells sent forth their musical peals, many of the buildings were illuminated, and in numerous ways the population demonstrated their loyalty to the Queen and the throne of these realms. At nine o'clock the next morning the Royal party left the hotel and proceeded to the station, where they were received with a similar display of enthusiasm as greeted them on their arrival on the preceding evening. Her Majesty and the Prince took leave of the Duke of Devonshire, and then the train departed for the north. The engine, it may be stated, was driven by Mr. Kirtley, superintendent of the Locomotive Department. Thus ended a series of short and unofficial visits, which Her Most Gracious Majesty the Queen paid to this town and county, visits long remembered and appreciated by their loyal and devoted inhabitants, whose attachment to Her Majesty and the Throne is as ardent and sincere to-day as it was at that distant and early period of her most benign reign.

VISIT OF THE PRINCE AND PRINCESS OF WALES TO CHATSWORTH AND DERBY.

Twenty years passed away before Derbyshire had the proud satisfaction and distinguished honour of once more welcoming and receiving any Royal personage in her midst. It was on the 17th of December, 1872, that the Prince and Princess of Wales became the guests of His Grace the Duke of Devonshire, at Chatsworth. They also paid an official visit to Derby, having graciously condescended to honour Derby School—one of the oldest foundations in the country—with their presence at the annual Speech Day. The event was one of unalloyed happiness and rejoicing. "Never has there been such a day in Derby; never, probably, were rejoicings so general and enthusiastic; never, certainly, were the decorations and illuminations so elaborate, so costly, so universal; never in our memory were the thoroughfares so crowded and impassable. Flags there, bunting here, arches yonder, bannerets everywhere; the very eye became bewildered with beauty." Such was the graphic description of the scene presented in the streets on that auspicious and memorable occasion. The royal special train departed from London and entered Derby Station amidst loud applause. Mr. (now Sir James) Allport (General Manager of the Midland Railway Company at that time), the late Mr. Needham (Superintendent), and Mr. W. Kirtley accompanied the train. On the platform to receive the Royal visitors were the Duke of Devonshire, the Marquis of Hartington, M.P., the Hon. E. Coke, Mr. Price, M.P. (chairman), Mr. Ellis (deputy-chairman of the Midland Company), the Mayor and Mayoress (now Sir John and Lady Smith), the Recorder (the late G. Boden, Esq., Q.C.), the Town Clerk (the late Mr. John Gadsby), and others. The Prince and Princess shook hands with the party from Chatsworth and with the Mayor. The Mayoress presented the Princess with a bouquet, composed of the rarest and most beautiful flowers in cultivation, all of which were elegantly arranged. An address was next presented to their Royal Highnesses on behalf of the Litchurch Local Board, of which the late Mr. Henry Fowkes was chairman, and Mr. W. Harvey Whiston, clerk. The Prince of Wales being a Past Grand Master of the English Freemasons, and the Marquis of Hartington being Provincial Grand Master of Derbyshire, it was determined by the Provincial Grand Lodge to present a loyal address to their illustrious brother. This ceremony was gracefully performed by Bro. H. C. Okeover, Deputy Provincial Grand Master of Derbyshire, the

DERBY SCHOOL.
(*From a Photo. by W. W. Winter, Derby.*)

address having been previously signed by himself and Bro. William Henry Marsden, P.G.S. A procession, consisting of the Mayor and Corporation and many notable personages, was formed at the station and, preceded by an advance guard of the Fifth Dragoon Guards, passed through the principal thoroughfares of the town to the Market Place, where the Mayor presented to the Prince of Wales a magnificent album containing various addresses to their Royal Highnesses. A circuitous route was then taken to the Drill Hall, which presented a most effective picture of ornamentation. The School " speeches " had concluded when the Royal pair arrived at the hall, where they were enthusiastically welcomed by a large and distinguished assembly of ladies and gentlemen. A most interesting part of the memorable ceremony, nevertheless, remained incompleted. The successful students received from the hands of the Prince the rewards of their year's industry and success in the pursuit of their work. An address in Latin was delivered by the Captain of the School (Hobson, *primus*), who has since distinguished himself by becoming a Senior Wrangler and also a Deputy-Professor of his University. An ode, composed for the occasion by J. Harkness, a late captain of the School, and set to music by E. Tanning, Mendelssohn scholar of the Royal Academy, was very effectively rendered by the choir, Mrs. Osborne Bateman singing the solo. A prize poem, "The Visit of the Prince and Princess of Wales," was also read by the author, J. Harkness, and loudly cheered. Another interesting feature of these proceedings was the presentation by the Princess of Wales of two Queen's Prizes to Miss Turner and Mr. George Bailey, students of the Derby School of Art, a brief history of which Institution was narrated to their Royal Highnesses by the late Lord Belper.

The Royal visitors subsequently attended the Infirmary, the needed re-construction of which has now been the means of securing the first State Visit of our beloved Queen to Derby. On alighting at the Infirmary the Prince and Princess were received by H. Allsopp, Esq. (afterwards Lord Hindlip), the president for the year, Mr. Rowland Smith, M.P., and other gentlemen. The Royal Visitors were conducted up the staircase by the President and Miss Probyn (the late lady superintendent), and were accompanied by the Duke of Devonshire, Lady Frederick Cavendish, the Countess of Macclesfield, the High Sheriff, the Mayor and Mayoress, and others. In the Board Room their Royal Highnesses inscribed their names in the visitors' book—" Albert Edward ". and " Alexandra," after which they were presented with an address, signed on behalf of the Weekly Board by the President, and Mr. Samuel Whitaker, the Secretary. The Prince and Princess were afterwards conducted through the new Nightingale wing—first through the men's ward, which the Prince, at the request of the Board, named the "Albert Edward Ward," and afterwards through the women's ward, which was in like manner named by the Princess the "Alexandra Ward," by which names these wards are still known. Their Royal Highnesses made many kind and gracious enquiries respecting individual cases, manifesting very great interest in the sufferers, and taking special notice of the children whose bodily ailments confined them in the building. The Royal Party were then escorted to the Midland Station, and left for Rowsley amidst a lively demonstration of enthusiasm. In addition to the Fifth Dragoon Guards, military duty was undertaken by the First Derbyshire Rifle Volunteers, under the command of Colonel Sir Henry Wilmot, V.C., M.P., the field officers on duty being Major John Evans, Major Holmes, and Captain and Adjutant Balguy. The third battalion of Volunteers was commanded by Colonel Cavendish. Though the Royal Party left the borough in the evening, the rejoicings did not terminate. The town was brilliantly illuminated, and the festivities were continued throughout the night. With a princely liberality which had characterised the Mayor throughout these memorable proceedings, his Worship gave a banquet and ball. The banquet took place at the Royal Hotel, where his Worship had the pleasure of receiving 250 distinguished guests. The ball, by which the festivities at Derby were worthily and right loyally concluded, took place at the Drill Hall. About 800 ladies and gentlemen were present. The scene was most brilliant and effective, and the proceedings were conducted on that munificent scale which so worthily maintained the reputation of the Mayor.

The village of Rowsley, and likewise the station, had been artistically decorated in honour of the royal visit. The surrounding villages had also caught the spirit of loyalty, and there were decorations in the villages and at the residences lying on the road between Rowsley and the Palace of the Peak. Chatsworth was safely reached under a guard of honour, consisting

From a Photo. by the)   HARDWICK HALL.   *(London Stereoscopic Co*

of Volunteers, and the booming of the cannon and the tremendous cheers of the spectators terminated the eventful and doubtless pleasant day s journey of the illustrious visitors. At Chatsworth the preparations for the welcome and entertainment of the visitors were of a most elaborate and magnificent character. That evening a distinguished and select circle of guests, including, besides members of his Grace's family, the Dukes of Rutland and St. Albans, Earl Granville, and other members of the nobility, dined with their Royal Highnesses. On the following morning the Prince formed one of a shooting party of eight, including the Duke of Rutland, Lord Waterpark, Lord Berkeley Paget and Lord Hartington. The deep snow and still deeper mud, made walking a real toil, but some capital shots were made, and the sport did not cease until darkness began to fall, and the air had become humid. During her illustrious husband's absence, the Princess drove out in an open carriage, making a circuit of the grounds, and observing the numerous curious and interesting objects which displayed themselves to her view in the Duke's beautifully picturesque domains. In the evening a grand illumination of the building and a splendid display of fireworks was followed by a ball. The splendid suite of rooms, to which special decorative art had added its utmost charm to the permanent beauty of the apartments, were still further embellished by "the living pictures of the youthful, the fair, the noble, and the dignified guests," and a writer of the time, altering Byron's well-known words, said—

"The Peak's Palace halls had gathered then
Their beauty and their chivalry."

The ball itself was a great success, and there are doubtless many who had the privilege of being present who still remember its joyousness and magnificence. Next day the Prince joined another shooting party, and the Princess spent her time in a less exciting fashion. Besides visiting the Conservatory, with the splendid surroundings of which she was delighted, she drove out in a pony carriage with Lady Louisa Egerton. In the evening there was a dinner party, consisting of Lord and Lady George Cavendish, the High Sheriff of Derbyshire, Mr. (now Sir William) Evans, Colonel Cavendish, and some fifty guests. A private ball followed, at which the Prince and Princess and most of the guests were present.

A visit to Derbyshire would be incomplete unless it comprehended the fine old baronial mansion of Haddon Hall, especially when the visitors are in the immediate vicinity of that mediæval mansion, which is one of the special attractions of the Peak. Accordingly, on Friday, Dec. 20th, their Royal Highnesses proceeded thither, and were entertained by the noble owner (the late Duke of Rutland). The ancient mansion, with its weird surroundings, produced a striking contrast in comparison with the magnificence and palatial surroundings of Chatsworth. And the contrast was designed to become even more marked, inasmuch as the entertainment was arranged to represent, as far as possible, the habits of three hundred years ago, when Dorothy Vernon eloped with Sir John Manners, from which pair the noble owner of Haddon was descended. The old pewter plates were brought into use; the spacious fireplaces blazed with immense logs; and the high table, worm-eaten and decayed, and one of the finest relics with which Haddon abounds, was brought into requisition. The *pièce de resistance* on it was a boar's head, the crest of the Vernon family. There was a large peacock pie, on the summit of which the bird, the crest of the Manners family, displayed its wealth of gorgeous plumage, and spread the vast circumference of its tail. The Buxton Band was stationed in the Minstrel Gallery, at one end of the Banqueting Hall. Over the fireplace there was a grand old heraldic frieze, containing a large number of shields bearing the arms of the Vernons and of various families allied with them, with the motto in large ancient letters, " Drede God and honour the Kyng," as well as the inscription " A.D. 1545. Monseigneur de Vernon." After a most interesting visit to this ancient pile, the Royal party drove back to Chatsworth, passing through Rowsley. On their way to Haddon in the morning the Royal visitors passed through Bakewell, which was splendidly decorated, and received a most enthusiastic reception, Mr. Nesfield, Mr. Taylor-Whitehead, Dr. Knox, Mr. Gratton, Mr. Greaves, and other well-known inhabitants taking a prominent part in the preparations and festivities. On the following day their Royal Highnesses left Chatsworth for Marlborough House, London, on their way to Sandringham. The return was made so as to afford the inhabitants of Chesterfield an opportunity of showing their loyalty to the guests of the Duke of Devonshire, and they did it in a manner worthy of the best traditions of our county. Triumphal arches, elaborate decorations, and bunting everywhere abounded; addresses were presented from the Corporation and other public bodies, and there was as great a display of loyalty as was witnessed when the Queen passed through the town many years before. The Royal party shook hands with the Duke of Devonshire, the Marquis of Hartington, Lady Louisa Egerton, and Lady Edward Cavendish on entering the train at Chesterfield Station, and the kindly tone of voice and genial manner told that the Royal guests, in bidding adieu to their Chatsworth friends, were terminating a most pleasant and memorable sojourn.

THE PRINCE OF WALES' VISIT TO DOVERIDGE HALL AND DERBY.

Friday, July 15th, 1881, was the date of the Prince of Wales' next visit to Derby. His Royal Highness (as the representative of the Queen) came to the Royal Agricultural Show, which was being held in Osmaston Park, and though to some extent the visit was primarily intended to be of a private nature, it was impossible for the respected Mayor (the late Sir Abraham Woodiwiss) to allow the occasion to pass without offering the Prince a formal reception. Though but little time or opportunity was afforded for preparation, the decorations were exceedingly tasteful and effective. His Worship, with that unbounded generosity which was one of his chief characteristics, erected at his own cost ten triumphal arches, which were massive and well-executed works of art, bearing appropriate mottoes boldly displayed. The Midland Railway Station, together with Messrs. Smith and Sons' bookstall (under the charge of Mr. Gallop), were neatly and effectively decorated, without any pretension to elaborate display. There was also a perfect wealth of ornamentation along the entire line of the Prince's route to the Show ground, as well as into the centre of the town. The Royal train was drawn by one of the Midland Company's finest and most powerful engines, and consisted of a saloon carriage and five coaches. It was accompanied by Mr. Noble (General Manager) and the late Mr. E. M. Needham; the excellent arrangements at the Station being carried out under the able supervision of Mr. Pakeman. His Royal Highness was received by a distinguished assembly of noblemen and gentlemen, including the Duke of Devonshire, the Marquis of Hartington, the High Sheriff of Derbyshire (Mr. F. Sumner, of Glossop), the Mayor of Derby (Mr.—afterwards Sir A.—Woodiwiss, J.P.), Mr. Bass, M.P., Mr. (now Sir) T. W. Evans, M.P., and Mr. Wells (Chairman of the Royal Agricultural Society). His Royal Highness's escort from the Station consisted of a squadron of the Derbyshire Yeomanry Cavalry, and immediately behind the Royal carriage were General

Cameron (of York), Col. Sir Henry Wilmot, V.C., M.P., Colonel Thompson, and other officers, upon whose breasts were the marks of favour bestowed by their Sovereign for deeds of valour in the service of their country. On reaching the Market Place, an address from the Corporation was handed to the Prince, who gave the Mayor a written reply, referring to his deep interest in agriculture, and expressing his pleasure at being able to again visit this ancient borough and renew his acquaintance with its inhabitants. The procession then passed along some of the principal streets, and by way of London Road to the Show Ground, a portion of the route being kept by the Derby Volunteers. A most enthusiastic welcome was accorded to the Prince at the Show Yard, where there were thousands of visitors from different parts of the country, and His Royal Highness seemed delighted with his reception, both in the Park and previously in the town. The Prince was entertained by the Mayor at a luncheon, consisting of the choicest delicacies in season, in a magnificent pavilion of very noble proportions. The internal furnishing and decorating had been entrusted to Messrs. Topham and Hamlet, of Derby. The floral decorations were skilfully executed by Mr. E. Cooling, and were worthy of his reputation. Mr. Towle, of the Midland Hotel, was the purveyor, his name alone being a sufficient guarantee for the excellence of that department. Some remarkably choice plaques which decorated the walls were supplied by the Derby Crown Porcelain Company; and Messrs. Elkington, of Birmingham, expressly manufactured a service of plate of extremely chaste design, which contributed not a little to the complete beauty of the luncheon table. There was an influential list of guests, including the Duke of Devonshire, the Duke of Sutherland, the Earl of Leicester, Lord Colvile, Lord Vernon, the Mayor, Sir H. Wilmot, M.P.; Rev. Sir G. Wilmot-Horton, Bart.; Mr. Bass, M.P.; Sir William Harcourt, M.P. (who was then Home Secretary); Mr. T. W. Evans, M.P.; Mr. Alderman Sowter, and Mr. Alderman John Smith. During luncheon the proceedings were diversified by a pleasing incident. Three young native girls from Hindostan, who were being educated at the cost of the Prince, and were in the charge of Miss Sutherland of Derby, were taken to the pavilion to be presented to His Royal Highness. The children, who were very prettily dressed in native costume, were presented to the Prince, who expressed himself pleased with the interview, and received from the eldest girl a very fine bouquet. Immediately after luncheon the Royal party drove to the Grand Stand, a portion of which had been specially reserved for their accommodation. The prize cattle were paraded, and His Royal Highness inspected the different breeds with all the interest of an adept. After the completion of the cattle parade, the Prince drove to the sheep pens, in several of which he was an exhibitor. He appeared to take special interest in this department, and entered into a discussion with several farmers as to the relative merits of their exhibits. The horses were afterwards paraded, and attracted a good deal of attention from His Royal Highness, who also made a complete inspection of the ground. Before leaving, the Mayoress, Mrs. (now Lady) Woodiwiss, and Mrs. (now Lady) Smith, were presented to His Royal Highness by Sir William Harcourt, M.P. The time occupied at the Show necessarily caused a hurried departure to the station, which the Prince left amidst the acclamations of the assembled multitude. Thus terminated a memorable and important visit in which "the first gentleman of these islands" had evinced his sympathy with the two staple branches of our industry—viz., agriculture and commerce.

DERBY SCHOOL RECEIVES THE PRINCE A SECOND TIME.

It was neither in an official nor yet in a representative capacity that His Royal Highness next came amongst us, but as the guest of Lord Hindlip, at Doveridge Hall. This was in November, 1888. When it became known that the Prince would attend the Derby Races, and that he had condescended to accept an invitation to Derby School, the Corporation dutifully endeavoured to ascertain his views with regard to a public reception. Singularly enough, this visit was paid during the mayoralty of Mr. Alderman Woodiwiss, J.P., eldest son of the late Sir Abraham Woodiwiss, whose munificent hospitality on the Prince's former visit imparted so much *éclat* to that memorable occasion. His Royal Highness expressed a desire, through Lord Hindlip, that as this was a private visit, undertaken for pleasure only, no formal notice of it should be taken by the municipal authorities. The inhabitants, nevertheless, decorated their houses with bunting, and turned out in their thousands to welcome their future King. The Prince (accompanied by General Sir C. Teasdale, his equerry, and one or two personal attendants) arrived at the Great Northern Station, Friar Gate, which was handsomely decorated, and was received by Lord and Lady Hindlip. After conversing with them for a few minutes, the party descended into the street, her ladyship having meanwhile presented the Prince with "a card of the races," specially printed for His Royal Highness by Mr. James Harwood, of Derby. The party drove to the Grand Stand on the race course, where they were received by Sir Henry Wilmot, Bart., the Hon. W. M. Jervis, Mr. Henry Boden, J.P., Mr. Walter Boden, J.P., and Colonel John Evans. The Prince lunched with the Doveridge Hall party in "the ancient dining-room," prepared for His Highness's reception, with appropriate taste, under the supervision of Mr. Henry Boden. Never before had there been a more aristocratic or distinguished company assembled on the Grand Stand on the race course than on that occasion, Lord and Lady Hindlip, Lord and Lady Burton, and other members of the nobility having brought distinguished parties from their respective seats in the county. The Prince remained until the last race, and then returned to Uttoxeter by special train, driving the remainder of the distance to Doveridge. On the second day of the Prince's visit a portion of the programme was spoiled by the rain. The Earl of Harrington, the noble master of the South Notts. Hunt, had made arrangements for an early meet to take place at Breadsall, and it was hoped that His Royal Highness would be able to attend, but this was found impossible. The Prince, however, went to the races, and on that occasion the Mayor of Derby (Mr. Woodiwiss) was introduced by Lord Hindlip to His Royal Highness, who pleasantly conversed with him for a short time. The great event of the day was the splendid victory of the Prince's own horse, "Magic," which, after running a waiting race, along an exceptionally difficult steeplechase course of three miles, won the contest amidst loud cheers. The *Derbyshire Advertiser's* account of the race said, at the time—"For the Prince of Wales' horse to win the Prince of Wales' Stakes in His Royal Highness's presence was as happy and appropriate an event as could possibly have happened, and the Prince was accordingly delighted alike with the victory of his horse and the applause he received."

The Prince, accompanied by a distinguished following, attended Derby School on the third day of his stay in Derbyshire. The School was effectively and tastefully decorated, and in the large class-room about 500 prominent inhabitants of the town and county assembled to give His Royal Highness a suitable welcome. On his arrival, the Prince was received by the head master (the late Rev. Walter Clark, B.D.), accompanied by Miss Clark, and the following governors of the School, who were introduced to His Royal Highness by the late Lord Belper—viz., Sir William Evans, Bart.; Sir John Smith, Knt.; Mr. F. C. Arkwright, J.P.; Mr. Ald. J. G. Crompton, J.P.; Mr. Ald. Hobson, J.P.; Mr. C. Bowring, J.P.; Mr. Ald. Roe, M.P.; Mr. N. C. Curzon, J.P.; and Col. Delacombe. The Prince inspected "The Prince of Wales's Class Rooms," erected in commemoration of the visit made to the School by His Royal Highness and his beloved Consort in 1872. The foundation-stone of these splendid buildings was laid by the Duke of Devonshire in 1874. The Prince inspected with great interest both the exterior and interior of the buildings, and asked various questions respecting the boys and their studies. The ceremony at the School was of short duration. From the Head Master His Royal Highness received a list of honours—a long and distinguished one—gained by Derbeians during the previous twenty years. This list was elegantly printed in gold letters over white satin. The Captain of the School (Henry Graves) accompanied by the Senior Præpositor (Raymond C. Jourdain) next presented a Latin address to the Prince, who also received a well-written ode (specially composed for the occasion) from Graves, the author, at whose request His Royal Highness graciously secured from the Head Master a perpetual holiday on the 14th of November. This boon was granted to the boys in celebration of this Royal visit. Before departing, the Prince delivered a brief address, saying that he should always take a deep interest in the prosperity of Derby School. He then drove away to the races amidst the music of the band and the plaudits of an assembled multitude.

THE PRINCE AT BURTON-ON-TRENT.

The busy, enterprising, and rapidly developing town of Burton-on-Trent had the honour of receiving its first visit from the Prince during his stay at Doveridge. The primary object of his entry into Burton was to inspect the brewery of Messrs. Allsopp and Co., the head of which important undertaking was at that time Lord Hindlip, who was entertaining the Prince with such generous hospitality. The arrangements made by the brewery officials for the reception and comfort of the Prince were upon a most appropriate and extensive scale. The directors' room was transformed into a luncheon room of great beauty; other rooms were also furnished and decorated for the ladies forming a portion of the party, while the various passages and approaches were also suitably adorned. Lord Hindlip, with his Royal and other guests, journeyed by special train from Uttoxeter to Burton, and the progress through the streets of the Beer Metropolis was made amidst the cheers of thousands of spectators, and the merry peals of the church bells. The Prince was conveyed through the extensive brewery, where he inspected the various operations through which the celebrated beverage of Burton passes in its manufacture. He was also entertained at a sumptuous lunch, and left the brewery after a very pleasant sojourn there. The pretty town of Uttoxeter participated in the rejoicings inseparable from the Royal presence. The station was elaborately dressed with flags and bunting, under the supervision of Mr. Dawson, the station master. The houses and streets of the old town, as well as the route to Doveridge, were also decorated. The railway traffic arrangements were under the able charge of Mr. W. D. Phillips, the North Staffordshire Company's traffic manager, and were all that could be desired.

This brief account of the Prince's visit to Derbyshire concludes our sketch of former Royal visits. It will be observed that our county has been singularly honoured by the presence of Royalty during the past sixty years, and there cannot be the least doubt that these visits have greatly endeared our gracious Sovereign and her illustrious family to the hearts of Derbyshire people.

PRINTED BY BEMROSE AND SONS, DERBY AND LONDON, FOR W. HOBSON, "ADVERTISER OFFICE," DERBY.

www.ingramcontent.com/pod-product-compliance
Lightning Source LLC
Chambersburg PA
CBHW021733220426
43662CB00008B/838